French Infantry During the Seven Years War 1756–1763

Volume 1: Organisation

Jean-Louis Vial

Helion & Company

Helion & Company Limited
Unit 8 Amherst Business Centre
Budbrooke Road
Warwick
CV34 5WE
England
Tel. 01926 499619
Email: info@helion.co.uk
Website: www.helion.co.uk
X (formerly Twitter): @Helionbooks
Facebook: @HelionBooks
Visit our blog at http://blog.helion.co.uk/

Published by Helion & Company 2024
Designed and typeset by Mach 3 Solutions (www.mach3solutions.co.uk)
Cover designed by Paul Hewitt, Battlefield Design (www.battlefield-design.co.uk)

Cover: Royal Roussillon Regiment fusilier and Saint Chamond Regiment grenadier (1757), by Sergey Shamenkov © Helion & Company. Background: Jean-Antoine Watteau, 'Recrue allant joindre le Régiment' (1710), Anne S.K. Brown Military Collection

ISBN 978-1-804514-36-8

British Library Cataloguing-in-Publication Data.
A catalogue record for this book is available from the British Library.

Contents

Note on Units of Measurement

In order to avoid confusion with units of measurements, such as the old French pied and the modern English foot, measurements are kept in eighteenth century French pieds and pouces. Official texts only used the reference measure known as pied de Roi or pied de Paris.

Here is a list of measurements translated into the metric system that can be found in eighteenth century texts and decrees:

Toise = 6 pieds = 1.949m
Aune = 3 pieds, 7 pouces, 8 lignes = 1.188m (used for fabrics)
Pied = 12 pouces = 325mm
Pouce = 12 lignes = 27.07mm
Ligne = 12 points = 2.25mm
Once = 30,48g
Gros = 3.8g

1

Introduction

> The habit of seeing the army only increased the astonishment which had struck me the first time on seeing it: indeed what a marvel should not be such an assemblage in the eyes of a man who would think that, in the midst of the perpetual conflict of passions, society only subsists by a continual miracle? Thousands of men, almost none of whom were born to be soldiers, live together under the harshest and most austere of all disciplines; everyday, they are exposed to being killed for a piece of bad bread, they are two hundred leagues from their country, looking for an enemy who has come from even further away to meet them; and then with the courage and intrepidity of a father who defends his legacy, they fight for a glory that does not survive them one moment.[1]

At the declaration of war in 1756 , according to the military records, the French regular infantry consisted of the Gardes françaises and the Gardes suisses who were part of the *Maison du Roi*, of the Grenadiers de France, 80 French regiments and 32 foreign regiments: including nine Swiss, 12 German, six Irish, two Scottish, and two Italian. The strength of regular troops was broken down as follows:

- The Régiment des Gardes françaises totalled 4,530 men and that of the Gardes suisses, 2,400 men.
- In 1756, the Grenadiers de France formed four battalions of 540 men each, for a total of 2,160 men.
- The Régiment du Roi, which had a particular organisation, consisted of 3,080 men. For the 79 other French regiments: 11 had four battalions, 52 had two battalions, and 16 had one battalion; for a total of 164 battalions. After the augmentation of August 1755, 155 of these battalions were increased to 925 men and nine battalions remained at 525 men. These latter battalions belonged to the regiments which had detached one of their battalions to the colonies, prior to the augmentation of 1755, and

1 Pierre Jean Grosley, *Mémoires sur les campagnes d'Italie de 1745 et 1746. Auxquels on a joint un journal des mêmes campagnes, tenu dans le bureau de M. le maréchal de Maillebois avec une explication de tous les passages et cols du Dauphiné versants en Savoie et en Piémont* (Amsterdam: chez Marc-Michel Rey, 1777), p.2.

would thus remain on an establishment of 12 companies per battalion throughout the war.

- The very theoretical total strength of this French infantry was 157,930 men.
- For the foreign infantry regiments, the nine Swiss regiments totalled 12,960 soldiers, the 12 German regiments 7,600 men, the nine Scottish and Irish regiments 6,345 men, and the two Italian regiments 1,370 men.
- The foreign infantry consisted of 28,275 men, or nearly 18 percent of the total strength of the infantry regiments in 1756.

It was only during the first two years of the conflict that new regiments were created. Thus in 1757, six additional regiments were raised: two German regiments, Bouillon and Royal Deux-Ponts, two Liégeois regiments, Vierzet and Horion; as well as the Régiment Royal Lorraine and the Régiment Royal Barrois, which were raised among battalions of the Lorraine militia. Finally, in 1758, only one levy was made, the Swiss Régiment d'Eptingen.

France, like other nations, maintained foreign regiments in its pay. About them minister Étienne-François de Choiseul wrote: 'The acquisition of a foreign soldier is equivalent to three men: the one we buy, the one we prevent the enemy from buying and the Frenchman that we keep for agriculture.'[2] The historical origins of these troops differed depending on the country from which they came.

The Swiss represented the first contingent of foreign troops in the service of France. They constituted a special case, they could be found in the service of France, the United Provinces, Spain, and the Kingdom of Naples amongst others. This strong presence of Swiss troops in the main armies of Europe ensured both the recognition of the Swiss Confederation and guaranteed its security. At that time, the canton of the Grey Leagues (Grisons in French) was not yet an integral part of the Confederation, which is why we see mentions of Swiss and Grisons. Recruitment was done through a capitulation, which was a contract between a canton and a sovereign; the regiment was then said to be acknowledged by the canton. Some of these capitulations were binding. Like that of the Régiment d'Erlach in 1672 where one can read: 'we will not use this regiment at any time against the powers of the same religion as the city of Bern.'[3] This caused some difficulties when Swiss regiments had to participate in the occupation of the states of certain Protestant princes during the Seven Years War. The Revocation of the Edict of Nantes, in 1685, provoked in the following years the departure of Protestant officers from the French service. At the beginning of the Seven Years War, the Régiment de Lochmann gives us another example of the intricacies of these capitulations, refusing to cross the Rhine on the pretext that the capitulation regulating

2 Quoted in Albert Babeau, *La vie militaire sous l'Ancien régime* (Paris: Firmin Didot, 1889), vol.2, p.351. Étienne-François de Choiseul Beaupré Stainville, duc de Choiseul was Minister for Foreign Affairs from 1758 to 1761 and Minister of War from 1761 to 1770. It seems important to note that his father, the marquis de Stainville, was Minister of the Emperor Charles VI of Austria and ambassador to the King of France before Starhemberg.

3 Beat Fidel Zurlauben, *Tableaux de la suisse* (Paris: Lamy, 1784), vol.1, p.346.

their service prohibited them from entering Germany. Beat-Fidel Zurlauben in his *Code militaire des Suisses* writes about this that: 'one of the first things that Swiss officers learn on entering the service is that the troops of the nation serving in France must not serve at sea or cross the Rhine.'[4]

The only Swiss infantry regiment attached to the French navy, the Régiment de Karrer (Hallwyl in 1752), was not governed by a capitulation. This regiment took part, along with the land forces, in the defence of the coasts of France. Thus, we see it in September 1757, alongside the Bigorre and Béarn regiments, occupying the Fouras Peninsula to protect Rochefort from the British threat.

German troops reflected France's quest for influence on its north-eastern borders, especially among the small Catholic and even Protestant states of Germany, seeking by this means to thwart the influence of Austria. Recruitment here was very different from that of the Swiss. For the latter, these were individual commitments of Swiss citizens, while in the case of German troops it was the prince who entered the service of the King of France and who recruited in his own lands. Even if troops returns showed a great diversity of origin, soldiers were mainly from across the Rhine. The colonel proprietors at the head of these regiments were most often general officers. The troops from Liège, who entered the service of France in 1757, must be placed in a similar context. From 1694 to 1763, three members of the House of Bavaria, loyal allies of France, had succeeded each other at the head of the Bishopric of Liège.

Irish and Scottish troops come to France because of a common enemy, the English. The arrival of Irish troops had been particularly important when Catholic James II had to cede his throne to William of Orange following the Glorious Revolution. Troops loyal to James II joined the French, Spanish or Austrian armies.

Even though France had often been involved in the provinces of northern Italy during previous wars, the contingent of Cisalpine troops maintained by France under Louis XV was very modest. If, under Louis XIV, there had been many Piedmontese or Savoyard regiments in French pay, in 1757, there were only two Italian regiments: Royal Italien, which had been raised in 1671 under Louis XIV; and Royal Corse which was created when France had conquered the island from the Genoese in 1739.

Capitaines of foreign regiments were forbidden to engage French subjects in their companies. If there were any, *capitaines* of French regiments were entitled to claim that they be given back and incorporated for six years in a French regiment. Troop returns and numerous decrees recalled the rule. The decrees of 1730, 1748, 1750, and the last in May 1752 demonstrate to us that the obligations faced by *capitaines* imposed opposite practices on them.

The rank and order of precedence of the regiments were determined by their seniority of creation. The concept thus stated seems simple, but, in reality, seniority was a complex question to settle. During the seventeenth and eighteenth centuries, many infantry units were constantly raised,

4 Beat Fidel Zurlauben, *Code militaire des Suisses, pour servir de suite à l'Histoire Militaire des Suisses, au service de la France* (Paris: Vincent, 1758), vol.1, p.151.

reformed, or disbanded, then restored or even reduced to a single company, making it very difficult to determine the exact seniority of the corps. The *colonels propriétaires* or *colonels lieutenants* were very finicky on this subject. Disagreements were not limited to simple court quarrels, disputes took place on the battlefields or during sieges, resulting in real insubordination. Examples are very numerous of regiments refusing to yield precedence as they were marching to the trench or taking position in the line of battle. For example, this forced Louis XIV to avoid grouping La Marine and Rambure, or Picardie and Piémont, in the same army corps. In December 1653, to settle these quarrels, Louis XIV asked to receive all relevant documents supporting the seniority claims of each of the regiments. He then published, on 1 April 1654, a decree which definitively settled the rank and rotation of each regiment. Nevertheless, some claims were not definitively settled. In 1684, during the brief War of the Reunions, Louis XIV needed additional troops. He assembled the garrison companies and transformed 26 of them into new regiments. But, to avoid quarrels of seniority, he issued their decree of creation on a daily basis, from 1 to 26 September 1684. Thus, the Régiment de Flandre was officially created on 1 September and the Régiment de Luxembourg on 26 September.

The Gardes françaises and the Gardes suisses, both attached to the *Maison du Roi*, were at the head of the infantry of France. Then came the six *Vieux* which were the first permanent regiments of the French infantry, originating from the 'Old Bands' of the sixteenth century. They were followed by the six regiments of the *Petits Vieux*. Finally, all other regiments were ordered according to their seniority of creation. On certain occasions, some regiments more recently created, in particular princely regiments, managed to fit in this hierarchy. By a game of musical chairs, the more senior regiment disappeared and was replaced by the other regiment. In such a case, the *colonel*'s company of the old regiment, guardian of its tradition and seniority, was preserved, becoming the colonel's company of the new regiment. Similarly, the *colonel*'s company of the new regiment became its second company, losing its rank and its white colour.

Other characteristics differentiated regiments between them. Thus, there were royal regiments of which the King was the *colonel* with at their head a *colonel lieutenant*, these were: Du Roi, Royal, Royal des Vaisseaux, Royal la Marine, Royal Comtois, La Couronne, Royal Roussillon, Royal Lorraine, Royal Barrois, Royal Pologne, Royal Deux-Ponts, Royal Italien, Royal Suédois, Royal Bavière, Royal Corse and Royal Écossais. Then came the regiments of the Queen and of the Dauphin (heir apparent), and those of the prince of the blood, also commanded by a *colonel lieutenant*. Then those of gentlemen, belonging to the nobility, and finally the provincial regiments. The end of the Seven Years War and the reforms undertaken by Belle-Isle and Choiseul marked the disappearance of the regiments of gentlemen in favour of provincial regiments.

To this regular infantry of hired soldiers, we must add the infantrymen from the provincial and coastguard militias. In particular the 11 regiments of Grenadiers royaux which totalled 11,880 men and 595 officers. As the Grenadiers of France, they were always at full strength. The 107 battalions of the provincial militias had a very theoretical strength of 63,130 men. If the Grenadiers royaux drawn from the militias participated in campaigns of the Seven Years War, only about 20 fusilier battalions of the provincial militia were sent to Germany and served to cover the rear positions of the army and the convoys. In 1758, they served as regiments of recruits to replenish the ranks of regular regiments. The remaining militia battalions were employed for the defence of the coasts or to replace regular regiments in garrison places.

There were also the coastguard militias, in particular the detached companies, with a total strength of 45,000 men. We could also mention the companies of invalids employed in places, but they were not real combat units.

The French Infantry

Most regiments had one or two battalions, exceptionally they had three or four battalions. The Seven Years War, like the previous ones, highlighted the weakness of regiments made up of only one or two battalions. This problem was one of the reasons for the reorganisation of the army in December 1762, which reduced the number of regiments while strengthening them. From 1749, at the end of the War of the Austrian Succession, all battalions had been reduced to 12 fusilier companies and one grenadier company. On 1 August 1755, each battalion was increased to 16 companies of 40 fusiliers and one company of 45 grenadiers.

The staff of a regiment included: one *colonel*, one *lieutenant colonel*, one *major*, one *aide major*, one *aumônier* (chaplain) and one *chirurgien* (surgeon), two *enseignes* per battalion with the rank of *lieutenant*, destined to carry the colours and one *maréchal des logis* (quartermaster). When the regiment had more than one battalion, a commander (the most senior *capitaine*) and an *aide major* were added to each additional battalion.

Fusilier companies consisted of one *capitaine*, one *lieutenant*, two *sergents*, three *caporaux* (corporals), three *anspessades*, 31 fusiliers and one drummer. The grenadier company consisted of one *capitaine*, one *lieutenant*, one *sous lieutenant*, two *sergents*, three *caporaux*, three *anspessades*, 36 grenadiers and one drummer.

The theoretical strength of a battalion was 685 men and 35 officers; however, companies were never at full strength. Insufficient recruitment, the killed, wounded and sick, deserters or prisoners markedly reduced its strength. In May 1757, at the very beginning of the war, a report by M. de Cornillon, *major général* of the infantry, estimated an average strength of 550 men per battalion in the field, a shortage of nearly 20 percent. To complete battalions, a decree of 1 May 1757 authorised the enlistment of up to five foreigners in the French infantry regiments. This measure seems to have been difficult to apply if we are to believe the King's instruction to *maréchal* de Richelieu in July 1757: 'it is true that this augmentation has had little effect up to now, either by the difficulty that these regiments claim to have experimented in recruitment, or by the ill will of *capitaines*, who find it to their advantage not to complete their companies.'[5] This weakness was linked to the lack of recruitment, and was compounded during the campaigns by the various detachments made by regiments and their battalions to create Volontaires de l'Armée ad hoc units, and to occupy conquered towns, fortresses and places, and to a lesser extent, the creation of chasseur companies in 1760 which were sometimes detached from their regiments of origin. Furthermore, from 1757, there were 16 fusiliers assigned to the service of the regimental guns.

Exceptionally, the Régiment du Roi had four battalions with companies of 45 men. The King also maintained five supernumeraries in each battalion, for a total of 770 men. In these battalions, there were also one *lieutenant en second* and one *sous lieutenant en second*, who only benefited from housing, but had no salary. From July 1758, a *major en second* and four *sous aides majors* were added to the regiment. The *colonel lieutenant*, who reported only to the King was a general officer. The *lieutenant colonel* and the battalion commanders all had the *colonel*'s patent. The Régiment du Roi, the Grenadiers de France and the Gardes françaises were the only French regiments where the *colonel* was a general officer.

In January 1760, the Régiment de Piémont, which had returned to France to recover, saw its organisation modified by the decree of 1 February 1760. It now consisted of four battalions of nine companies: one grenadier company of 45 men and eight fusilier companies of 80 men, excluding officers. This increase in the strength of the basic unit, which was the company, without any increase of the number of officers, lasted only one year. On 1 February 1761, a second decree re-established the previous organisation of the regiment.

Some regiments had the privilege to administer their own military justice, a privilege known as provostship or great staff. Provostship added one *prévôt*, one auditor, one registrar, one justice executioner and one or two *archers* (assistants to the executioner) to the staff of a regiment. In 1757, 34 infantry regiments had this privilege: Picardie, Champagne, Navarre, Piémont, Normandie, La Marine, La Tour du Pin, Bourbonnais, Auvergne, Belsunce, Mailly, Du Roi, Royal, Lyonnais, Dauphin, Anjou, Eu, La Reine, Royal des Vaisseaux, Orléans, La Couronne, Artois, Royal Roussillon, Condé, Bourbon, Royal Marine, Royal Comtois, Rohan Rochefort, Nice, Penthièvre, Chartres, Conti, Enghien and the Gardes Lorraines.

Regiments Destined for the Colonies

The organisation of the regiments destined for colonial service during the Seven Years War was the subject of specific decrees. The still unofficial war broke out in the colonies of Canada in 1754. The first regiments selected to embark for Québec did not apply the increase stipulated by the decree of August 1755 and preserved their organisation of 1749; namely 525 men

5 Philippe-Henri Grimoard, *Correspondance particulière et historique du Maréchal duc de Richelieu, en 1756, 1757 et 1758, avec M. Paris du Verney, ... suivie de Mémoires relatifs à l'expédition de Minorque, en 1756, et précédée d'une notice historique sur la vie du Maréchal* (London, Paris: Buisson, 1789), vol.1, p.32.

divided into 12 fusilier companies and a grenadier company. The first battalion of each of these regiments remained stationed in France while the second battalion embarked for the colonies. The regiments selected for colonial service were: La Reine, Artois, La Sarre, Royal Roussillon, Languedoc, Béarn and Guyenne sent to Canada and the single battalion of Angoumois destined for Louisiane. A first contingent set sail for Canada in August 1755: La Reine, Guyenne, Béarn and Languedoc. Eight of these companies were intercepted and captured by British vessels during their transfer to Canada, these were four companies from La Reine and four companies from Languedoc. To compensate for this reduction, a decree of 28 January 1757 established four new companies for each of these regiments. In April 1756, two new battalions sailed for Canada, they belonged to the La Sarre and Royal Roussillon regiments. In February 1757 a decree increased the strength of the companies of the battalions serving in Canada:

> ...orders that the said 13 companies, which form each of the said regiments of La Reine, La Sarre, Royal Roussillon, Languedoc, Guyenne and Béarn, which His Majesty has sent to Canada, will be brought to, namely: those of the said grenadiers of 45 men to 50, and those of fusiliers which are only 40 men, to the same number 50 men; the said increase making for each of the said battalions that of 125 men, which will put them at 650 men instead of 525...[6]

After the loss of Canada in 1760, the battalions were taken prisoner and then sent back to Europe. On their return to France, the battalions of the decimated regiments were reorganized by the decree of 1 February 1761, applicable from 1 April 1761. Thus, the regiments La Reine, La Sarre, Royal Roussillon, Languedoc, Guyenne, and Béarn saw their numbers reduced to one company of grenadiers of 40 men and 12 companies of fusiliers of only 20 men.

The regiments of Lorraine and Berry applied the augmentation to 17 companies, which had been stipulated by the decree of August 1755. Since part of their battalions were destined to be sent to India, they were reorganised in a particular way in November 1756. Their second battalion was subdivided to form the second and third battalions of their respective regiment, each of these battalions now consisting of eight fusilier companies and one grenadier company, each of these companies having a strength of 60 men. At the beginning of 1757, they embarked for the East Indies, with the first companies disembarked at Pondichéry in September 1757.

By a decree of 30 April 1762, the regiments of Boulonnais, Foix and Quercy, garrisoning Saint-Domingue, incorporated the colonial troops of Saint-Domingue. On this occasion, the latter troops were increased to 51 companies: three grenadier companies of 45 men, and 48 fusilier companies of 40 men each. These new companies were divided in groups of one grenadier company and 16 fusilier companies, each group forming a second battalion for the three regiments of Boulonnais, Foix and Berry (Quercy).

6 Henri Raymond Casgrain, *Lettres de la cour de Versailles au baron de Dieskau, au marquis de Montcalm et au chevalier de Lévis* (Quebec: Demers, 1890), p.56.

Shortly afterwards, on 31 January 1763, six other colonial picquet companies (50 men each), the so-called 'Trois Cent', were disbanded and incorporated into the regiments of Boulonnais, Foix, Quercy and Angoumois.

The Reform of 21 December 1762

The reform of December 1762 reduced the number of regiments while reinforcing them.

> His Majesty wanting to give permanent names to his French infantry regiments which do not have one, to ensure knowledge and remembrance of their actions, his intention is that in the future: the Régiment de Boisgelin takes the title of Béarn; the Régiment de Rougé that of the province of Flandre; the Régiment de Chastelux that of Guyenne; the Régiment de Vaubécourt that of the province of Aunis; the Régiment de Rosen that of the Dauphiné; the Régiment de Montmorin that of the province of Isle de France; the Régiment de Briqueville that of the province of Soissonnais; the Régiment de Montrevel that of the province of Berry; the Régiment de Montmorency that of the province of Haynault; the Régiment d'Aumont that of the province of Beauce; the Régiment de Puységur that of the province of Vivarais; the Régiment de Bouillé that of the province of Vexin; and the Régiment de Lastic that of the province of Beaujolais. And above all wants His Majesty that, notwithstanding the change of names of the said regiments, they currently retain the rank which they currently enjoy in the infantry.[7]

Thus, it was not Vivarais which gained some ranks, but simply Puységur which became Vivarais. Ten of the reformed regiments saw their soldiers placed on absolute leave, and three others were used to bring three other regiments up to four battalions. Thus, Guyenne was integrated into the Régiment du Dauphin, Flandre into the Régiment de Touraine and Berry into the Régiment d'Aquitaine.

The Swiss and Grison Infantry

The Swiss and Grison infantry comprised nine regiments at the outbreak of war in 1756, then 10 regiments after the creation of the Régiment d'Eptingen on 25 February 1758. Since the decree of 1 April 1756, the Swiss regiments had two battalions of six companies and each company numbered 120 men, including the five officers. This brought the theoretical strength of Swiss troops up to 14,400 men in 1758, including the newly raised Régiment d'Eptingen. Each company consisted of one *capitaine*, one *capitaine lieutenant*, one *lieutenant*, one *sous lieutenant*, one *enseigne*, three *sergents*, one *fourrier*, one *porte-enseigne*, one *capitaine d'arme*, one *prévôt*, four *caporaux*, four *anspessades*, 98 fusiliers and two drummers.

7 Acte royal, 10 December 1762, *Ordonnance du roi, concernant l'infanterie françoise du 10 décembre 1762* (Paris: Imprimerie royale, 1762).

The Swiss regiments, with their rank in 1758 were: Jenner No. 49, Boccard No. 50, Reding No. 51, Castella No. 52, Wittmer-Waldner No. 55, Planta-Darbonnier No. 63, Diesbach No. 90, Courten No. 91, Salis Mayenfeldt No. 102, Lochmann No. 117, Eptingen No. 122. The Swiss Regiment d'Hallwyl was destined for service with the navy and the colonies. It was placed under the authority of the Secretary of State of the Navy and did not rank among infantry regiments.

The German Infantry

At the outbreak of the Seven Years War in 1756, there were 12 German regiments of one, two or three battalions and the battalions had six or eight companies. Orders were given in German. The German regiments, with their rank in 1756, were: Alsace No. 36 at three battalions, Bentheim-Anhalt No. 46 at two battalions, La Marck No. 66 at two battalions, Royal Suédois No. 95 at two battalions, Royal Bavière No. 101 at two battalions, Lowendhal No. 106 at two battalions, Bergh No. 108 at one battalion, Nassau Ussingen No. 110 at one battalion, Nassau Saarbrück No. 111 at one battalion, Saint Germain No. 114 at one battalion, La Dauphine No. 115 at one battalion, Royal Pologne No. 116 at one battalion.

The decree of 16 September 1756 increased the companies of the six first German infantry regiments to 85 men: Alsace, Bentheim, La Marck, Royal Suédois, Lowendhal and Royal Bavière. The same year, another decree of 23 October extended the same measure to the remaining German regiments: La Dauphine, Nassau Saarbrück, Nassau Ussingen, Saint-Germain, Bergh and Royal Pologne. These regiments, which had only six companies per battalion were brought up to eight companies by the same decree. Therefore, by the end of 1756, all the German battalions had an identical composition of eight companies and each company numbered 85 men. The staff consisted of: one *colonel* and one *lieutenant colonel*, both having their own company, one *major*, one *aide major* per battalion, one interpreter, one chaplain, one surgeon, one auditor, one *prévôt*, one clerk, two *archers*, one justice executioner and one *tambour major*. The commanders of the second and third battalions had a company.

Each company was commanded by: one *capitaine*, one *capitaine en second*, one *premier lieutenant*, one *second lieutenant* and one *lieutenant en second*. The latter in the first and second companies acted as *enseignes* and carried the colours. The company consisted of three *sergents*, one *fourrier*, one *capitaine d'arme*, one *fourrier schutz*, three *caporaux*, one professional carpenter, two drummers, six *anspessades*, six grenadiers and 61 fusiliers. As we can see, for the German infantry, there was no separate grenadier company. However, in manoeuvres and in war, the grenadiers of the different companies were assembled to form a separate company.

At the beginning of 1757, two new German regiments were raised, bringing up to 14 the German regiments in the service of France. First of all, the Régiment de Bouillon raised in January 1757, which took the 118th rank. It had two battalions and each battalion had eight companies and the company had 85 men, excluding officers. The Royal Deux-Ponts, raised in February 1757, took the 119th rank in the infantry. It had three battalions, each of six companies and the company had 113 men, excluding officers. As we can see, the latter adopted a different organisation from the other regiments.

The comte de Saint-Germain, in a letter addressed to the marquis de Paulmy in January 1758, wrote:

> The difficulties encountered by the German regiments in recruiting come from the fact that the number of regiments has been increased too much; because they only have Alsace and a part of Lorraine, whereas formerly they had Flandre and all of new France, because the King currently has cartels [agreements for the exchange of prisoners and deserters] with all the princes of Germany.[8]

And in 1760: 'His Majesty, having recognized that in his German infantry there are several regiments too weak to be able to sustain themselves in the field, has deemed it appropriate to reinforce them by the incorporation of other regiments of this nation.'[9] Thus, the decree of 18 January 1760 completely reorganised the German infantry: the regiments Alsace, Anhalt, La Mark, Royal Suédois, Royal Bavière, Nassau and Royal Deux-Ponts received an additional battalion, while Lowendhal, Bergh, Saint-Germain, La Dauphine and Royal Pologne were abolished. The first battalion of Lowendhal was incorporated into Anhalt, the second battalion was incorporated into La Mark. Similarly, Bergh was incorporated into Alsace, Saint-Germain into Nassau, La Dauphine into Royal Bavière and Royal Pologne into Royal Suédois. The Régiment d'Alsace then consisted of four battalions, while the other German regiments had three battalions.

The decree of 21 December 1762 reorganised the foreign infantry on the same footing as the French infantry, each battalion being composed of eight fusilier companies and one grenadier company. The regiment Alsace, Anhalt, La Mark, Royal Suédois, Royal Bavière, Nassau and Royal Deux-Ponts were reduced to two battalions. Each battalion consisted of nine companies, including a grenadier company of 52 men and eight fusilier companies of 79 men. The grenadier company comprised one *capitaine*, one *lieutenant*, one *sous lieutenant*, two *sergents*, one *fourrier*, four *caporaux*, four *appointés*, 42 grenadiers and one drummer. The fusilier company comprised one *capitaine*, one *lieutenant*, one *sous lieutenant*, four *sergents*, one *fourrier*, eight *caporaux*, four *appointés*, 60 fusiliers and two drummers.

Henceforth, there were only three officers left in each company, namely: one *capitaine*, one *lieutenant en pied* and one *sous lieutenant*. However, as the *colonels propriétaires*, *lieutenant colonels* and *colonels commandants* of battalions kept a company, the King gave each of these companies a *capitaine lieutenant* who enjoyed the prerogatives of a full captain. The *capitaines en second* and *seconds lieutenants* previously attached to each company remained

8 Léon Mention, *Le comte de Saint Germain et ses réformes* (Paris: Clavel, 1884), p.284.

9 Acte royal, 18 January 1760, *Ordonnance du Roi, concernant les régimens d'infanterie allemande qui sont à son service du 18 janvier 1760* (Paris: Imprimerie royale, 1760).

in place, but they were not replaced, 'the intention of His Majesty being to let these functions die out.'[10] The regiments retained their great staff, that is to say their provostship, and a *sous aide major* was added to each battalion. The Régiment Royal Deux-Ponts had a *colonel lieutenant* in addition to the *colonel propriétaire* and to the *colonel commandant*. His Majesty also created two *enseignes porte-drapeaux* per battalion, they were drawn from the corps of *sergents* and ranked as officers.

The Irish and Scottish Infantry

At the outbreak of the Seven Years War, there were six Irish and two Scottish regiments in the service of France. They all had a single battalion. Orders were always given in English, even though anglophones did not represent the majority of the soldiers. The Irish and Scottish regiments, with their rank in 1756, were: Bulkeley Irish No. 92, O'Brien de Clare Irish No. 93, Dillon Irish No. 94, Rooth Irish No. 98, Berwick Irish No. 99, Royal Écossais No. 107, Lally Irish No. 109, and O'Gilvy Scottish No. 113.

Since the decree of 20 December 1756, battalions consisted of 12 fusilier companies of 55 men and one grenadier company of 45 men, excluding officers. Then the decree of January 1757 brought each battalion up to 705 men distributed in 13 companies: one grenadier company of 45 men and 12 fusilier companies of 55 men, excluding officers. The staff of each regiment consisted of one *colonel* and one *lieutenant colonel*, who had no company, one *major*, one *aide major*, one *aumônier* (chaplain), one *chirurgien major* (surgeon major), one *maréchal des logis* and an interpreter and two *enseignes* per battalion.

The regiments Rooth and Berwick obtained, by the decree of 25 December 1758, the privilege of provostship, which added one *prévôt* and his lieutenant, one clerk, five *archers*, and one justice executioner to its staff. The regiments also had 12 cadets, who served as soldiers but received higher pay.

Each fusilier company consisted of: one *capitaine*, one *capitaine en second*, one *lieutenant*, one *lieutenant en second*, three *sergents*, four *caporaux*, four *anspessades*, 43 fusiliers and one drummer. The grenadier company consisted of: one *capitaine*, one *capitaine en second*, one *lieutenant*, one *lieutenant en second*, two *sergents*, three *caporaux*, three *anspessades*, 36 grenadiers and one drummer.

The Italian Infantry

The regiments Royal Italien and Royal Corse were each reorganised by the decree of 29 January 1757 to a single battalion of 685 men, in nine companies: one company of 45 grenadiers and eight companies of 80 fusiliers. The staff of these regiments consisted of one *colonel* and one *lieutenant colonel*, who

10 Acte royal, 21 December 1762, *Ordonnance du roi, concernant les régimens d'infanterie allemande du 21 décembre 1762* (Metz: Collignon, 1763).

had no company, one *major*, one interpreter, one chaplain and one *tambour major*. They had provostship since the decree of 25 February 1758 and this privilege added one *prévôt* and his lieutenant, one clerk, five *archers* and one justice executioner to their staff.

Each fusilier company consisted of: one *capitaine*, one *capitaine en second*, one *lieutenant en premier*, one *lieutenant en second*, five *sergents*, five *caporaux*, seven *anspessades*, 15 *appointés*, 46 fusiliers and two drummers. The grenadier company consisted of: one *capitaine*, one *lieutenant*, one *lieutenant en second*, three *sergents*, three *caporaux*, five *anspessades*, 33 grenadiers and one drummer.

The Liégeois Infantry

In 1757, the Bishopric of Liège, administered by the House of Bavaria allied to France, supplied two regiments. These were two regiments raised according to the decree of 25 March 1757 and commanded by the comte de Horion and the Baron de Vierzet. Each regiment had two battalions and was organised as the German infantry, the only difference being the presence in the two first companies of an *enseigne* charged to carry the flag instead of a *lieutenant en second*. Each battalion had six companies and the company had 85 men. The staff comprised one *colonel*, one *lieutenant colonel*, each commanding a company, one *major*, one *aide major* per battalion, one chaplain, one surgeon, one auditor, one *prévôt*, one clerk, one *tambour major*, two *archers*, and one executor of justice. Each company was commanded by one *capitaine*, with one *capitaine en second*, one *premier lieutenant*, two *lieutenants* and one *lieutenant en second*, who in the first and second companies served as *enseignes* to carry the colours, three *sergents*, one *fourrier*, two *capitaines d'arme*, one *fourrier schutz*, three *caporaux*, one professional carpenter, two drummers, six *anspessades*, six grenadiers and 61 fusiliers.

The Grenadiers de France

The Régiment des Grenadiers de France was created by the decree of 15 February 1749, by grouping in a single corps all companies of grenadiers of the infantry regiments, which had been disbanded after the Treaty of Aix-la-Chapelle 'to continue to maintain in His Majesty's service troops so precious to preserve.'[11] At its creation, the regiment occupied the 137th rank, after the Scottish Régiment d'Albany, and before the Volontaires de Flandre. This elite regiment could not remain at the end of the list of infantry regiments as the rule, where seniority determined the rank, would have it. Consequently, the decree of 15 September 1750 gave it rank no. 40, immediately after the Régiment de Bourbon. To achieve this result, the day of the official creation of the first grenadiers in the French infantry in 1667 was chosen as the

11 Acte royal, 15 February 1749, *Ordonnance du roy pour la formation d'un régiment sous le titre de Grenadiers de France du 15 février 1749* (Paris: Imprimerie royale, 1749).

reference date. By this decree, the regiment acquired 83 years of seniority. In 1762, it took the name of Corps des Grenadiers de France and was disbanded in 1771.

The establishment of the regiment was 2,160 grenadiers, distributed in four brigades of 12 companies each. As noted previously, all grenadier companies were always at full strength.

A *lieutenant general* was placed at the head of the regiment with the title of *inspecteur commandant*. The marquis de Saint-Pern commanded from the creation of the regiment in 1749, and the comte de Choiseul-Stainville succeeded him in March 1761. The staff also included a second in command, ranking as *colonel*, a chaplain, a surgeon and a treasurer. Surprisingly, this elite corps did not have provostship. Until July 1756, there was a single *major* for the entire regiment, when he was temporarily replaced by a *major* for each of the four brigades. 'His Majesty regulates by his decree dated 8 July 1756, that each brigade is commanded by a *colonel*, a *lieutenant colonel* and a *major de brigade* and that the staff of each brigade is composed of one *sergent major* and one *aide major*, where the places of *sergent majors* would be filled by the present *aides majors*.'[12] Just four months later, the decree of 6 October 1759 re-established the previous organisation and the *majors de brigade* were suppressed.

The creation of the regiment following the reform of many infantry regiments led to an overabundance of officers. Originally, the brigades were commanded by sixteen *colonels* at the rate of four per brigade. By 1756, there were 24 *colonels* attached to this corps, at a rate of six *colonels* per brigade; and regularly some supernumerary colonels: two in 1759, one in 1760. This number of *colonels* entailed a particular constraint: they could only command each brigade 'par quartiers' – in this case only two months a year. And we find the same situation for the *lieutenant colonels* who, on the basis of two per brigade, served on a semi-annual rotation. In the *Mémoires pour servir à l'histoire de notre temps*, which reported the campaigns of *maréchal* de Broglie between 1759 and 1761, there is a complete instruction of the marquis de Saint Pern in which he organises the tours of duty of these 48 companies with the army, for detachments as well as for honour guards, camp service, etc.

In his memoirs, the Prince de Montbarrey informs us that this regiment was also a 'military school for young people who, by their birth or by the services of their fathers, claimed to obtain the *colonel*'s patent, and who however were too young to be entrusted with the chief administration of a regiment.'[13] Of the 16 *colonels* at the creation of the regiment, eight came from disbanded regiments and eight were young men of good family; including the Prince of Montbarrey himself, then only 17 years old.

The decree creating the regiment specified that each brigade had a flag with one *enseigne* per brigade. Therefore, there were only four colours for this

---

12 Acte royal, 8 July 1756, *Ordonnance concernant le régiment des grenadiers de France du 8 juillet 1756* (Paris: Imprimerie Royale, 1756).

13 Alexandre Montbarrey, *Mémoires autographes de M. le prince de Montbarrey* (Paris: Eymery, 1826), p.89.

regiment, and these were all ordinance colours, the regiment has no colonel company, nor a colonel colour. This is confirmed by the 1757 manuscript of the Musée de l'armée, which represents only two ordinance flags under the figure of the *Grenadier de France*.

Each of the 48 companies was composed of 45 men: two *sergents*, three *caporaux*, three *anspessades*, one drummer and 36 grenadiers. It was commanded by a *capitaine*, a *lieutenant* and a *sous lieutenant*. 'One of the two *lieutenants* is usually a soldier of fortune, whom his merit and his services have raised to the rank of officer.'[14] Each brigade also had a small corps of carpenters attached to it. It was composed of a *sergent* and a *caporal* at the head of 11 grenadiers-carpenters.

Height was an important factor to join the Grenadiers de France; from 1753, it was fixed at at least five pieds five pouces (1.76m). Part of the soldiers were drawn from the Grenadiers royaux de la Milice, 'it is a singular distinction and an honour that the King wanted to make to his *grenadiers royaux* to admit them in a corps such as the Grenadiers de France, which was made up of the elite of his troops.'[15] But to avoid depleting the corps of the Grenadiers royaux, it became necessary to change this recruitment rule. From 1 May 1757, the Grenadiers de France could only recruit among the grenadiers postiches, that is to say the recruit companies of the Grenadiers royaux. Then, from the decree dated 21 December 1762, recruitment was made among the grenadier companies of each of the French infantry regiment.

The Grenadiers de France took part in of all the campaigns of the Seven Years War, where they were brigaded with the Grenadiers royaux. With the reorganisation of December 1762, they became the Corps des Grenadiers de France. They were still organised in four brigades of 12 companies, but the brigade flags were suppressed.

The staff of the Corps was composed of one *colonel*, one *colonel commandant*, two *lieutenant colonels*, two *majors*, four *aides majors*, four *sous aides majors*, one treasurer, one quartermaster, one chaplain and one surgeon. A band was attached to the regimental staff: one *tambour major* and 12 musicians, including three bassoons, three oboes, three clarinets and three hunting horns. The staff of a brigade was composed of one *lieutenant colonel* and one *major* for two brigades. Each of the 48 companies was commanded by one *capitaine*, with one *lieutenant* and one *sous lieutenant* and consisted of two *sergents*, one *fourrier* (quartermaster sergeant), four *caporaux*, four *appointés* replacing the *anspessades*, 40 grenadiers and one drummer.

---

14 *Encyclopédie Méthodique, Art militaire* (Paris: Briasson, David, Lebreton, Durand, 1757), vol.7, p.936.

15 Jacques Gebelin, *Histoire des milices provinciales (1688–1791) Le tirage au sort sous l'Ancien Régime* (Paris: Hachette, 1882), p.157.

2

The Hierarchy of an Infantry Regiment

The Staff of the Regiment

The Colonel

The *colonel* was proprietor of his charge, and the price of each regiment varied according to its hierarchical place in the infantry. With the exception of the charge of *colonel lieutenant* in the Régiment du Roi, all other regiments could be bought. To obtain a regiment, it was necessary to obtain the approval of the King; rank and money conditioned its obtention. Until the decree of July 1661, the *colonel* was designated by the title of *mestre de camp d'infanterie*, which was suppressed by this decree. His company became the *colonel*'s company and first company of the regiment. With this same decree, the King arrogated to himself the appointment of the *lieutenants colonels*, without having to take into account the seniority of the *capitaines* from whom they came.

In the royal regiments where the King was the nominal *colonel*, he who commanded the regiment in his name was called *colonel lieutenant*. That was the case for the regiments Du Roi, Royal, Royal des Vaisseaux, Royal La Marine, Royal Comtois, La Couronne, Royal Roussillon, Royal Lorraine, Royal Barrois, Royal Pologne, Royal Deux-Ponts, Royal Italien, Royal Suédois, Royal Bavière, Royal Corse and Royal Écossais. Similarly, the princes' regiments were also commanded by a *colonel lieutenant*: Dauphin, Aquitaine, Eu, La Reine, Orléans, Conti, Condé, Bourbon, Penthièvre, Chartres, Enghien, comte de la Marche and La Dauphine. The same was true for the Gardes Lorraine*s* of the King of Poland, when it served with the army.

From 1749, the *colonels* had no more companies, in other words, they were no longer *capitaines* of their company. When he assumed effective command of his regiment during a battle, which was still often the case during the Seven Years War, the *colonel*, distinguished by a gorget and a spontoon, took his place three paces in front of the *capitaines*. This position in front of the regiment explains the heavy toll they paid in battle. In peacetime, *colonels* were only required to be present at their regiment for three months a year.

The Lieutenant Colonel

The *lieutenant colonel* was a non-venal office (not one sold by the state), which was given by the King to experienced *capitaines* who were not wealthy enough to acquire the charge of *colonel*. In his choices, the King did not necessarily follow the seniority of the patents of the *capitaines*. It was the *lieutenant colonel* who commanded in the absence of the *colonel*, this happened frequently, especially in peacetime. This function had initially been essentially honorary then, when the position of *colonel général de l'infanterie* was abolished in 1661, it became a real military appointment. The decrees of 1 December 1661, 27 March 1664 and 25 July 1665 set its prerogatives, in particular in relation to other *capitaines* who contested its authority.

According to Bombelles, a good *lieutenant colonel* had to be regarded as the father of the regiment, and should have deserved by his valour, his exactness, his integrity and his merit the trust, respect and friendship of officers and soldiers.[1] He and the *major* were the two essential cogs of the regimental staff, they were in fact forbidden to be on leave at the same time.

The Major

The *major* was a very special officer. First of all, he was a *capitaine* and his seniority rank was that of his *capitaine*'s commission, not that of his appointment as *major.* Just like the *lieutenant colonel*, it was the King who appointed him and, theoretically, he could not be promoted to *major* in the regiment where he had previously served as *capitaine*. As his authority extended to all companies, he did not command any. He did not wear the gorget like other officers. Here is what Boussanellles writes in his *Observations Militaires* in 1761: 'the *officiers majors* of a regiment are the pivot, the axis, the master wheel; they are in a nutshell the main springs.'[2]

The *major* was charged with the 'detail' of the regiment, cumulating a number of responsibilities such as the management of the public funds of the regiment, the keeping of accounting ledgers, ensuring the use of the deductions made by the *capitaines*, as well as the dispatching of furloughs and leaves, and of correspondence with inspectors and with the Ministry of War. He was also responsible for keeping the registers, such as information on the officers of his regiment: the date of their commission, their furloughs, their place of residence, etc.

The *major* supervised the general training of the regiment, in particular drill, manoeuvres and weapon handling. He had to perfectly know all regulations. And, as we will see about infantry tactics during battles, he was charged to stand in front of the regiment to transmit orders. He kept a diary where he transcribed all details of the daily life of the regiment: officers commanding on that day, guard duties, detachments, *étapes* (the daily allowance for soldier upon the march), the organisation of bread and meat distributions, and much more.

1 Henri François, comte de Bombelles, *Mémoires pour le service journalier de l'infanterie* (Paris: Delatour, 1744), p.317.

2 Louis de Boussanelle, *Observations militaires* (Paris: Jombert, Cellot, 1761), p.32.

In garrison, the *major* was charged with troop discipline, and he liaised with the mayors, aldermen and syndics of the cities. In a court martial, he read the judgement. He summoned and inspected the guards and took the orders of his *colonel* or *lieutenant colonel*. He organised guards, parties and detachments to escort convoys. He received 'Le Mot' – the password of the day – from the staff and transmitted it to the *sergents* and *maréchaux des logis*. On campaign, he received the orders transmitted by the *major de brigade* of the staff and referred them to his *colonel* and *lieutenant colonel* for their execution by the *capitaines* and *sergents*.

The *aide major* assisted the *major* in his tasks. He often had a commission of *capitaine* but did not enjoy the rights and salaries attached to this rank. Only when his seniority finally allowed him to join the group of *capitaines* could he assume the rank that his commission had given him. He was chosen by the *colonel* among the *lieutenants*. He ranked with the *lieutenants* according to the date of his patent of *aide major*. There were also some *garçons majors*, who were in fact *sous lieutenants* occupying this function, which was created during the Seven Years War to allow each detachment of a regiment to be always accompanied by an *officier major*, as prescribed, for example, by the instruction of the Prince de Soubise in 1761: '…when the gentlemen commanding a battalion will be in service, a *garçon major* will accompany them.'[3]

Since the *major* regulated the details of all companies, *sergents* were subordinated to him. This was the reason why there were *sergents majors*, who informed the *major* of the regiment of everything happening in their companies, for example the progress of the training of recruits, or the state of the sick. 'In this capacity they must give him an exact account everything that comes to their knowledge, and which relates to the service, without excepting even what their own officers could do which were contrary to it.'[4] The decree of 1762 confirmed them this authority: 'He [His Majesty] wants that in the future the charge of *major* be in all infantry regiments a higher rank than that of *capitaine* …'[5]

The Capitaine

The *capitaine* was the pivot of the regiment due to the responsibility he had for recruits and the maintenance of his company. But this also represented a major flaw, as the comte de Saint-Germain wrote in December 1757:

> The method of assigning the troops to the captain is pernicious, and as long as it remains, there will be no subordination. The captains get their recruits only by paying for them, because they compete with each other for them. One does not want to lose a recruit who costs a lot, and to keep him, one avoids giving him the

3 Anon., *Instruction pour l'infanterie de l'armée du roi commandée par M. le maréchal prince de Soubise* (Publication details unknown), p.7.

4 Louis Hippolite Bacquet, capitaine d'infanterie, *L'infanterie au 18e siècle, l'organisation* (Paris, Nancy: Berger Lervrault, 1907), p.22.

5 Acte royal, 10 December 1762, *Ordonnance du roi concernant l'infanterie françoise du 10 décembre 1762* (Paris: Imprimerie Royale, 1762).

> slightest displeasure, one allows him everything. It is only a question of being able to present men to the commissary; but as discipline could displease them and make them desert, one does not get any. The *lieutenant* of a company would not dare say a word to a soldier; that would be like cutting down a fruit tree in the *capitaine*'s farm.[6]

Since 1654, the *capitaine* no longer held a venal office (one that could be purchased), therefore he was not officially the owner of his company as the *colonel* was of his regiment. In this regard, Héricourt recalls 'that it is not permitted to sell any company office in the infantry',[7] while at the same time it was possible to buy a cavalry company. The reality was quite different and unofficially these infantry companies could be sold, since they were an important element in the hierarchical progression of the career officer.

Maintaining a company required an officer to be sufficiently wealthy. In 1757 the marquis de Mailly, *colonel* of his own infantry regiment gave recommendations for choosing a good *capitaine*:

> It is of the utmost consequence to put at the head of the companies only wealthy officers, who can get good recruits and do not spare money to have handsome men, who can maintain their soldiers cleanly in clothing, shoes… and who is able to remedy accidents that happen all too frequently. The income of an infantry *capitaine* is not sufficient for this; and, when he has no resources from home, his troops are always very bad, their recruits acquired on the cheap and his soldiers, poorly maintained.[8]

The *capitaine* dressed and equipped his soldiers, he collected the pay of his troops according to the review made by the commissaries. He took deductions from this pay for the upkeep of uniforms, shoes, tents, bread, and other necessaries. These sums constituted what was called the 'masse et l'ustensile.' He paid the meagre remainder to the soldiers, who used it to supplement their daily meals, to go to the cabarets of the garrison or to the food vendors who followed the army. To encourage the *capitaine* to have the most complete company possible, in addition to his salary, he received a bonus according to the size of his company. Thus, he received eight livres 10 sols per month for 38 men, 25 livres 10 sols if he had 39 men and 42 livres and 10 sols if his company was at full strength. This was the reason for fake soldiers or 'passe-volants'. To avoid abuse, it was recommended to the commissaries of war, during reviews, to count the soldiers by having them pass over a bridge or through the gate of a city.

It was the *capitaine* who created the *sergents*, *caporaux* and *anspessades* in his company. He kept a record of his company. The place and dates of enlistment, ages, and general descriptions of the troops were recorded.

---

6 Claude-Louis comte de Saint-Germain, *Correspondance particulière du Comte de Saint-Germain avec M. Paris du Vernay* (London, Paris: Buisson, 1789), vol.1, p.173.

7 Nicolas d'Héricourt, *Elémens de l'art militaire* (La Haye: Pierre Gosse, 1748), vol.2, p.140.

8 Louis Tueytey, *Les officiers sous l'ancien régime* (Paris: Pion, 1908), p.130.

A major element of the reform of December 1762 related to the organisation of infantry regiments was the removal of the burden of recruitment by the *capitaine*, this responsibility now falling to the State. This reform, if it was an advantage for the army, was less advantageous for the general condition of the soldier. Until then, the *capitaine* was concerned about the fate of the soldier in his company. He had, out of interest, a sometimes-attentive ear to his grievances. From Choiseul's reform, the soldier's interlocutor became the *colonel*, more interested in the proud appearance of his regiment and the perfect execution of manoeuvres than the daily life of the soldier.

When companies were at full strength, a *capitaine en second* was sometimes added to assist the *capitaine* in his duties. It was often a *capitaine* whose company had been disbanded. There were also *capitaines postiches* who were temporarily appointed to command a company in the absence of a *capitaine* taken prisoner of war. In regiments of several battalions, for each battalion with the exception of that containing the *colonel*'s company, there was a *capitaine commandant de bataillon*. He was also designated as *premier capitaine*, and was provided with a letter authorising him to exert command and was counted in the staff of the regiment. These *premiers capitaines* were abolished in 1762 and re-established by the decree of 11 June 1774.

The *capitaine* of the grenadier company was privileged because he had no difficulty with recruitment. His company always having to be complete, he was permitted to take the men necessary to him, from among the fusilier companies of his battalion. He had to pay compensation of 25 to 30 livres per man to the *capitaine* of the fusilier company.

Junior Officers

The Lieutenant

The *lieutenant* had the same functions as the *capitaine*, and in his absence he commanded the company. The regulation of 1753 required him to inspect weapons on a daily basis to make sure that they were in good condition with dry ammunition, flints in sufficient quantity, and all kit was complete. They ordered any repairs and reported the results of the inspections to the *colonel* of the regiment. It was a venal office.

The Enseigne

Only the *colonel*'s company and that of the *lieutenant colonel* had *enseignes*. The *enseigne* was the 'custodian of the honour of the regiment; the *enseigne* must prefer death a thousand times to the shame of abandoning his colour or to surrender it cowardly to his enemy' wrote Du Bousquet.[9]

There were two *enseignes* per battalion, attached to the two first companies. They ranked as *lieutenants* and were subject to the same duties as *lieutenants*. It was the decree of 10 February 1749, reforming the French

9 Louis Du Bousquet, *Instructions militaires sur le service de garnison et de campagne* (Rouen: Besongne, 1769), vol.1, p.146.

infantry at the end of the War of the Austrian Succession, which regulated the new organisation.

> Article V: The King's intention being that in the future there would be only two flags per battalion, including a white one attached to the company designated as the *colonel*'s company, two *enseignes* per battalion will be maintained to carry these flags [...], which *enseignes* shall have the rank of *lieutenants*; [...] On the day of battle, they are responsible for carrying the flag, at their side an old *sergent* is placed to defend it and raise the flag in case the *enseigne* is killed or wounded.[10] When the *enseignes* are absent, the last *capitaine* carries the white flag.

By the decree of December 1762, *enseignes* were replaced by *porte-drapeaux*, drawn from the corps of *sergents* with the rank of *sous lieutenants*.

The Maréchal des Logis

In the infantry, unlike the cavalry, *maréchal des logis* was more of a function than a rank and the one who occupied it would, depending on the period, occupy a higher or lower rank, he was often an *aide major*, that is a *lieutenant*. If the name was retained in the cavalry or the *Maréchaussée*, in the infantry, he became *sergent fourrier* at the end of the *Ancien Régime*. The *maréchal des logis* of the infantry was responsible for marking the camp of his regiment, and he distributed the quarters to the *fourriers* of each company.

Other Personnel of the Staff

The Prévôt of the Regiment

The *prévôt* assumed a judicial function and he was present only in the regiments which the King had allowed to administer their own justice. Regiments having provostship were said to have a *grand état-major*. In such a case, the *prévôt*, one *lieutenant*, one clerk, five *archers* (soldier of military justice) and one justice executioner were added to the regimental staff. As *prévôt* of the army, he began proceedings to court martial deserters, marauders and others. He interrogated and confronted the witnesses then he submitted the case to the *major* who made his own conclusions. Staff officers assembled in a tribunal to pass judgment.

The *prévôt* of the regiment fixed the price of the foodstuff sold by the vivandiers in his quarters, and he established butcher shops. *Prévôts* were non-combatants, and on the day of a battle they remained with the baggage. They disappeared with the reform of December 1762.

The Trésorier of the Regiment

The *trésorier* (treasurer) made their official appearance only by the decree of December 1762, but their existence is attested much earlier in the numerous texts regulating the organisation of regiments, in particular for the

10 Acte royal, 10 February 1749, *Ordonnance du Roy concernant les régiments de son infanterie françoise du 10 févier 1749* (Lyon: Valfray, 1749).

management of the various deductions. He was a civilian and was presented by the *colonel*, the *lieutenant colonel* and the *major* of the regiment, to the Secretary of State for War, who, if he agreed, established a patent for him.

The Aumôniers and Chirurgiens of the Regimental Staff

Clerics were chosen by the *colonel* or the *mestre de camp* of the regiment, who proposed them to the Secretary of State for War. They did not belong to a particular congregation. There were many Recollets, but also Oratorians and others. The *aumônier* received a salary and their ministry extended only to military personnel. For the navy, a seminary had been created at Rochefort in 1686 to train chaplains for naval vessels. In the French regiments, there was no religion but that of the King, that is Roman Catholic. The Protestant religion was recognized in the Swiss and German regiments such as the Gardes suisses, who maintained two clerics: a Protestant pastor and a Catholic priest. Exceptionally, the Régiment suédois maintained only a Protestant pastor.

'The chaplains have their complete chapel which the King provided them on entering campaign.' Just as parish registers constituted the civil status of the *Ancien Régime*, in military hospitals, *aumôniers* kept registers of death 'which they have signed at the end of each month by two officers of the hospital and by the commissaries to war, which has to be in accordance with that of the contractor. He draws from this register two certificates, signed and legalised by the commissaries of war, to send one to the regiment, and the other to the family of the deceased; and for foreign troops, to send one only to the regiment.'[11]

The military surgeons of the sixteenth and seventeenth centuries were still often the barbers of the regiment. Physicians and *chirurgiens* had civilian training. There was a training body specific to military medicine, as shown by one of the articles of the regulations for military hospitals of 1747. The first amphitheatres for teaching specific to military medicine were formalised only in 1775 and the school of the military health service was created in Lyon only in 1888. Before the decree of 2 May 1781, it was the *mestre de camp*, the *colonel*, who chose the *chirurgien*. From 1781 only licensed surgeons were admitted, appointed by the Minister.

The Non-commissioned Officers of the Regiment

Non-commissioned officers derived their authority from the *colonels* and above all from the *capitaines* who appointed them.

The Sergents

The *sergent* or *sergens* is one of the oldest military ranks in the army. They were chosen by the *capitaine*, and the Gardes-Françaises was the only regiment where the King had to approve this choice. Most often a *sergent* had spent

11 François-Alexandre Aubert de La Chesnaye Des Bois, *Dictionnaire militaire* (Paris: Gissey, Bordelet, David, 1745), vol.1, p.76.

his entire military career in the same company of which he was one of the pillars, and where he had often entered as a private and had been noticed for his abilities. Du Bousquet in his class prepared for the students of the École Royale Militaire writes: 'it is infinitely important for a *capitaine* to have good *sergents*, since they are the soul of his company and the first motive which sets it in motion: he must choose them brave, intelligent, of good morals: it is good that they have size, strength and good figure: it is useful that they know how to write and number.'[12]

Sergents had both an administrative role and the role of instructor. They were in charge of the administration of the company – dates of enlistment, terms and prices of enlistment, the state of the sick, of the absences and other paperwork. They had to know perfectly the handling of weapons, the evolutions, and the manoeuvres that he had to teach to the *caporaux* and soldiers of their company. They made sure that the soldiers were well behaved. 'There must be a *sergent* of the week for each company, who must be the first to get up and the last to go to bed.' 'That whenever it is found that at the said time [9:00 a.m.] the stairs will not be swept, the rooms clean, the beds not made, that there will be rubbish behind the doors, under the beds, or on the stairs, the *sergent* will pay ten sols for the poor.'[13]

The King also created *sergents majors*, to whom he issued a commission to hold the rank of *capitaine*. They were subordinate to the *capitaine* of their company, but also to the *major* of the regiment to whom they had to report on the state of their company.

By decrees, besides the marks of his rank which were threads of real silver or gold rather than false silver or gold, the *sergent* had always benefited from special consideration as to the quality of the cloth and the making of his uniform. He was also distinguished by his halberd.

The Fourrier

The function of *fourrier* (quartermaster) is very old, but it was only formalized in 1758 by a decree which created a *fourrier* in each infantry company: 'they were the stewards, the bursars of each company.' They ranked with the *sergents* according to the seniority of their appointment. They had to know how to read and write, they were in charge of the administration of the company of which they held the muster roll, relieving in this the *sergent* who could devote themselves to military training. He was also responsible for distributing accommodation tickets to soldiers. In 1776 he became a *sergent major*, previously he was only equivalent to that rank (decree of 1 March 1768).

The Caporal

A company was divided into three or four squads placed under the command of a *caporal*. *Caporaux* assisted the *sergent* in their tasks. They had to be

12 Louis Du Bousquet, *Instructions militaires sur le service de garnison et de campagne* (Rouen: Besongne, 1769), vol.1, p.39.

13 Pierre Briquet, *Code militaire ou compilation des ordonnances des Rois en France, concernant les gens de guerre* (Paris: Durand, 1761), vol.4, p.356.

educated enough to keep a muster roll by company and by barrack room. The *caporal* of the day controlled the clothing and armament of the soldiers, he was head of the barrack room. He was responsible for the chores – getting coal, wood, peat, and candles – and for the equipment of the guardhouse: torches or lanterns, for the hooded canvas great-coats to protect the guards in winter, for shovels and tools, etc. He was also responsible for the training of his squad, which he reported to his *sergent*. A squad was said to be 'broken' when it was made up of soldiers from different companies to perform a service. The *caporal* posted and changed the sentries, he had to ensure good order in the guardhouse, he commanded a squad, received the word of the rounds when they passed near his unit. During rounds, it was he who organised the guard posts and who controlled the changing of the sentries. He received the rounds with his sword in hand, the thumb of his left hand resting on the point of his sword which he put on the stomach of whoever was arriving, who at the same time gave him the password. In the cavalry, he was known as a *brigadier*.

The Anspessade

The *anspessade*, sometimes also written *lansepessade*, was not a non-commissioned officer, but a private, who received slightly higher pay as a form of reward for seniority and bravery. In the reviews of the war commissaries, he took the name of *appointé*. Often, he served as an instructor and replaced the *caporal* in his absence. This title was abolished in 1776, then restored in 1788 before being definitively abolished in 1793.

3

The Soldier, his Recruitment and Training

Recruitment and Enlistment

From the beginning of the eighteenth century, recruitment was less and less constrained, voluntary enlistment tended to become the rule. But until the end of the *Ancien Régime*, there would always be the touts, a 'man who by his cleverness induces young people to take part … they make men on the cheap and resell them to *capitaines*. There are such touts in Paris who do no other job all year round.'[1] It was easier to recruit in towns where the number of young people making a living from makeshift and small trades was larger. As *capitaines* were asked to maintain their entire company and they received a bonus proportionate to the number of soldiers present, they therefore had every interest in not being too fussy about the conditions by which enlistment was obtained. 'One of the greatest in this matter is that of agreements, that is to say the price that an officer demanded to release a family child.'[2] Forced recruitment, by trickery or violence, was one of the causes of the significant rate of desertion, despite the galley or death penalties incurred by the deserter. This is why sanctions against forced engagements became more and more severe over the course of the century: 'His Majesty expressly forbids all *capitaines*, and other officers, not to enlist any cavalry, dragoons and soldiers, who is not a volunteer'[3] This was repeated in all the successive decrees from Louis XIV up to the end of the *Ancien Régime*. At a certain point, enlistment had to be confirmed, in the presence of the person who contracted it, before a commissary of war or a sub-delegate of the intendancy. The eighteenth century also saw of the appearance of recruitment advertising by means of illustrated posters. Under the ministry of Belle-Isle, a small revolution began during the war in 1760, with the creation of recruit battalions.[4] It led

1 La Chesnaye, *Dictionnaire militaire*, vol.2, p.282.
2 Anon., *Code municipal* (Paris: Prault, Vallat-Lachapelle, 1756), p.190.
3 Pierre Briquet, *Code militaire ou compilation des ordonnances des Rois en France, concernant les gens de guerre* (Paris: Nyon, 1761), vol.5, p.184.
4 Auguste de Foucquet, duc de Belle-Isle, was Minister of War from March 1758 to January 1761.

to the decree of December 1762, then of February 1763 for the creation of regiments of recruits and to the end of recruitment by *capitaines*.

Most soldiers were illiterate, and at the bottom of certain forms one can read: 'not knowing how to write, made his mark' or 'declared not knowing the use of writing and made his ordinary mark.' But that was not always the case, as shown by the rare, but touching letters written to their families by enlisted soldiers or militiamen. And, if he was educated enough to be able to keep a book, he became a *caporal* and then a *sergent* or a *fourrier*.

Enlistment was for six years. Those who obtained promotions to the ranks of *anspessade*, *caporal*, *sergent*, or who became grenadiers, had to serve three additional years. They were free to renounce to these promotions. At the end of these six years, they could re-enlist for a shorter period, the minimum being in theory one year. Alsatians could serve in French or German regiments, but until 1727 they could not be admitted to the Gardes françaises. Finally, by a rare but costly privilege, the subjects of the Comtat Venaissin and of the state of Avignon had three days to retract from their enlistment, but in addition to the bonus they had to return, they had to pay an indemnity of 30 livres to the *capitaine*.

Upon enlistment, the soldier took a sobriquet, and was known by this new name, which appeared on the muster rolls. This sobriquet might evoke a place of origin, a city, a province such as Provençal, Poitvin, or Lorrain, or a saint, such as Saint-Louis, Saint-Briac, or Saint-André. It could also allude to the soldier's physiognomy, for example Lagrandeur (large), Belair (good-looking), Bellerose (good-looking and ruddy), or sometimes retain the original or slightly modified surname. Many had humorous nicknames: Sansregret (with out regrets), Belhumeur (cheerfulness), Brindamour (crumb of love), or Vuydebouteille (emptier of bottles). Reading the muster rolls shows a certain repetition, sometimes several recruits of the same company even had the same sobriquet. It seems that the sobriquet was not chosen by the soldier but given by the *capitaine* or the *sergent* of the company during enlistment and its recording in the register of the muster rolls.

A few regiments retained a regional identity over the decades, despite changes in *colonels* and the renewal of *capitaines*. This was the case with the Régiment Royal Corse where the *capitaines* were always Corsican and where recruits were drawn from the island. The same was true for the Régiment Royal Roussillon as Guignard writes in *L'École de Mars*: '...in the Royal Roussillon, which was similarly mixed: command was made in Catalan jargon where nobody understands anything, if he is not natural of this country,'[5] or the Régiment Royal Cantabres which had to be composed of officers and soldiers from beyond the Adour River and from the County of Armagnac. For most regiments, the province names they bore no longer reflected the geographical origin of their recruitment. However, the responsibility of each *capitaine* to recruit his own company led to the formation of groups of recruits originating from the same village or the same geographical area.

---

5 Pierre Claude de Guignard, *L'Ecole de Mars* (Paris: Simart, 1725), vol.1, p.716.

The enlisted soldier found himself uprooted and sent to garrisons in the border regions, which changed regularly. Military families were created, married soldiers who would serve for a lifetime and would have one or more sons who would in turn enlist. Families for whom the regiment became their roots and village. Several examples found in the archives show us the solidarity that existed for the widows and children of these families of soldiers. Historian Xavier Audoin writes on this topic:

> By a laudable tolerance, the regiments had received the children of the soldiers, six years old, with a fusilier's half pay. At sixteen, they granted them the price of the enlistment, and the full salary. If at this age, they refused to enlist, they paid to the *masse* [deductions retained by the company] one hundred *livres* in compensation. They were employed either for music or for making clothing and equipment. The council [in 1778] wanted the number of children brought up in this way to be reduced to sixteen per regiment.[6]

Attempts were made to limit the marriages of soldiers as well as officers, who had to ask permission from the commander of their regiment. Similarly, it was forbidden for priests serving in the army to celebrate a marriage under penalty of being punished as perpetrators and accomplices in the crime of kidnapping. Some of these soldiers' wives followed the army on campaign. Thus in 1758, the commissioners of war in the army noted the requisition of several houses to accommodate the eight wives of troopers of the Régiment de Fumel Cavalerie. They also followed them when they were taken prisoner. In 1797, we can still read in the *Encyclopédie* about the marriage of soldiers: 'The fifteen or twenty women who are today in the train of each military corps give more trouble on the roads and in the establishment of lodgings than a quadruple number of soldiers…'[7] The paintings of Watteau, Parrocel or Vernet, and the gouaches of Becher show us these families following the army with women, babies and children.

The enlistment of women as soldiers, if sometimes anecdotal, was very real. Marie Bertrand, nicknamed La Douceur, was discovered after having served several months in the Régiment d'infanterie d'Enghien. We also find women in the cavalry. Establishment tables show us that the enlistment of free black soldiers from Africa or the Caribbean was rarer in the infantry than in the dragoons or the cavalry.

The decrees did not mention the height required to serve in the French infantry, whereas it was fixed at five pieds for militiamen. The tendency of certain *colonels* to favour proud appearance and good stature was the occasion for a call to order in 1728 by M. d'Angervilliers, then Secretary of State for War, who ordered them not to dismiss recruits who would be below five pieds two pouces (1.678m) provided they were 'well-legged, of build, age and strength suitable for service.' Recruitment posters also give us some information. Thus, a poster of the Régiment de Rouergue indicated that it

---

6 Xavier Audoin, *Histoire de l'administration de la guerre* (Paris: Didot l'ainé, 1811), vol.4, p.247.

7 *Encyclopédie Méthodique, Art militaire* (Paris: Agasse, 1797), vol.4, p.763.

recruited from five pieds two pouces, and the Régiment de Navarre recruited from five pieds one pouce, but also from five for teenagers.

The letters of Guillaume de l'Église de Lalande, *capitaine* in the Régiment de Champagne, show us that in this regiment 'below five pieds two pouces we do not receive them' and when he asks his brother for help in recruiting two men, he tells him: 'make sure the height gauge is good.'[8] Height remained an important element for the recruiter and the recruit; the latter received a bonus for drinking allowance proportional to his height. This gratuity given to the soldier is the origin of the word 'pourboire' (tip). Recruits would receive the pour-boire as soon as they signed their enlistment. With the decree of 25 March 1776 on the administrations of units, this pour-boire became a sum systematically given in addition to the soldier's enlistment bonus.

The age of recruits had to be over 16 and even 18 for the Gardes françaises. The establishment tables display a wide age range in the regiments. Recruits were aged between 17 and 35 years old, and more rarely over 45 years old, and the re-enlisted could reach 45–50 years old.

Another method to find recruits was to involve the officers of the regiments. Thus, officers going on leave were obliged to recruit a certain number of men. If successful, they received a bonus, otherwise they paid a fine. In October 1758, before winter quarters and leave for certain officers, *maréchal* de Belle-Isle wrote to Contades:

> I believe, Monsieur le *Maréchal*, that you are rendering a great service to the state, by very seriously encouraging gentlemen *colonels* to get recruits, I am not saying that they will have absolutely no militias; but I say those who by their negligence will not have made possible recruits; will pay the militiamen, whom the King will give them to complete them, double what it would have cost them, if they had worked; and the prize shall be proportioned to the laziness or negligence of the *capitaines*; which will seem to you, I believe, very fair.[9]

The correspondence of the Prunelle brothers during the Seven Years War teaches us that Prunelle de Saint Didier, *cornette* in the Royal Dragons, had to recruit three men and, but bringing back only one, he was deducted 100 écus from his salary. And his brother Prunelle de Roisson, *lieutenant* in the Régiment d'infanterie de Berry, preferred not to leave on furlough in order to avoid the fine.[10]

The repurchase of prisoners was also an important element in recomposing the regiments. Thus, to recover 'eight to ten thousand old soldiers,' Belle-Isle wrote to Contades in October 1758: 'I hope that the thousand *écus* that M. de la Salle will bring, to pay the account of what is due to the Chancellery of Hanover, will be satisfying, and that in addition to what remains due, will not prevent the application of the cartel.'[11]

---

8 J. Dufresne, 'Lettres de Guillaume de L'Eglise de Lalande, *Revue de Gascogne*, vol.37, p.362.
9 Belle-Isle, *Lettres*, p.60.
10 René Lacour, *Les frères Prunelle de Vienne témoins oculaires de la guerre de Sept Ans* (Lyon: de la Guillotière, 1952).
11 Belle-Isle, *Lettres*, p.42.

Desertion was one of the scourges of all the armies of this period, and the causes were numerous: forced enlistment, ill-treatment of soldiers, punishments, discipline which in certain regiments wanted to be Prussian, maintenance beyond the term of the enlistment, forced enrolment of militiamen, delayed pay, and daily difficulties tempting men to maraud. Officers were well aware of the causes, thus Bohan writes: 'Desertion has more real causes in our country, and those who have studied them are only waiting to reveal them to find a minister in place who can or wants to hear them.'[12] At the start of the Seven Years War, *capitaine* Mercoyrol de Beaulieu of the Régiment de Picardie put it this way '…after seven years of peace, when at least two-thirds of the soldiers are new and have only seen gunpowder in peace drill, you should expect to see their honour compromised.'[13]

In garrison, the soldier was considered as a deserter if he was found, without leave, more than two lieues (eight kilometres) from his garrison. In wartime, during campaigns, it was forbidden to move more than a quarter of a lieue away from the camp, except for special service or by authorisation issued by the *prévôt*; to get vegetables for example. The death penalty for desertion, reinstated under Louis XIV, was only abolished by Saint-Germain in 1778 and the 'punition de la chaine' – four years hard labour, with one of their feet attached to a ball and chain – was suppressed in 1786. When caught, the deserter was quickly tried and condemned to have his nose and ears cut off, and his cheeks branded with the fleur de lys. He was then taken to His Majesty's galleys to be convict for life. Despite this cruel punishment, nothing stemmed the flow of these soldiers fleeing the royal armies. A list of soldiers reputed to be deserters was regularly drawn up. During the war, rolls were published every four or six months bearing the names, regiments, and descriptions of deserters. They were distributed to intendants, commanders of places, commissaries of war, *majors* of regiments and to all the *maréchaussées* of the kingdom. In each of their departments, the *maréchaussée* had to make monthly visits to the birthplace of deserters. The descriptions of the deserters were taken from the muster rolls of the regiments to establish these rolls of deserters. The entries in the muster roll were made on the basis of the declarations of the enlisted, the only acts of civil status of this time, which were the parish registers, were not used. In cases of failure to return at the expiration of a limited leave, the *prévôt* of the army issued a summons, and if the soldier did not return within three months, he was condemned in absentia as a deserter.

It should be noted that, until the middle of the nineteenth century, there was never any mention of the desertion of officers. In 1743, the comte d'Argenson replied in this sense to the marquis de Bissy about the *maréchaux des logis* of the cavalry, who at that time were still considered officers: 'they mount and dress at their own expense and when they leave their service, they

12 François Philippe Loubat, baron de Bohan, *Examen critique du militaire françois* (Genève: publisher unknown, 1781), vol.1, p.220.

13 Jacques de Mercoyrol de Beaulieu, *Campagnes de Jacques de Mercoyrol de Beaulieu, capitaine au régiment de Picardie 1743-1763* (Paris: Renouard, 1915), p.119.

are not subject to the penalties of desertion.'[14] The nobility was considered to have a born military function, so they were allowed to serve abroad without betraying their nation. As a rule, they asked the King for permission to serve a foreign prince, and if by the game of alliances, the latter became an enemy, nothing prevented them from continuing to serve this prince. A number of French officers remained in the service of Frederick II during the Seven Years War.

Amnesty was another solution found by the government to recompose its army; clearly showing the impotence of the state both to raise new recruits in sufficient numbers and to reduce the flow of deserters. In April 1757, the King published a decree granting amnesty to deserters from the War of the Austrian Succession, which had ended nine years earlier, who had enlisted 'in the troops which are at present employed in disturbing the tranquillity of the Germanic Corps,' if they joined the Armée du Bas-Rhin. This decree targeted the French soldiers of the Prussian and Hanoverian armies. A correction of this decree was published in May 1757, specifying that, of course, if the deserters had enlisted in the service of the new Allied powers, in particular Austria, these deserters would be granted amnesty and could return to France without being worried, once they had completed their enlistment there and had been granted regular leave from this Allied army.

The School of the Soldier

As they arrived in the companies, the new recruits were entrusted to the *sergents* who took care of their military training. Since recruits were considered the property of a *capitaine*, new recruits from different companies were not grouped together for common basic training.

In *L'école du soldat*, published in 1753 as an instructional text concerning the execution of the decree of 7 May 1750, we can see the creation of the soldier classes and of the squads.[15] First class soldiers were selected from among the most experienced and well-trained privates, *anspessades* and *caporaux*; they were responsible for instructing the so-called second-class soldiers, the latter having to pass a practical examination to be admitted to the first class. When the whole regiment or its greater part was formed of first-class soldiers, it organised itself in squads required to meet regularly for drill and weapon handling. The squad was a new sub-unit of the company, it was not a combat formation, but only a training unit. It was really only from the decree of 1764 that the individual and collective training of the soldier and the company was really specified in detail becoming the company school, and later in 1774, these routine exercises took the name of 'exercices de détails' (detailed exercises).

---

14 Joseph Margerand, 'Mélanges, Le grade de maréchal des logis', *Carnet de la Sabretache, Revue militaire rétrospective*,1934, pp.308–309.

15 Acte royal, 1753, *Instruction pour l'infanterie concernant l'exécution de l'ordonnance du 7 mai 1750* (Paris: Imprimerie royale, 1753).

Individual training took place daily in the morning, it was led by the *caporaux* and *anspessades* under the control of the *sergents*. Squad training took place once a week on Sunday mornings. Finally, each entire battalion exercised manoeuvres once a week, from 1 May to 1 September and every 15 days during winter. In the garrisons, the *major* of the place required all the troops of the garrison to perform a general exercise once a month.

To begin their training, recruits learned to march individually at cadenced step, then two by two, then four by four, etc. in order to acquire cohesion in the execution of manoeuvres. Then they were taught all the manoeuvres and conversions to form in three lines, and in column, always in cadenced steps. Meanwhile, they also learned the different drum signals and the signals used by the *majors* to transmit orders.

The weapon handling exercises were only the mechanical repetition of the 15 steps of reloading, without effective firing. After this individual training, soldiers practised collective fire drills to accustom themselves to fire together; by section, by platoon, and by ranks, most often without powder and with wooden 'flints' or with empty cartridges. There was some firing at targets, but it was very little practised; largely due to the cost of gunpowder and lead, which were not permanently allocated to regiments or companies, but had to be requested from the Corps de l'artillerie. Target shooting was mainly practised during training camps.

Camps of instruction had existed on an occasional basis since Louis XIV. During his reign, they were also often associated to important construction projects; the King utilising a large and cheap workforce. Under Louis XV, these camps became more regular, and the opportunity was taken to train the troops in the new regulations, results were analysed, and the general officers reported them to the ministry. Some camps served both as assembly and mobilisation camps in anticipation of war and as training camps, as in 1727 and 1756. These were also camps where tactical tests were carried out, such as at the camp near Sarrelouis in 1754, where 200 men from the Régiment de Touraine were trained in Prussian manoeuvres and then executed them in the presence of general officers like the duc de Belle-Isle. Writing to comte d'Argenson in May 1754 Bombelles concluded about this experimentation: 'I assure you Sir that it would be desirable for all officers of the King's troops to observe, as we have done, that the Prussian fire is only a terrible thunder which can only produce a mediocre effect, whereas ours, served according to our ancient usage, is infinitely more murderous and consequently superior.'[16]

In 1753, at the camp of Beaucaire under M. de Crémille, 543,000 cartridges were fired by only 10 infantry battalions, or a little more than 5,000 men. Most of the cartridges fired were blanks, without bullets, during attack and defence simulations, only a very small part of the firing was made with balls and on targets. Mauvillon writes: 'First, to shoot really well, you need fairly

16 Archives départementales des Yvelines, Minutes des lettres écrites par M. de Bombelles, commandant à Bitche: au maréchal de Belle-Isle ; au maréchal de Noailles ; à M. d'Argenson, ministre de la guerre, etc (Cahier In-folio, papier, 50 feuillets). Marc Pierre de Voyer de Paulmy, comte d'Argenson was Minister of War from January 1743 to February 1757.

continuous practice. Ten or 12 rounds fired a year are not enough for that.'[17] It was only the regulation of 1769 that prescribed training mainly grenadiers and first-class soldiers in target shooting, 'in order to teach them to aim well and to shoot correctly: it will be distributed for this purpose, a prize to the one who will have fired the best.'[18]

The perception of the armies of the *Ancien Régime* is not always flattering, they are often viewed in the light of the victorious armies of the Revolution and the Empire. However, there was already a certain modernity in the organisation in divisions or during training manoeuvres. Thus, reading the regulation of 1 May 1769 is interesting and similar training had already been practised during the training camps of 1755 and 1756. Here is an example of an exercise which aimed to teach the soldiers to reform ranks after each enemy salvo.

> On days of small war [here in the sense of training], one-third of the rank and file were given playing cards on which a number was written. Each hung his card on one of the buttons of the coat; chance presided over the distribution of these numbers, which ranged from one to six and which were intended to designate those of the men who would be supposed to be put out of action. Two battalions were placed in line facing each other within musket range; one of them was intended for marching for the charge, the other for executing fires; at the first salvo, the marching troop was reduced by all the men bearing the number one; they remained on their knees and the serrefiles filled the empty places with men in the third row; at a second salvo the places occupied by the men bearing the number two became vacant in their turn, and so on, so that at the end there was only two ranks left.[19]

Similarly, safety was considered, the provisional regulations of 1744 for the service of the infantry in the field specifies: 'Great care will be taken to inspect the weapons by company before the exercise, in order to be assured that there will be no loaded ones. Soldiers will be forbidden to have bullets on them on days of exercise, and all necessary precautions will generally be taken to avoid accidents.'[20]

At the Sarrelouis training camp in 1754, commanded by M. de Chevert, troops simulated manoeuvres and combats with empty cartridges. The flash from the barrel of a musket of a soldier of the Régiment de La Tour du Pin, added to the unexpected tear, during the action, of the silk of a standard of the Régiment de Beauvilliers Cavalerie put a stop to the exercise. All weapons and pouches were checked to ensure that loaded cartridges had not been distributed, without any error being found; it was a false alarm, a defect of the musket or some other incident.

---

17 Jakob Mauvillon, *Essai sur l'influence de la poudre à canon dans l'art de la guerre moderne* (Lieipsic: Haug, 1788), p.143.

18 Mauvillon, *Essai sur l'influence de la poudre à canon*, p.143.

19 Étienne Alexandre Bardin, *Dictionnaire de l'armée de terre* (Paris: Corréard, 1843), vol.5, p.1398.

20 Acte royal, 1744, *Règlement provisionnel pour le service de l'infanterie en campagne* (Paris: Imprimerie Royale, 1744).

A worm was used to ensure that the weapons were always properly unloaded, especially in case of misfire. A technique to make sure that the musket was unloaded consisted of quickly dropping the iron rod into the barrel, if it was empty the rod would make a metallic sound when it hit the bottom of the breech. But in the midst of action, accidents still remained numerous.

4

Officer Training and Careers

Wealth, the Key to a Military Career

Wealth determined the arm; the court nobility bought companies or regiments of cavalry; the less well-off provincial nobility made a career in the infantry. Unlike technical arms, where it was their abilities and interest that directed the future officer to the artillery or engineering schools.

Most of the nobility, especially in the provinces, was getting poorer. Income from land was dwindling and at the same time the venality of public offices, including military offices, continued to grow. Saint-Simon writes about military offices: 'this venality of the sole door by which one can ascend to the higher ranks is a great sore in the military. It is a gangrene that has long corroded all the orders and all the parts of the state, under which it is difficult for it not to succumb.' In his memoirs, the comte de Saint Germain makes an even more critical analysis of it:

> A pernicious distinction has been introduced between the nobility of the court and the nobility of the provinces, which is almost always worth better, between the rich and the poor, so that one has everything, without deserving anything, and the other have nothing, whatever it deserves; that everyone has pretensions, and that few people take it upon themselves to justify them with services and talents.[1]

A few years after writing these words, and becoming Secretary of State for War from 1776, he had many colleges opened in the provinces, entrusted to religious orders, to welcome and train this impecunious young nobility.

There were exceptions to this rule, where merit was rewarded with promotion, even to the rank of general officer. François de Chevert, who reached the rank of *lieutenant général*, is one example of career advancement that resulted from military valour. Soldiers too could become officers and be made *lieutenants* based on their seniority of service and their merit.

The impoverishment of the nobility of the sword was one of the reasons for the increasing numbers, in the army, of officers from the developing

1 Comte Claude-Louis de Saint-Germain, *Mémoires de M. le Comte de Saint-Germain* (Amsterdam: M.M. Rey, 1779), p.45.

bourgeoisie or from the wealthy judiciary; with the help of a good or elegant appearance and above all of a sufficient fortune to enable them to live nobly. Even in a prestigious corps like the Maison du Roi, wealthy nobility was lacking. The lifestyle of a Garde du Corps or a simple trooper in the Chevaux légers was such that sometimes some officers left these corps for lack of financial means. This clemency vis-à-vis commoners varied according to circumstances, tolerated in times of war, but more difficult to accept during periods of peace, when opportunities in the army were reduced.

This job market in the army led to the reduction of the role of seniority for promotions, favouring the installation of concordats in the mechanism of military promotion. The concordat was a financial agreement, it was concluded to obtain the withdrawal of an older officer – a kind of early retirement bonus. The officers constituted a common fund to make the oldest leave, each of them then climbing a level towards a possible promotion. All these practices were prohibited by regulations and decrees. As soon as he arrived at the ministry in March 1758, Belle-Isle once more denounced these abuses in a circular addressed to all *colonels*. There were some severe penalties to serve as an example, but he did not manage to eradicate the practice.

Officer Training

Royal power has always sought to support the training of young nobility in the profession of arms. Training was soon imposed and structured for technical corps such as the navy, artillery or engineers, with the creation of specific schools in Rochefort, La Fère, and Mézières. However, for the army, with the infantry and cavalry, it was not until the middle of the eighteenth century that the first military schools were established, or riding schools created.

Future officers all went through much the same apprenticeship cycle. It began in early childhood with the acquisition of reading and writing with a tutor. Then, at around 10 years of age, the young boy was sent to one of the many colleges in the kingdom; usually as a boarder. There he learned the basics of mathematics, drawing, geography, and sometimes horse riding. These colleges were managed by religious communities, often Jesuits, but also Benedictines, Barnabites, Doctrinaries, and Minims. Since Henry IV, the Jesuits had obtained permission to open schools; for example the Royal College of La Flèche, founded and given to the Jesuits by Henri IV in 1603. After the suppression of the Jesuit congregation in 1761, the Collège de la Flèche became a military college in 1764, 'a boarding school to serve as a seminary at the École Royale Militaire.'[2] If his family was rich enough, the young man benefited, during these three to five years of college, from the services of a tutor or a coach. As he grew older, he also attended the lessons of one of the many fencing halls of the kingdom where he was introduced to fencing.

2 François Marchant de Burbure François, *Essais historiques sur la ville et sur le collège de La Flèche* (Angers: Pavie, 1803), p.304.

Then around 15–17 years old, the young man entered a regiment as a cadet, and for one or two years, he learned weapon handling, exercises, and military discipline. If he belonged to the high nobility, and was destined to be provided with a regiment, it was with the Mousquetaires de la Maison du Roi or in the Régiment d'infanterie du Roi that he joined the army. If he was less wealthy, one appealed to the many relations of his relatives to find a *capitaine*, a *major* or a *colonel* who would agree to take him into his regiment. His expenses would keep increasing; he needed two or three horses, a valet, and much more. He also had to face the costs of life in garrison, and of gambling. In the absence of money, he joined a regiment as a volunteer, he then had to live and equip himself at his own expense. At the end of his training as a cadet, he became *sous lieutenant* or his family bought him a lieutenancy or a company and he became a *capitaine*.

Some fairly wealthy young men, before joining as a cadet, attended classes for one or two years in one of the rare academies of the King, in Paris, or Lyon, where 'one learns the exercises suitable for the nobility and military people.'[3] In these institutions originally dedicated to horse riding, they attended classes more specifically oriented towards the profession of arms. There were language lessons, such as in German or Italian, and fencing masters. Military drill was also taught there, as well as drawing and dancing.

It should be noted that, on several occasions since the seventeenth century, cadets had been grouped in companies of cadets or gentlemen cadets. The last formations of this type, before the Seven Years War, were established between 1726 and 1733. Even though some excellent officers had come out of these units, they were never more than sporadic attempts. The company of gentlemen cadet of the King of Poland established in Lunéville constituted an exception, it was maintained from its creation in December 1738 until the death of the King of Poland in February 1766. In 1776, the young men destined to become officers were once more brought together with the creation of companies of gentleman cadets.

The École Royale Militaire

Richelieu, Mazarin then Louvois had already considered the creation of a military school, but these projects never came to fruition. In 1724, Jean Pâris Montmartel, Garde of the Royal treasure and banker to the Court, planned a polytechnic school, but his project, too ambitious and too expensive, was abandoned. A few years later in 1749, his brother Joseph Pâris Duvernay, general administrator of the military supplies, proposed to the King the establishment of an academic college, which should enable the vast majority of the penniless nobility, who supplied most of the army officers, to ensure the future of some of their children. The edict creating the École Royale Militaire was promulgated in January 1751 under the ministry of Argenson. On this occasion, Pâris Duvernay had known perfectly how to use the influence of

3 *Almanach Royal année 1755* (Paris: Le Breton, 1755) p.377.

Madame de Pompadour with the King to carry out his project. The marquis de Salières, *lieutenant général* and *inspecteur général* of the infantry was the first governor of the school. Without waiting for the construction of the school buildings next to the Invalides, classes began at the Château de Vincennes in 1753 before moving to the first buildings in July 1756. In theory, the school was supposed to accommodate 500 students, but only half this number were admitted when it opened. The first students came out of the institution at the beginning of the Seven Years War and joined regiments, most often as *sous lieutenants* or out of service *lieutenants* attached to a regiment. When they left the military school, they received an annual pension of 200 *livres* until they could adequately support themselves. Even if he did not receive a salary, the out of service officer was considered as active, and this period was counted in his seniority of service. At that time, seniority was fundamental for promotion and career.

The uniform of the students of the military school was a black cocked hat trimmed with silver lace, a blue coat with red cuffs and a yellow collar, a red waistcoat, and white buttons. In 1776, 10 new military schools were created throughout France.

The Recruitment of *Colonels*

Until the middle of the eighteenth century, no quality, qualification, or experience were required to become *colonel* of a regiment. A brief stint as a cadet in the company of the Mousquetaires and here was our young man ready to lead his regiment into battle. This was how '*colonels à bavette*' multiplied; and Voltaire to ridicule this custom had his hero say, in *L'indiscret* published in 1725: '*Colonel* at 15, I think with reason, that at 30 I can be honoured with the baton.'[4] The King, not to be outdone, set a bad example, when in 1758 he gave the Régiment Royal Carabiniers to his grandson, who was only three years old. And this at the same time his Minister of War, *maréchal* de Belle-Isle, obtained directions from the King that an officer who had not already served as a *lieutenant* and then as a *capitaine* could not be admitted to the command of a regiment.

The duc de Croÿ learned of Belle-Isle's opinions through painful experience. In March 1758, he took his 13-year-old son to M. de Jumilhac to enrol him in the Mousquetaires. A few weeks later, he presented his son to the King and to the Court. There he met for the first time *maréchal* de Belle-Isle, who was quite upset that the young man had been admitted to the Mousquetaires when he was not over 15 years old. And during a meal the next day, here is what the duc de Croÿ reported:

> But, on leaving the table, the *Maréchal* began precisely to declare all his projects, which were to be a captain for five years and not to be able to have a regiment until the age of 23. I was counting on my son to be one at 17, and he would have been,

4 François Antoine Chevrier, *La vie politique et militaire de M. le maréchal duc de Belle-Isle* (Bruxelles: Boubers, 1762), p.175.

> if things had remained on the old footing. I represented that we did not deserve to set such an example, but the *Maréchal* was deaf, and there were too many people for me to speak loudly… I saw my son's collar broken by the new regulation of having no regiment before being 24, a reasonable regulation in certain respects, but which, mixing up everything, deprived the court nobility of all its advantages.[5]

A few weeks later, with the publication of the regulations of 29 April 1758, the decision became final: 'Consequently, H.M. has decided that henceforth no officer can be provided with a regiment that he has not previously served with for at least seven years, two of which as a *lieutenant*, *enseigne*, *sous lieutenant* or *cornette*, and five in that of *capitaine* in the infantry, cavalry or dragoons.'[6]

The aristocracy of the *Ancien Régime* was in full evolution; the duc de Croÿ is the archetype of this old court nobility for whom rank gave prerogatives and social priorities. Thus, one bought a company or a regiment like property or land. Here is what we can read in the journal of the marquis de Dangeau on Tuesday, 16 September 1710, in Versailles: 'M. le Duc de Mortemart has lost a considerable sum at gambling against the Prince d'Isenghien and gives him his regiment to sell to pay most of it. M. de Beauvilliers, father-in-law of this duke, wants to make it easier for his son-in-law to pay as he wishes and hopes that such an adventure will correct M. de Mortemart from gambling.'[7]

In 1714, Louis XIV once again fixed the price of regiments and prohibited 'to exceed the said sums on pain of deprivation of the regiments.' The six Vieux cost 75,000 livres, the six Petits vieux cost 50,000, the Régiment de Poitou and those that followed it until the creations of 1684 cost 40,000 livres, all other regiments, created from 1684, cost 30,000 livres. Despite the decree of Louis XIV, the amounts remained variable, in particular for the gentlemen's regiments. The decree of 1762, which transformed them into provincial regiments, again fixed their price.

The Sacrifices of Service in the Army

For the officers of the regimental staff, service in the army was a very heavy financial burden from which one did not derive benefit, but on the contrary high losses and often debts accumulated, especially during war. The King even published notices to stay the seizure of property, and exemptions from the taille (a direct land tax) for some of the debts that officers and soldiers were forced to incur during war. These measures were often not enough to keep them out of poverty.

5 Emmanuel-Henri de Grouchy, *Journal inédit du duc de Croÿ, 1718-1784* (Paris: Flammarion, 1906), vol.2, p.427.

6 Acte royal, 29 April 1758, *Règlement que le Roi a jugé à propos de faire sur l'ancienneté de service que devront avoir les officiers qui seront proposés pour commander les régiments du 29 avril 1758* (Paris: Imprimerie Royale, 1758).

7 Philippe de Courcillon marquis de Dangeau, *Journal du Marquis de Dangeau* (Paris: Firmin-Didot, 1858), vol.13, p.244.

The officer had to provide himself with everything from his personal funds: uniform, equipment, horses, lodging and valets, grooms, and more. In March 1757, M. Mopinot de la Chapotte, a cavalry officer from the nobility of the robe wrote:

> Reason tells me that as soon as I have arrived in Paris, I will have to leave to put myself in a position to beat a Frederick, King of Prussia, who has done me neither good nor harm; it also tells me that I will have to spend the short time I stay there buying horses, building tents, beds, cooking utensils, borrowing money, ruining myself to serve a king. who may never serve me and the country which will never show me the slightest gratitude.[8]

From the army, the officer received rations of fodder and bread proportional to his rank and his servants; if he renounced them, the purchasing department paid him the counterpart in money. To illustrate the precariousness in which out of service officers, burdened with debts at the end of a war, could find themselves, here is what Barbier wrote in his diary in March 1749, after the War of the Austrian Succession:

> There have been several decrees which are reported in excerpt in the Gazette de France, for the disbandment of the troops which is stronger than has ever been done in this country. At least twelve regiments have been completely suppressed and all the others have been greatly reduced. This puts on the streets a large number of young people who had served for some years in the troops as *lieutenants*, *sous lieutenants* and even *capitaines*, and who are embarrassed after having been officers, to take any other occupation and who have neither pay nor quality anymore, and who find themselves without property. This should teach young people from bourgeois families, who are able to choose different professions to earn their living, not to indulge so imprudently in the military profession which flatters them first with brilliance and laziness, and in which one easily obtains offices in time of war when troops are needed. There is not the same disadvantage for the soldiers who can more easily return to their villages, resume their first occupation and work in the lands which become untilled during war. The King gives a month's salary to all out of service officers to return home. Two stories are told in Paris, one of a *lieutenant* who, having only 35 *livres* to return to his country which was very far away, and having no other coat than that of ordonnance, put cheese to sell in the town where his regiment was; on the reproach which was made to him by his former comrades and on the reprimands of the commander of the place, he answered them quite simply that he did nothing against honour, that he preferred to do this little trade than asking for alms on the way and that he had no desire or disposition to steal; that when he had earned something for his journey, he would leave for his country.
>
> The other, of a well-built *lieutenant*, who, having done some brilliant action, had been honoured with the Cross of Saint-Louis; not knowing where to turn, had contacted a *capitaine* in the Gardes françaises who accepted him as a soldier.

---

8 Jean Lemoine, *Sous Louis le Bien Aimé, correspondance amoureuse et militaire d'un officier pendant la guerre de sept ans* (Paris: Calman-Levy, undated), p.11.

> Having hidden his cross, being of the detachment to mount guard at Versailles, he paid his *sergent* a bottle; he asked him to post him in the most conspicuous place to see the King and all the Court pass by, since he had never seen the Court. Thus posted, hearing the drums because the King was going out, he put his cross of Saint-Louis on his coat. The Duc de Chartres was the first to notice it, he was surprised because it should not be. He spoke of it to the King, the soldier was asked by what right he had the cross; he gave an account of his adventure, of what had procured him the cross and of his present condition. It is said that he had a pension of 600 livres.'[9]

At the end of the Seven Years War, we find the same suffering, the same misery, amongst the out of service officers. Even the lucky officers who retired no longer received their pension, or it was reduced.

9 Edmond-Jean-François Barbier, *Chronique de la Régence et du règne de Louis XV (1718-1765) ou Journal de Barbier* (Paris: Charpentier, 1858), vol.4, p.354.

5

The Housing of Soldiers, and Marches

Housing Troops in Times of Peace

Troops were said to be cantoned when soldiers lived in tents or barracks as opposed to quartered troops, who were hosted in private homes or lived in 'casernes' (stone buildings) in a garrison town. In times of peace, the regiments were garrisoned in cities and walled towns in the border or coastal regions. In order not to impose this charge on the same city for too long, the troops regularly changed garrison. Two systems were used, billeting and casernes. In 1716, a decree was published, prescribing that: 'The king having seen fit to relieve his subjects of the personal accommodation of his troops, he orders the selection and renting of empty houses, suitable for quartering the soldiers.'[1] This measure was taken pending the construction of casernes in the main cities of the kingdom. The communities still had to provide beds, tables, benches, gun racks, hooks, and other equipment for the stables. When troops changed location, they had to return this equipment and to compensate for what had been destroyed or lost. But in 1724, faced with the cost of this method and the impossibility of building enough casernes in a reasonable time, the preference returned to billeting. Some communities paid for casernes to be exempted from housing soldiers. Another way these communities found was to rent houses to quarter the troops there. Officers, for their part, rented a room and a stable from the inhabitants by mutual agreement. Upon presentation of receipts, they were reimbursed; up to 1,800 livres per year for a *lieutenant général*, 1,200 for a *maréchal de camp*, 900 for a *brigadier*, 800 for a *commissaire ordonnateur*, 300 for a *capitaine d'artillerie*, and so on.

In the middle of the eighteenth century only a very small portion of the garrison towns had a caserne, which meant that when not in service the soldier stayed with the locals. The inhabitants had to provide him with a bed lined with a sheet, a pot, a bowl, a hanging board for bread (a precaution

1 Chennevières, François de. *Détails militaires dont la connoissance est nécessaire à tous les offciers, et principalement aux commissaires des guerres* (Paris: Charles-Antoine Jombert, 1750), vol.3, p.59.

against rodents), a candle and a place for his fire. This constituted part of the 'ustensile' which was a tax in kind. It was the war commissary who, with the advice of the mayor or the aldermen, issued the billeting tickets. There were exemptions for military quarters, but they were intended to be limited as the needs in the garrison towns were great. Gentlemen making a profession of arms or having retired and obtained the Cross of Saint Louis were exempt, but the title of nobility did not exempt one from quartering. There were additional exemptions for clergymen, mayors, aldermen, tax collectors (for the taille and gabelle, for salt and saltpeter), 'étapiers' (an officer appointed to give the soldiers their allowance upon the march), postal clerks, financial clerks, and others. In theory these exemptions were only valid for the accommodation they occupied and not for other dwellings or outbuildings where their valets, farmers or other of their household lived. The multiplication of offices, exemptions, and abuses placed the burden largely on craftsmen. If the stay was extended, the landlord was partially compensated. One easily imagines the complications and the slowness of a gathering of troops scattered in all districts of a city.

In times of peace, in garrison, the soldier was authorized to work on his own account to earn a few sols allowing him to improve his daily life, to buy a few pints at the cabaret or even to pay for the firewood of the seven months deemed as summer – April to October inclusively. It was the *capitaine* who could 'give them an opportunity to earn a living, when they can without failing in service.'[2]

The construction of caserns decided under Louis XIV was only done very slowly. For lack of means, many caserns were still houses and buildings rented to quarter the troops. In 1726, the Bishop of Metz, the duc de Coislin, relieved the population of his city of the housing of soldiers and had a casern that could accommodate nearly 2,000 men built at his own expense. It was inaugurated on 8 June 1731, in the presence of the comte de Belle-Isle and the comte de Bavière, as mentioned in the *Mercure de France*. D'Argenson had the first casern in Paris built in 1745; it was intended for the Gardes françaises.

Belidor in his work *La science des ingénieurs* gives us a good idea of the design of a casern in the middle of the eighteenth century. The barrack rooms; all with a fireplace, were designed for four beds or 12 soldiers, they were mostly located on the first floor, the ground floor being usually reserved for stables. The part of the casern where the officers lived was called the officers' lodge. Rooms were for two officers, or for an officer and his family, with a kitchen for the servants. Often the officers, their families and their servants alone occupied the new caserns, when they were not allocated to civilians protected by the intendant; this situation kept soldiers in precarious living conditions. Most often there were as many beds as the room could hold, along with a table, two benches and a fireplace. There was one berth for two soldiers, but in the statements of supplies of the war commissaries, we see that it was rather two *sergents* or three soldiers per bed. Dragoons, cavalry and the Royal Artillerie only slept in pairs. The NCOs did not sleep with

2 Charles Sevin de Quincy, *Maximes et instructions sur l'art militaire* (Paris: Mariette, Delespine, Coignard, 1726), p.266.

soldiers. The beds provided were those in use in the garrison place, but if the communities could not supply them, they were ordered on the local market. The decree of 25 October 1716 gives us details on the dimensions of the beds that had to be provided by the tenderers, as well as a straw mattress, the straw of which had to be replaced twice a year, a mattress and a bolster stuffed with well-carded wool and covered with a washed cloth, a pair of sheets which were changed every 20 days in summer and every month in winter. The bed should be made of oak, and in regions where oak was rare, of walnut or elm or even fir. Elevated from the ground 12–15 pouces (32–40cm) and measuring five pieds nine pouces (1.87m) long and four pieds (1.3m) wide. The white wool blanket should measure eight pieds six pouces (2.7m) long by seven pieds four pouces (2.4m) wide; the sheets should be of a similar size. There had also to be tables, benches, and racks for depositing weapons.

For comparison, here is what Héricourt said for officers in 1758:

> Supplies for the lodges are composed of a bedstead with column, with a tester, furnished with bergamo fabric attached to the tester or sliding on curtain poles, a straw mattress, a mattress, a blanket, a bolster and a pair of sheets renewed every 15 days from 1 April to 1 October and from three weeks to three weeks during winter. The room is furnished with a rack for clothes, a table and four chairs, the hearth with one or two andirons, a pair of tongs and a shovel. A copper candlestick is given with a platter, two plates, and a pewter chamber pot; moreover a tablecloth and two napkins which are changed weekly; the servants' supplies are like those of the soldiers. Usually, two *lieutenants* or *sous lieutenants* are accommodated in one room.[3]

Officers lived alone in their room, except in times of war. The fate of cavalrymen or mounted dragoons was often more enviable than that of foot soldiers. The absence of caserns with sufficient stables most often meant that mounted troops had to be housed outside the cities, scattered in the surrounding villages, among the peasants and sharecroppers where the fodder cost the King nothing.

Marches of the Army and of the Infantry during Campaigns

Before considering the encampment of the army, let us follow the raising of the camp and the marches between two camps.

The day before departure, the *général* and his staff held a last council of war, then the *maréchal de camp* of the day transmitted the order of march to the *maréchal général des logis* of the army. It is he who then took charge of all the organisation of the raising of the camp, the composition of the columns, and the routes to follow until the installation of the new camp. He established a detailed order of march for the various brigades and regiments, he took into account the conditions of the troops and the number of columns, planned

3 Nicolas d'Héricourt, *Elémens de l'art militaire* (La Haye: J. Neaulme, 1739), p.234.

the different routes to follow, determined if he could anchor his positions on a village, or use the natural defence of a river or swamp. Finally, he had his document validated by the staff, and after approval, he transmitted the detailed marching orders to the various *majors*: including the *major général* of the army, *major général* of the cavalry, and of the infantry, who in turn transmitted them to the particular *majors* of divisions, regiments, and battalions, and to *vaguemestres* (baggage-masters). From that moment, he also sent hussars, dragoons, and light troops to scout for the different columns and to occupy and secure the passes, fords, and bridges. In the morning, a vanguard detachment, composed of light troops, cavalry and grenadiers was ready with the *maréchal de camp* of the day and a *maréchal des logis* of the army, and they left at least an hour before the rest of the army.

On the morning of the day of march, the drummer and the bugler on guard duty at the headquarters began to beat *La Générale* and to sound *Le Boute-Selle* at the time indicated by the *major général*. They left headquarters beating and sounding to join the nearest infantry and cavalry regiment, where in turn the drums and bugles started beating and sounding. Before the instruction of *maréchal* de Broglie in 1760, the drummers of each regiment assembled and had to cover the front of their regiment twice, while beating, which represents nearly 550 yards (500m) for a regiment of four battalions. Broglie modified this rule by having the drummers of each battalion assemble, alongside their colours, and had them beat firmly, *La Générale* 25 times, taking care that they all began and ended at the same time. Picquet officers mounted their horses and took up position at the head and tail of their battalion. During this time the officers and *sergents* lined up their companies, their front aligned on the piles of arms. The camp was broken up and small baggage loaded with the tents, stakes, and pots. Heavy baggage had been loaded the day before as soon as the warning order had been transmitted. Then, when *L'Assemblée* was beaten, the baggage and the servants of the officers joined the *vaguemestre* at an agreed place, where they assembled near the camp-colour of the baggage of each brigade. Servants were forbidden to leave the camp-colour under penalty of flogging. At the same time that the baggage was assembling, the soldiers of the companies lined up in the main streets of the camp.

When the drums beat *Aux Drapeaux*, the companies marched forward, in battle array in three open ranks. All the companies of the same brigade advanced about 40 paces in front of their camp and halted. When the general officers arrived, the *major* closed ranks and split the battalion to the right or left to form the marching columns. The soldiers marched in platoons at three paces from each other. The colours were placed in the middle of the column of each battalion. If the carts of the battalions were placed at the rear of the column with all the small baggage, the horses of the platoon walked on the flanks of the column and of their battalions, but it was forbidden that they could enter the column. Note that in his instruction of 1760, Broglie made the horses of the platoon march with the columns, although in the same text we can read that 'no car, nor pack-horse, nor mules may march with the columns.'[4]

4 Victor François Broglie, *Instruction pour l'armée du Roi* (Francfort: Van Duren, 1760), p.40.

Jean-Antoine Watteau, 'Recrue allant joindre le Régiment' (Recruit joining the Regiment) (1710). (Anne S.K. Brown Military Collection)

When the grenadier company was present, it placed itself at the head of its battalion and the picquet company at the rear. If the grenadier company had been detached, the picquet company took its place. Here again de Broglie's instruction of 1760 brought some changes, the grenadiers and chasseurs of each infantry division gathered to advance 100 paces in front of the camp of the first line of their division. Similarly, the carabiniers of the different cavalry regiments that composed each wing came together to form a squadron that was placed in front of the first line of the wing.

The guards who were at the outposts left them at *La Générale* and either joined their regiment or assembled together to be employed in the rearguard. At the head of each column, workers and about 50 men, who had been drawn from each brigade, were sent to spot difficult passages and to look for small detours to avoid them, 'to mend the communications or bridges which could have been spoiled.'[5]

The army usually marched from sunrise to sunset, with a maximum of 14 hours for the longest summer marches and only a maximum of eight hours of march during winter. The distance covered depended on the state of the roads, the weather conditions, the state of the troops. As a rule, the cavalry opened and closed the infantry columns and marched on the wings of the centre column composed of the artillery and the heavy baggage. Dispositions also varied depending on whether the army was close to the enemy, and whether the latter was on a flank or in front.

5 Broglie, *Instruction pour l'armée du Roi*, p.32

An infantryman travelled at about one lieue to one and a half lieue per hour, or four and a half to six kilometres per hour. Halts were made regularly, so that the columns did not stretch too much, with a final stop when approaching the camp so that the army could regroup and encamp in good order. If the halt was prolonged or the enemy was near, the platoons mustered into battalions 12 paces apart, ready to form line with a quarter turn right or left. *Sergents* took roll calls during halts. During the halt, sentries and cavalry vedettes took position along the columns, less to guard against an enemy attack than to prevent the soldiers from leaving the columns to maraud or desert. To restart after a halt, the drums beat *Aux Champs*. Depending on the roads and the adjacent fields, the infantry could march in four, six or eight rows abreast. The *capitaines* and *sous lieutenants* marched at the head of their company, the *lieutenants* at the rear, and the *sergents*, one at the right wing of the first rank, the other at the left wing of the last. The *majors* continually rode from the head to the rear of the column of their regiment, in order to ensure good order and discipline.

The regimental route books are rich sources of insights. The book of Baron de Plas, *capitaine* in the Régiment Du Roi Infanterie, gives an idea of the distances covered by this regiment during the three campaigns of 1757, 1758, and 1759.[6] Most stages were between three and five lieues (13–22km), sometimes seven to eight (31–38km). In June 1758, they covered 10 lieues (45km), which took them more than 18 hours. A letter from M. Mopinot explains the circumstances of this laborious march:

> The army set off on the 14th at midnight, artillery, mobile hospital, baggage, cavalry, infantry and provisions in two columns; it passes through Uerdingen [near Krefeld] without stopping [...] it continues its march as far as Neuss where it encamps; the first troops did not arrive in this camp until the 15th at 11:00 p.m., and the last on the 16th at 10:00 a.m.; they suffer a lot from the rain and the cold during this long march.[7]

A march of 15 lieues (66km) was an exception. During the campaign of 1757, from March to December, from Abbeville in Picardie to Neuss in Westphalia, the regiment covered nearly 450 lieues, or approximately 2,000km. For the campaign of 1758, from June to November, from Neuss to Aix-la-Chapelle (Aachen), the regiment covered 161 lieues (700km), much less than the previous year, but this 1758 campaign hastily started only in late June, after the breach of the Convention of Klosterzeven. Finally for the campaign of the year 1759, from May 1759 to January 1760, from and to Aix-la-Chapelle, where the regiment returned to take up its winter quarters, it marched 329 lieues (1,450km). During these three campaigns, between two days of march, the army often established itself in the villages, it also set up camps, but without unpacking everything as it would for a camp of position. Simple bivouacs under the stars between two walking days were quite rare.

---

6 L'abbé Paul Legrand, 'Livre des routes du baron de Plas capitaine au régiment d'infanterie Du Roi (1757–1759)', *Bulletin et mémoires de la Société archéologique et historique de la Charente*, 1905–1906, p.169.

7 Lemoine, *Correspondance*, p.180.

The location of camps of position during campaigns were dictated by the movements or positions of the enemy army, but they were above all imposed by the distribution of bread which was done every four days. Each time, the Intendance (commissary) had to establish ovens, and organise convoys and distributions. When it became necessary to continue the march of the army, the intendancy distributed biscuits to soldiers to free them from distributions.

The army was a single body and always moved together with infantry, cavalry, artillery and all the baggage to go from one encampment to another. Therefore, the *maréchal général des logis*, and the geographers and all the small staff attached to him, had a key roles in planning and preparing the roads and the future camp. The mass of troops, horses, cattle, baggage and paraphernalia, and all the civilian personnel, carters, butchers, sutlers, caterers, and launderers represented by the whole army when it moved required the use of multiple routes, in four to six columns. Broglie in 1760 relied on the divisional formation he put in place to determine the composition of the columns. He set up a vanguard column equipped with artillery. Artillery convoys, supplies and baggage took the widest and best-maintained roads, infantry and cavalry progressed either on roads and paths, or in columns through fields. The state of roads in the bad season was another factor, with the difficulties of the supply of fodder, which limited campaigns between May and October. The arrival of rain or snow in autumn and winter which significantly degraded the condition of roads and slowed the speed of the transport of supplies and of the army itself.

The march of the baggage was done under the authority of the *vaguemestre général* of the army, a function occupied by a general officer. He coordinated the movement of the baggage with the *vaguemestres généraux* of each brigade, and the latter with the particular *vaguemestres* of each regiment. Baggage set off according to the rank that the regiment held in the brigade and in each regiment by battalion, and in each battalion according to the rank of each company. The function of *vaguemestre* was created in 1692.

In December 1761, *maréchal* de Broglie had an instruction sent to the *majors* of the infantry to try to standardize the march of the soldiers:

> It should be noted that, when the battalion has been placed in column and marching to move forward, the soldier must nevertheless carry his musket according to the regulations, march in line in his rank, and mark time with the battery as long as the drums continue to beat, and that it is only when the *major* has made these stop that they can carry their musket as they wish and in the way that will be most convenient for them, chat, sing, not having to be subject then to any other precaution than that of following exactly the file in which he is, and not increasing the interval of two steps which must be between him and the soldier who precedes him. For the same reason, as soon as the drums begin to beat again, he will fall back exactly into his rank, line up there, carry the musket and march at the pace marked by the drums.[8]

8 Broglie, *Correspondance*, vol.4, p.655.

Among the first to arrive at the new camp with the vanguard, there were the *maréchal de camp* of the day and the *maréchal des logis* of the army. They determined the final location of the encampment and had it covered by dragoons and light troops. The *maréchal des logis* then instructed the detachments of infantry, cavalry, or dragoons and their *fourriers* who accompanied the vanguard, to delimit with small stakes stuck in the ground the positions occupied by each of the battalions or squadrons, but also the width of streets and location of tents. Soubise in his instruction of 1761, indicates that each regiment provided a detachment of five men, which is 'composed henceforth of two *sergents*, three *caporaux* and a private to carry the tracing-line.'[9] The regulations required the use of a tracing-line and wooden pegs to ensure the alignment of the tents inside the space intended for each regiment, then it was the *sergents* and *caporaux* of the regiments who had to mark the streets, tents, kitchens, and other locations. The tracing-line for the tents was marked by small cordons sewn at equal distances, and of different colours to make it possible to quickly mark on the ground with a stake, either the position of the forked tent pole, or that of the corners of the tents, allowing a perfect alignment. The soldiers then had 'the wooden camp' (poles and crosspieces) placed on the ground to ensure proper alignment. All this when the space on the ground allowed it or when the rain and humidity had not reduced the length of the tracing-line. In the texts of this period there were two types of pace measurement: the infantryman's pace with its variations and the camp pace which was used as a measure for the camps, or the spaces occupied by a troop in battle, and which was three pieds (97.5cm) which was the measure of a horse's pace. In theory the encampment was traced with a tracing-line, but in the draft regulation for the service of the armies in 1812 one can read: 'the regulation of 1778 proves that although they were prescribed by the regulation of 1753 [the tracing-lines], only the pace of the *fourriers* were used to mark out the camp during the war of 1756.'[10]

When the rest of the troop arrived at the camp, it took about three hours for the soldiers and servants of the officers to set up the tents, provide themselves with wood, straw and water at the sutlers, get vegetables, dig the kitchens and make the soup, before finally taking at least six hours of rest. In the absence of a planned march, on waking in the morning, the soldier had one hour to dress and take up arms if he was on duty. Then there were periods of rest while waiting for the distribution of bread or between days of march, during which soldiers shaved (once a week as a rule), had fun at the travelling cabaret, wrote or had letters written, or made fascines and gabions.

Night marches were infrequent and were carried out mainly during spring or summer. But not always, as here is the report of a night march, made during the winter of 1757, the report of which can be read in the memoirs of Mr. Mercoyrol de Beaulieu, *capitaine* of the Régiment de Picardie:

---

9 *Maréchal* de Soubise, *Instruction pour l'infanterie de l'armée du roi commandée par Mr le Maréchal Prince de Soubise* (Place and publisher unknown, c.1761), p.37.

10 Claude Antoine Hippolyte, vicomte de Preval, *Du service des armées en campagne* (Blois: Aucher–Eloy, 1827), p.48.

> The evening order was given at 6:00 p.m., where it was said that at midnight (it was Christmas Eve) all troops would start moving towards the bridge where they were destined to cross the river… Imagine the soldier clad in gaiters, as he is all year round, most of them without stockings and the flesh of the legs showing through the buttonholes of these gaiters, as I saw an infinity of them; imagine, to pity them a little more, that the cold was so bitter that, when at daybreak we arrived at the bridge to cross it, where we stopped for half an hour or three quarters of an hour when soldiers and officers alike wanted to eat something, all breads were frozen, both those of the soldiers and those in the canteens of the officers; and that that to satisfy this pressing appetite, fires were soon and quickly made to thaw the bread. The wine was also chilled in the flasks; the officers were obliged to present them to the fire to make it drinkable. The smoke from those cursed fires was stirred by contrary winds and our bread was soaked with it; yet I saw not a single delicate one; all ate their bread, and with appetite, and far from being surprised by this necessity, it caused us laughter and everyone was joyful, each one thinking better to endure the circumstance than his neighbour… Our whole army spent the rest of the day and the following night in the camp previously occupied by the enemy army; big fires were made there and that night, just as cold as the previous one, was spent at the bivouac.[11]

Undernourished and poorly protected from the cold, it is not surprising that chronically more than 10 percent of the soldiers of an army stayed in hospitals, nor that the number of deaths by disease – especially respiratory infections and diarrhoea – was greater than the number of men killed in battle.

Making Camp

The army encamped according to the order of battle; this order was immutable. It resulted from a set of rules dictated by the conditions of the troops, the number of brigades, squadrons, battalions, and especially the seniority of both the regiments and the *capitaines* of the companies. Dupain de Montesson tells us about this:

> When all regiments of infantry, cavalry and dragoons are encamped so that each according to his seniority occupies the place due to its rank, either in the first or second line; this is called being encamped in order of battle, because it is in the same order that one keeps, when one presents battle to the enemy on the plain or when he himself comes to give it.[12]

The articles devoted to the procedures for setting up a camp were prominent in the military regulations of the time. 'The chief object in the distribution or arrangement of a camp being to afford the facility for the officers and soldiers

11 Mercoyrol de Beaulieu, *Campagnes*, p.168.

12 Louis Charles Dupain de Montesson, *Les amusements militaires* (Paris: Desprez, 1757), p.120.

to proceed easily and promptly to the head of the camp...'[13] The encampment of French troops was established hierarchically from right to left and from rear to front of the camp. It was done in two lines, or sometimes three lines, depending on the nature of terrain. Positions were set by the *maréchal général des logis* of the army. The classic formation put the cavalry on the wings, the infantry in the middle and the Maison du Roi, when it was present, in the second line. Cavalry encampments were placed on the wings and separated by at least 50 paces from the infantry encampment in the centre.

The nature of the terrain also dictated the disposition of the camp, with natural features being used to strengthen its position. In particular on the wings where it was sought to lean on a village, a river, a wood occupied by infantry or, failing that, to place dragoons 'en potence' on the wings. Reading the plans drawn up for the campaign of 1757 by Sieur Du Bois, an engineer geographer, shows us for example how, depending on the configuration of the terrain, most of the camps were arranged along broken lines, in a sawtooth pattern, but always respecting the same hierarchy in the positioning of troops. In view of a battle, the encampment was established on a relatively straight line, each body of troops being from the outset in line of battle.

The front of the camp was also called the 'front de bandière' and was the line on which the first tents of the regiments of the first line were placed. 'Bandière' is a term that comes from old French and means banner, yet during the Seven Years War the colours were no longer placed there, but 20 meters in front of this line.

Between the regulation of 1753, which contained some calculation errors, and the various contemporaneous authors such as Le Blond, d'Espagnac, Rochefort, and Tricano, we sometimes find differences as to the extent of the camps described. They are mainly due to the intervals that some authors make more or less wide between battalions, regiments, and brigades. They only constitute variations on an organisation of the camp which was always similar. Le Blond, professor of mathematics for the Pages of the King's stables, then tutor to the Children of France, is undoubtedly one of the most instructive authors for the period of the Seven Years War. His work *Éléments de tactique* is purely educational, it does not defend a theory or a system, it simply exposes the tactical rules of its time or confronts the opinions of different authors. Of additional interest, its 1758 edition is one of the rare texts to take into account the increase to 17 companies of the infantry regiments decreed in August 1755.

Hereafter, we describe the general layout of the camp for a battalion of French infantry which included 16 companies of fusiliers of 40 men and one company of grenadiers of 45 men. The front of the camp of the 17 companies extended 110 pas (paces) (107m); the line of the tents was 90 pas (87.75m), to which was added on its left a free space of 20 pas (19.5m) separating it from

13 Guillaume Le Blond, *Éléments de tactique ,ouvrage dans lequel on traite de l'arrangement & de la formation des troupes ; des évolutions de l'infanterie & de la cavalerie ; des principaux ordres de bataille ; de la marche des armées & de la castramétation, ou de la manière de tracer ou marquer les camps par règles & par principes* (Paris: chez Charles-Antoine Jombert, 1758), p.335.

the next battalion; in depth, the six tents of each of the companies extended over 17 pas (16.5m). The depth of a line of the encampment, between the first tents of the soldiers and the tents of the officers at the rear, extended 80 toises (150m) and the distance between the front of the first line and that of the second line was usually 150 to 200 toises (285–380m).

The guards of the battalion were placed 100 pas in front of its encampment. It was composed of 16 fusiliers, one man per fusilier company. At the camp, they were the only ones to be armed with a permanently loaded musket, even the picquets, who policed the camp, were without muskets most of the time. Note that Broglie, in his instruction of 1760, increased this distance to 130 pas. Similarly, a guard was posted at the rear of the encampment of the battalion, 100 or 130 pas behind the soldiers' last tent. These guards provided the sentries who ensure that no soldier left the camp unless accompanied by an officer or *sergent*. There were two sentries posted at each wing of the battalion and a third near the arms. These guards had a tent to allow them to rest between each guard duty which lasted two hours: the tent was taken from those of an incomplete company. They made a fire there, around which the soldiers could warm up and sit down, but always with their weapons 'in their arms, making sure that they sit around the fire opposite their post, without sleeping, and that they cover the lock of their musket, so that neither rain nor dew could drench it.'[14] In October 1759, near Giessen, faced with the intensity of the cold, the guard posts were barracked, the tents being sheltered under a rudimentary wooden frame, covered with planks or with turf and branches, and the sentries were only on guard for an hour at a time before going to warm up by the fire of the barracks.

Still in the front of the camp, there was a rack which was used to deposit and protect the weapons of the 48 fusiliers of the picquet. It was placed to the right of the battalion encampment, across the tents of the grenadiers and one step in front of the pile of arms of the grenadiers. The rack was constructed with two poles five pieds (1.62m) long with a circumference of seven pouces, joined by two crosspieces 10 pieds (3.25m) long by 10 pouces around. The first crosspiece was placed at a height of two meters and the second, on which the muskets rested, at about 1.30 meters. The rack was protected by canvas cut and arranged in the shape of a mansard roof unlike the conical shape of the piles of arms of the companies. The rack was guarded by an armed sentry. At camp, the picquet soldiers were unarmed; the internal police service of the camp provided by the picquet was carried out without arms. The picquet also provided the guards who were placed near the *colonel*'s tent. To limit soldiers' fatigue, after their day of picquet duty, they could not be subsequently assigned to camp guard duty.

Since the decrees of 1749 and 1753, there were only two colours per battalion. They were placed opposite the main street in the centre of each battalion. Each of these colours, separated by two toises (four metres), was guarded by a sentry, sword in hand, his musket loaded and placed next to the

14 Pierre Briquet, *Code militaire ou compilation des ordonnances des Rois en France, concernant les gens de guerre* (Paris: Nyon, 1761), vol.5, p.70.

colour on two small wooden crutches stuck in the ground. The colours were placed 10 toises (20m) beyond the front of the encampment.

The piles of arms, where all soldiers deposited their muskets, were aligned in front of the battalion. They stood 10 pas (9.75m) in front of the line of tents of the companies to which they belonged. The piles were conical in shape and covered with a cloth bell of arms to protect the weapons from the elements. To build a pile, the *fourrier* of each company drew a circle approximately 2.60m in circumference. He had a furrow about eight centimetres deep and 15 centimetres wide dug, and had the earth heaved in a bank against the pile, the furrow was filled with turf and small wooden stakes half a *pied* long were planted in the middle of the furrow to support the butts of the muskets and thus insulate them from the dampness of the ground. A stake 1.76m long and 13 to 16 centimetres in diameter was planted in the centre of the pile and conical-shaped bell of arms was stretched on this stake. This model of pile of arms was built only for instruction or residential camps, for temporary camps the circumference was simply lined with intertwined branches on which the butts of the muskets rested. There was one bell of arms per company. This bell of arms was made of a piece of canvas or ticking that was two meters high, 55cm round at the top and 5.7m in circumference at the bottom, including covering the opening. According to the instruction of 17 February 1753, the bell of arms and the tents were marked in black characters with the name of the regiment and the number of each company.

Since January 1757, the infantry had been provided with regimental artillery at the rate of one piece of cannon 'à la suédoise' per battalion. Not all regiments were equipped with them, and some had only one piece for two battalions. These pieces were located next to the pile of arms of the picquet of each battalion 'and not beyond them,'[15] on the left of the battalion in front of the picquet tents. The officer in charge of the artillery camped alongside the *major* of the regiment, and near his tent he assembled all the horses attached to this artillery 'in order to be within reach to make sure that they received proper care.'[16] The 16 soldiers responsible for the service of a piece, commanded by a *sergent*, were probably gathered under two tents close to the piece; but it has not been possible to confirm this in the sources.

The soldiers' tents were called 'cannonière' tents. According to the decree of 17 February 1753, the tents of the infantry measured: 10 pieds 4 pouces (3.35m) long including the apse, 6 pieds 6 pouces (2.11m) wide and 5 pieds 8 pouces (1.84m) high. They were supported by two 10 pieds (3.25m) fork-shaped poles and an eight pieds (2.60m) crossbar and stretched with 21 small pegs. The name of the regiment had to be inscribed in black on the canvas. The ridge of the tent was lined with a strip of canvas called a 'faîtière' which reinforced and protected this part, it measured the length of the crossbar and was 30 to 40 centimetres wide. Tents were made of unbleached, grey, or yellowish canvas or striped ticking; white and blue or white and brick red like those represented on certain plates of the 1757 manuscript or by Blarenberghe. More rarely, some regiments had tents coated with a mix of

15 Soubise, *Instruction pour l'infanterie de l'armée du roi*, p.29.
16 Soubise, *Instruction pour l'infanterie de l'armée du roi*, p.29.

resin and wax to make them waterproof. This type of canvas was mainly used to cover army wagons and carts, or the winter gaiters of soldiers. Along the bottom of the canvas, all around the tents were sewn 21 brailing loops through which the pegs were passed to stretch the canvas. Since the instruction of 1732, the tents were slightly larger, with length increased from 2.77m to 3.35m and width from 1.95m to 2.11m.

These tents, which were not very large, had to accommodate eight soldiers. Puységur in his *Art de la Guerre* has a plate which shows how to make nine soldiers sleep under a tent, which even if it is not exactly the model of 1753 makes it possible to judge the very rudimentary sleeping conditions of the soldier. In practice the tents always housed fewer soldiers; the companies were never complete due to insufficient recruitment, illness, or men on duty. When a company was under strength, the size of the camp was not changed, but one or more tent sites were left empty, taking care to place them in the centre of the alignment of the tents of the company. Thus, whatever its strength, the camp of a battalion almost always occupied an area of the same size.

There were six tents for the grenadiers and five tents for each company of 40 fusiliers. For a battalion, that made six tents for the grenadier company, 80 tents for the 16 fusilier companies and three tents for the drummers, who camped separately, for a total of 89 tents. The battalions being composed of 17 companies, this represented eight streets, with eight double rows of tents for the fusiliers and a single row on the right for the grenadier company.

A certain synchronisation was sought when setting up or striking tents, for example when breaking camp, when *La Générale* began to beat, two soldiers held the poles at each end of the tent and as soon as the drums stopped all the tents of the same regiment fell at the same time. A similar process was followed during the installation of a camp, so that all tents rose at the same time.

Tents, poles, and crossbars were transported on the regimental carts. The crossbar and the poles were renewed as needed by the Intendancy, which allowed for a certain homogeneity in the size of the tents. Pegs could be made from offcuts from the poles.

It was also the Intendancy that renewed the tents according to losses and destruction. Usually, tents did not last a winter and new tents were distributed each spring. Straw was an important concern for the Intendancy services, as it was used in tents to isolate soldiers from the ground. Each soldier received a bundle of straw weighing 10 pounds, renewed every 15 days in the residential camps or in the camps of position, and in the barracks during winter.

A *sergent* counted as two soldiers, one camped in the first tent of his company and the other in the last. The *tambour major* was considered a *sergent*. The *sergent* of the week in each company had to ensure that all the soldiers of his company were present. To make sure that the soldiers did not spend the night outside, he had to take a roll call at 4:00 a.m. in summer and 6:00 a.m. in winter.

The first tent of each company faced the front of the camp, the last the rear and the others faced the main streets. Between the tents of two companies was a one pied (32cm) wide space between them, called a small street where a furrow was made to carry off water, there was a principle of never occupying this space: 'As all the tents of the infantry are not always equal, if it happens that some regiments by the size of its tents cannot place their apse in the space of the small street then we will take a pied on each side of the main street.'[17] On each side, between each tent, there was also a small street about one pace wide. The tents of the grenadier company and that of the *colonel*'s company faced outwards in the direction of the neighbouring battalions; this space was called the great interval. There were nine pieds (three meters) between the poles of two side-by-side tents. The main street was 15 to 25 pieds wide (4.90–8.10m), it was the space used to adapt and fit the extent of the camp to the terrain.

The battalion was allowed to have a two-wheeled cart drawn by four horses. In his dictionary, Héricourt indicates:

> In several regiments the soldiers have their tents carried by mules that they buy with the remainder of the last loan of the month of February which the King pays for 30 days. In others, they entrust them the sutler of the company, whom they pay ten *sols* each on returning to winter quarters, the tents belong to the sutler at the end of the campaign.[18]

To this cart were added pack horses at the rate of one horse per platoon as indicated by de Broglie's instruction: 'There shall also be attached to the *chasseurs*, either alternately or permanently, as may be arranged by the *colonels*, one of the eight platoon horses to carry their tents; and those of the platoon which will have provided the horse will be distributed among the seven other platoon horses of the battalion.'[19]

All the kitchens, with the sutlers or butchers attached to the regiments, were located in the space between the last tents of the companies and the officers' camp. The soldiers' kitchens were 10 paces behind the companies' encampment, then 10 paces further from the kitchens were the regimental sutlers with their horses, carriages, their own kitchens, wood and fodder arranged around their tents. There were three sutlers per battalion, they lodged in three tents similar to those of the soldiers, but no regulation seemed to exist. Each double line of tents had a double kitchen, which is to say each single line of tents – grenadiers and picquets – had a single kitchen. On the same alignment as the kitchens, behind the first company of each battalion, stood the three tents of the drummers of the battalion and the sixth tent of the grenadier company.

A kitchen was built for each company and one for the drummers. The field kitchens of the armies of Europe were all similar in principle, they were stoves dug into the ground, much more efficient than an open fire. *L'Encyclopédie* mentions that they were 'holes that soldiers make to form a kind of stove

17 Anon., *Instruction concernant le service de campagne* (Metz: veuve Brice Antoine, 1733), p.6.
18 Nicolas d'Héricourt, *Elémens de l'art militaire* (La Haye: J. Neaulme, 1756) vol.2, p.23.
19 Broglie, *Correspondance inédite*, vol 4, p.655.

where they cook the things necessary for their food.'[20] Their principle differed little from the kitchen stoves of the time, except that they were made of earth instead of bricks. They were not replaced by mobile kitchens until very late in the nineteenth century, around the years 1850–1860.

To build these stoves, the soldiers dug a trench just over two pieds (75cm) deep aligned with the tents of their company. For a company, this trench was about three paces long and four pieds wide (1.3m) according to Héricourt. It had to accommodate all the stock pots of the company; at the rate of one stock pot per tent of five to seven men, which made five to eight stoves depending on the number of men, lined up behind each company. The earth from the trench was piled up in a mound opposite the small street, to raise a low earth wall to separate the kitchens of two adjoining companies. To make the hearth, they then dug a sufficient cavity 15–20cm above the bottom of the trench, they then drilled a chimney at the rear of this hearth. Finally, an opening was made just above the hearth to receive the stock pot. To improve the circulation of hot air, the stock pot usually rested on small turf briquettes, in order to leave a small space between the opening of the hearth and the bottom of the stock pot. Opposite the stoves, the soldiers cut a bench which served both as a step to descend into this small trench and as a seat for the soldiers to sit down. For the companies at the extremities of the battalion, the picquets and the grenadiers, the single kitchens were aligned with the tents and the hearths oriented towards the main street.

In order to protect themselves from sun, wind and rain, the soldiers set up a canopy of canvas or planks with a pole and two fork-shaped poles above the kitchens. The disadvantage of these kitchens dug in the ground was that they deteriorated very quickly as soon as the weather degraded. It should be noted that, influenced by the kitchens of the British Army, circular rather than linear kitchens were beginning to appear. The soldiers used the expression 'faire bouillir la timbale',[21] which meant to cook their mess tin in the larger stock pot. What did the soldier's mess tin contain? This question will be addressed in the volume dealing with the Intendancy services and subsistence.

Following the kitchens and sutlers came the encampment of the junior officers – *lieutenants, sous lieutenants* – 20 paces away from the sutlers, they were encamped behind their company, this interval of 20 paces was used for their valets, horses, kitchen, wood and fodder. Their tents were of a similar design as that of soldiers' (tente cannonière), but more spacious and above all they had a marquee which was a double roof. Note that by extension the term marquee tended to become synonymous with double-roofed tent or officer's tent.

Twenty paces behind the junior officers, came the tents of the *capitaines* and their valets and grooms arranged in the same way. The officers' tents measured 4–6.7m2, not including the apse and were seven to eight pieds (2.2–2.6m) high. They were tents with a double roof and double side, the

20 *L'Encyclopédie Encyclopédie ou Dictionnaire raisonné des sciences, des arts et des métiers* (Paris: Jaucourt, Blondel, Le Blond, Bellin, 1751), vol.4, p.539.

21 *Dictionnaire de l'Académie françoise* (Paris: Vve Bernard Brunet, 1762), vol.2, p.834.

vertical parts were called side walls. The space within this double-sided wall was large enough to store and shelter the officers' baggage.

Finally, at the very back of the camp, the staff was placed at 50 paces behind the encampment of the *capitaines*. The tents of senior and junior officers faced the front of the camp, and those of valets and servants faced sideways or rearward. The tents of the *colonel* and *lieutenant colonel* were in the centre of the regiment, the first on the right and the second on the left of the interval in the middle of the battalion. The *major* was on the right on the alignment of the grenadier company and the *aide major*, on the left on that of the last fusilier company. The surgeon was placed between the *colonel* and the *major*, the chaplain between the *lieutenant colonel* and the *aide major*.

Senior officers lodged in much more spacious tents than soldiers, with camp beds, tables, and chairs. If the army had a prolonged sojourn, they had wooden barracks built. Their tents did not have to conform to a regulated size, but contemporaneous paintings give us an idea of their proportions. They could be round or rectangular in shape and had a pavilion, a small awning, which covered the entrance. The inner tent walls were made of ticking and were lined with fine painted canvas or Indian silk. There are many representations of these tents, such as that of Blarenberghe, painted around 1760 on a snuffbox kept in the Hermitage Museum. To feed themselves, the officers, according to their wealth, called either on the cooks who were part of their retinue, or above all on the very many caterers who, with the sutlers, followed the army. Officers had theoretically to stay in the camp with their soldiers, but if there was a dwelling in this camp, they could stay there, after requisition by the *maréchal général des logis*.

The chapels were placed towards the centre of the regiment, near the camp guard in the first or second line. The butcher shops were located 50 paces behind the staff. The latrines were dug 150–200 paces in front of the battalion of the first line and 100 paces behind the staff of the last line. A shelter was built with two fork-shaped poles, four and a half pieds long, and a 12-pieds-long crossbar. But for the convenience of officers, Broglie had two latrines dug 20 paces behind the camp guard and two others 50 paces behind the last tents of the officers. Camp sentries were asked to see that 'no one goes anywhere but the latrines.'[22]

From 1760, Broglie, who had instituted the companies of chasseurs, had them camped apart, behind the battalion, probably on the alignment of the drummers' tents.

> From the first day of the campaign the chasseurs of the two companies which form a platoon will camp together, and they will be provided with a tent and a stock pot, one tent and one stock pot given by the two companies, they will camp separately at the rear of the battalions and will place themselves there at the place of the picquet every time we deploy in order of battle.[23]

22 Broglie, *Instruction pour l'armée du Roi*, p.21

23 Broglie, *Correspondance inédite*, vol.1, p.23.

When the army was encamped in two or three lines, the carts and mules carrying the gunpowder and ammunition of each brigade were placed between the lines, guarded by a sentry, sword in hand, and, when the army encamped in a single line, they were assembled near the guard at the head of the camp.

The headquarters were also called the King's quarters when he was present in the army. The general officers including the *général d'armée*, the *maréchal général des logis*, the *majors généraux* of the infantry and the cavalry, the commander of the artillery, the *prévôt*, the *intendant*, and the treasurer of the army were all to be found there. Headquarters were most often established in a village, preferably located at the rear and in the centre of the army camp. The place chosen for the headquarters gave its name to the camp.

Fallois tents for officers. (Private collection)

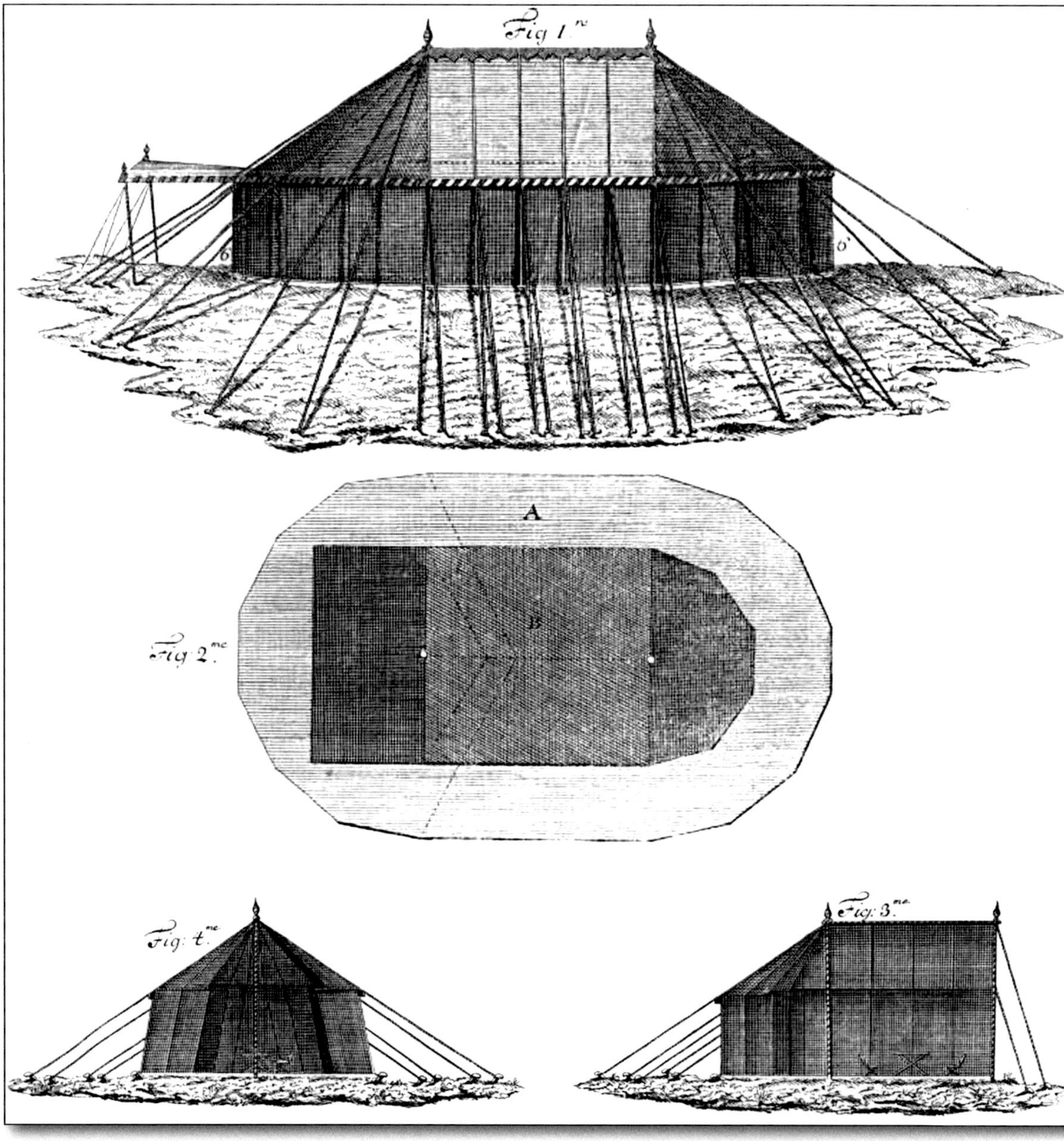

An army on the move was at that time a veritable ambulant city and, in camp, its headquarters were its centre. It was around the headquarters that all the merchants, sutlers, bakers, servants, grooms, butchers, distillers, launderers, repairers, and vendors of all kinds who followed the army set up their stalls. In an attempt to avoid marauding, it was also there that local farmers were authorised to come and sell their vegetables, after obtaining a passport from the *prévôt*, and market days were organized there. This ambulant city was also a good occasion for spies to get around the camp. *Maréchal* de Soubise tried to put some order into this by an instruction that he published in Germany. In a letter dated 17 May 1761, M. de Mopinot, *capitaine* in Dauphin Cavalerie gives us some details:

> M. de Soubise, by an effort of genius which well justifies the choice made of him to lead the best troops and the highest nobility of France, has found an easy and very ingenious means of getting to know everyone infallibly. By this famous decree, sutlers, bakers, merchants following the army, will wear on their clothes a tin plate, on which will be written: sutler, or baker, or merchant following the army of France. All lackeys or servants will wear the livery of their masters, or at least an aiguillette at the colours of the livery. Here is where wit shines: people employed in forage will wear a green cockade; those employed in butcher shops, a red cockade; those employed in provisions, a yellow cockade; those employed in hospitals, a black cockade; secretaries, valets, household officers, a blue cockade: such a decree and a retinue of seventy aides-de-camp, here is assuredly something to intimidate the enemy; so get ready to sing Te Deums for our victories or for peace.[24]

Soldiers could only come to get supplies accompanied by officers or non-commissioned officers. They were assembled at the head of their regiment at 7:00 a.m., when the first roll call was made, they were then led to the entrance to the headquarters, from there, they could then freely go and do their shopping with the merchants, sutlers and peasants. At 11:00 a.m., they had to be at the entrance to the headquarters, where a new roll call was made, before being escorted back to their regiments.

If the army stayed in one place for a prolonged period, a mobile hospital was set up in a village or houses near a river, but not too close to the camp that infection could spread.

The provisions quarter was the area where the bread-wagons were assembled for distribution. The bread was transported there from the neighbouring towns where the bakeries had been established. This area was located between the second line towards the centre of the camp.

However, everything did not always go as planned, thus on 25 August 1757, after three days of marching in pursuit of the army of the Duke of Cumberland which was retiring, the army of the duc de Richelieu set up camp near Verden. Tents were pitched and everyone got busy preparing the evening soup and foraging. Here is how the *Gazette de Vienne* reported what happened next:

24 Lemoine, *Correspondance*, p.287.

> Yesterday evening there was such a great hurricane that no one remembers in living memory having felt one like it. It did a lot of damage to our army, torn tents, and those that were not blown away by the violence of the wind were generally laid over on the ground, there were many overturned and broken baggage and ammunition wagons, and a great deal of ammunition was spoiled by the heavy rain which accompanied this terrible storm.[25]

A letter from *capitaine* Mopinot gives us another testimony to this summer storm:

> ...but at half-past five we had to fight the elements; hardly had the camp been pitched, many soldiers still being on the march, all the cavalry having gone to forage very far, the soldiers and servants scattered to collect straw, wood and water, that a terrible cloud appeared: wind, hail, fire wreaked terrible havoc, in an instant all tents were smashed and swept away, splinters flew everywhere and injured many people; riders, men, horses, troops were swept into the river, others were killed by lightning; horses, beds, equipment are scattered on all sides, the weapons are broken, all soldiers soaked by the rain and bruised by the hail have passed the night in water and without food, officers have fled into the houses neighbouring the camp, those of the princes have been singularly useful to them; finally, the army is in a pitiful state of decrepitude, everything is still in such great confusion that it is impossible to say exactly how much it is ruined. As for me, my dear friend, I was lucky enough to save my horses, which I brought into the makeshift room where I was lodged, but I came very close to paying dearly for this sort of good fortune; fire from the camp flew in the straw-covered roofs, and the wind shook the house so strongly that the less intrepid fled.[26]

It took several weeks before getting an army able to defend itself again.

In April 1759, a major change in infantry tactics was decided by *maréchal* Belle-Isle. A proponent of shock over fire for the infantry, he modified the arrangement of the order of battle of the army which he wanted to see deployed in column. The organisation of camps had to be modified accordingly.

> I have the honour to send you, Sir, a copy of the letter which I wrote by order of the King to *Maréchal* de Contades, on 9 April, to let him know that His Majesty's intention was that in the future all the infantry of the army he commands will only be formed in six ranks. In consequence of this decision to which His Majesty wishes all his infantry regiments to comply with, He ordered that in the future they would camp in platoons as explained in the attached memorandum. You will kindly give your orders accordingly to those within the reach of your command and keep an eye on their execution.
>
> Order in which the King wants the battalions to camp in the future, considering His Majesty's decision which obliges them to always form in six ranks. The front of each battalion will occupy 40 toises [78m]; namely:

25 *Gazette de Vienne*, N°.55 du mercredi 7 septembre 1757.
26 Lemoine, *Correspondance*, p.287.

two toises for the emplacement of the tents of the grenadier company.
four toises for a main street.
two toises for the emplacement of the tents of the two companies of the first platoon, which will camp on the same alignment in the depth of the camp, as well as those of the other platoons.
two toises for the emplacement of the third platoon whose tents will lean against those of the first platoon.
four toises for a main street.
four toises for the emplacement of the fifth and seventh platoons leaning against each other.
four toises for a main street.
four toises for the emplacement of the fifth and sixth platoons leaning against each other.
four toises for a main street.
four toises for the emplacement of the fourth and second platoons leaning against each other.
six toises for the interval from one battalion to the other.

Note. The first companies of each platoon will be encamped closest to the front of the camp and the second next on the same line. The main streets have been increased by one toise so that the platoons can form there in six ranks without hindrance.[27]

We know from testimonies and orders of battle that the deployment in column, if it was the subject of exercises, would not be used when forming for battle. With the exception of that taken in August 1759 at Minden by *maréchal* de Contades, where he placed his infantry in mixed order. After 1760, when *maréchal* de Broglie took command of the army, it returned to an arrangement in three ranks.

The Camp during Winter Quarters

The order of battle was preserved even when the army dispersed to take up winter quarters. La Roche Aymon after detailing the measures taken to enter winter quarters in 1759 writes: 'It will be noted that the army retained, although dispersed in its winter quarters, its order of battle, that is to say that the regiments were quartered in the same order as if the army had been encamped.'[28]

During the winter quarters, the season meant that there was no longer an abundance of fodder for horses, and the army had to live on reserves of dry fodder, with the troops were quartered in towns, villages or hamlets. The choice of cantonments was important; they had to be spread out enough not to ruin the country; but also had to be protected by a river or a fortified

27 'Vieille Tactique', *Carnet de la Sabretache, Revue militaire rétrospective*, 1895. p.43.
28 Guillaume marquis de la Roche Aymon, *Mémoires sur l'art de la guerre* (Paris: Corréard, 1857), vol.4, p.259.

place, and so sheltered from enemy light troops. Scouts were regularly sent out to reconnoitre and avoid any surprise raid. During the poor weather season, hostilities were most often suspended, being limited to skirmishes between hussars or light troops. The troops were barracked, that is to say, they lodged in rudimentary wooden shelters. These barracks were built on a piece of terrain seven to eight pieds (2.5m) long and six to seven pieds (2m) wide. Four large poles were used to carry four long crosspieces placed askew to support the roof which was of straw, or branches for the walls. If possible, planks were used, or for lack of anything better, wooden crosspieces interwoven with straw. Communities often complained that the soldiers destroyed the barns and other lean-tos to recover the planks. Soldiers then pitched their tents in these barracks for shelter, which did not prevent tents from becoming mouldy and justifying their replacement for each campaign. During the winter of 1759, the early arrival of abundant snow did not allow the timely construction of enough barracks, and, for a period, soldiers had to alternate every other day between tents and barracks.

Cormontaigne gives us drawings of such barracks built in a camp established near Metz in 1728 for fortification work.[29] This was an ideal barrack camp; it is not certain that during the campaigns of the Seven Years War all soldiers would have had such comfortable plank barracks. Most of the time, barracks were made of wattle and daub. The wattle consisted of interlaced flexible branches, such as hazel branches, between posts. Then the walls were sealed with a mix of mud and cut straw. The roofs were made of thatch or planks depending on what was available. Soldiers also weaved straw mats to insulate themselves from the ground.

From Colombier, a military doctor, we discover that barrack camps could be substantial:

> We make with tree branches, earth and manure, a sort of barracks that enclosed the tents. We make underground holes for the kitchen, for heating a kind of roof covers these holes, there are chimneys; and it sometimes happens that by making several of them touching each other with communicating doors, we make real apartments. Horses and cattle are similarly barracked and thus preserved … One can find fault with these [barracks] surrounding the tents; and although they hardly preserve from humidity, at least they are not dangerous. It is only very essential to build them solidly enough, so that there is no risk of being crushed in them, if they were to fall, and to make thatch roofs which allow water to flow. It must be forbidden to put embers in the midst of tents, as I have sometimes seen practised; because in addition to the fear of fire, one must have the fear of the smell of embers which is very pernicious, and goes especially to the head.[30]

The Intendancy was responsible for providing firewood, plus oil and wicks for the lamps.

---

29 Henri de Bousmard, *Mémorial de Cormontaingne pour l'attaque des places ...* (Berlin: Decker, 1803), p.359.

30 Jean Colombier, *Code de médecine militaire pour le service de terre* (Paris: Costard, 1772), p.227.

Winter conditions, with unsuitable equipment, poor food, and disastrous hygienic conditions, led to overcrowded hospitals and filled cemeteries. M. du Landey *major* in the Régiment de La Marche Infanterie writes during the winter of 1758–1759:

> We are as bad as we can be, with little food and so bad that without pressing hunger we would not dare to look at the meat we eat on our fat days … it is monstrous how many soldiers are dying, and how many officers are leaving. The man from Formigny died in the Brunswick hospital, his name was Hébert. We are losing our finest and strongest soldiers to pneumonia. Four grenadiers died on me, the smallest of which must have been five pieds six pouces and the oldest not yet thirty years old.[31]

The Bivouac

On the eve of battle, the camp was reduced to a minimum, the baggage remained at the rear, and the disposition of the troops who camped was made according to the planned order of battle. Most often, troops took shelter in tents, the use of the open-air bivouac, without shelter, as would be practised during the campaigns of the Empire was not yet in frequent use. But it was sometimes practised as Chevrier recounts in his *Histoire de la campagne de 1757*: '*Maréchal* de Richelieu, who feared some surprise, decided to make his army, which was still composed of only 44 battalions and 42 squadrons, spend the night at the bivouac.'[32] The company's muskets were gathered together in piles of arms, the butts isolated from the ground by branches, and a few steps behind, men spent the night around the fires.

Soldiers' Leisure

At the camp, soldiers, apart from exercises, chores, and guards had to pass time. Several contemporaneous paintings show us camp scenes. It is probably necessary to nuance these bucolic visions, when the camps were set up during a military campaign, the search for food remained a major concern for the soldiers. To combat foraging and desertion, there were four roll calls a day, two of which were at night, and officers were asked to regularly change roll call times throughout the day.

One key place to entertain the soldier was the local cabaret, with its distillers and sutlers, easily spotted from a distance. It was a very large and high tent with, at the end of the ridge pole, a piece of brightly coloured fabric which floated in the wind and where a crown of braided branches served as a

31 André Corvisier, 'Un officier normand de Louis XV. Le lieutenant-colonel Jean-François Le Parsonnier du Landey d'après sa correspondance (1714 -1785)', *Annales de Normandie*, 9e année n°3, 1959, p.205.

32 François Antoine Chevrier, *Suite des mémoires pour servir à l'histoire de notre temps* (Francfort: Publisher unknown, 1758), p.88.

sign. 'The love for wine is for the soldier, what the passion for gambling is for the officer: the mother of all disorders … And the women he finds in the lairs to which he is admitted destroy his health, ruin his temper, and debase his soul…'[33] This was where the soldiers spent what remained of their pay on beer, wine, and brandy. They played trading games or combination games as they were then called: checkers, dice, piquet, quadrille games, and ombre games. But also board games that resembled The Game of the Goose,[34] and outside, bowling, 'jeu de la grenouille' (a type of shuffleboard), horseshoes, and bocce; noting that there was not yet a jack, but a stake which marked the target.

Because these gambling games were also played by officers, causing quarrels and duels, very repressive decrees had been published since the time of Louis XIV to prohibit such games. Games of chance played for money were forbidden, for example the games of hocca, pharaon, barbacole, and basset. Fines were very heavy, up to almost 6,000 livres; split one third for the King, one third for the poor of the place where the infraction had been committed and one third for the informant. If the culprit could not pay the fine, he risked four months to one year in prison. If the soldiers gambled for a round of drinks or a few pints, officers could lose fortunes. Picquet patrols also served to ensure that no prohibited gambling was taking place.

Soldiers also danced and sang at the local cabaret, and there were popular songs that kept up with current events: *Trois jeunes tambours*, *Marlborough s'en va-t-en-guerre*, *Les adieux de la Tulipe*, *Fanchon*, *D'un grenadier à sa maîtresse*, to name a but a few. They often celebrated victories, but some song lyrics written on popular tunes made fun of princes, of the powerful, or of Madame de Pompadour.

The troops also attended shows, as in April 1759, when comedians were brought to Frankfurt to entertain the soldiers:

> M. le Duc de Broglie approves of the arrangements Messieurs Lot and Bersac will make to establish here the troupe of French actors whom he has engaged to come from Metz for this purpose. It asks these gentlemen to kindly grant the said troupe all the help it needs, and promote their performances and their establishment … I have the honour to inform Messieurs du Magistrat that the troupe of French actors, who are due to arrive from Metz, will begin performances next Sunday…[35]

There were also puppet shows.

Broglie's instructions of 1759, renewed by that of Soubise in 1760, indicated that it was forbidden for soldiers or valets to sell coffee, on the other hand they could sell brandy, tobacco, vinegar, cheese, and other products in the camp of their regiments. Coffee had only been introduced in the middle of the seventeenth century and was still a rare and expensive product. It is likely

33 *Encyclopédie Méthodique, Art militaire* (Paris: Panckoucke, 1787), vol.3, p.140.

34 A board game where players move their counters according to rolls of the dice and hope avoid hazards.

35 Elisabeth Mentzel, 'Die französische und deutsche Komödie von 1759 bis 1703 und ihr Einfluss auf den jungen Goethe' in *Archiv für Frankfurts Geschichte und Kunst* (Frankfurt: Völker, 1882), p.250.

Jean-Antoine Watteau, 'Soldats jouant aux cartes' (Soldiers playing cards) (1710). (Anne S.K. Brown Military Collection)

that troops used roasted chicory instead, a usage introduced by the Dutch. But such an instruction suggests that coffee had already taken hold in daily life. Still better, Becher in his series of gouaches he made on the armies he saw passing through his city during the war, shows us a drawing of a vendor of coffee and milk kept warm by embers. Coffee, like tobacco and salt, was subject to taxes and its exclusive trade entrusted to an outsourced tax collector. But, as we have already seen, tobacco could still be resold in the camp.

Paying Honours and Saluting

On a daily basis, soldiers during the first half of the eighteenth century did not salute their officers when they passed them, and officers did not salute each other. The saluting of officers among themselves was not a military courtesy, it was the one that nobles returned among themselves, according to their rank and their grade by removing their hats with more or less reverence. Circumstances in which honours had to be paid by presenting arms were few in number at the time. Honours had to be paid to the King, the princes of the blood, the legitimized princes, the *général* of the army and, in garrisons, the governors and *lieutenants généraux* of the provinces. On certain occasions, officers paid honours, and these occasions were well defined, for example every time the battalion or regiment took up arms to practice. When a general officer or a prince passed in front of a camp it was only the soldiers on duty, such as the various camp guards or the picquets, who paid honours, the other soldiers continued to go about their business. To pay honours, soldiers fixed their bayonet and stood in the 'Present Arms' position.

The Salute of an Officers Carrying a Spontoon

According to the decree of 14 May 1754, the salute of an officer carrying a spontoon when it was done halted with the officer resting on this weapon at the head of his unit, had to be made in four steps.

At the first, he would wheel to the right, carrying the spontoon at an angle, the butt spike ahead, raised only two from the ground, the arm extended at shoulder height, and the left hand grasping the spontoon about three pieds above the butt spike. At the second, the right hand leaving the spontoon, the left would be turned gently until the blade was lowered forward close to the ground, and the butt spike came to join the right hand, which would always remain at shoulder height. At the third, he would bring the spontoon back to the same position it was in at the end of the first step. At the fourth, he would wheel to the left, to adopt the same position he was in before saluting. He would then take off his hat with his left hand and would not put it back on until the person receiving the salute has passed him a few paces. The saluting officer had to pay attention to timely begin the movement so that, when he lowered the blade of the spontoon, the person to whom he was returning the salute was still three paces away, and that when he was front of him, he had taken back his initial position.

To salute with the spontoon while marching, with the officer carrying the spontoon on the left arm, he would, when he was approximately 30 paces from the person to whom the salute was due, transfer the spontoon to his right shoulder in three steps. At the first, he would grab the spontoon with his right hand at eye level. At the second, he would carry it in front of him on the right, holding it perpendicular, arm stretched forward. At the third, he would put it on the right shoulder, holding it horizontally, elbow at shoulder height. The officer making these movements had to take care to move three paces away from the first rank, so that by resting the spontoon on his shoulder, the blade could not injure the soldiers following him. He had to continue to walk in this position with an even step, until he was nine or 10 paces from the person who was to be saluted, and then the salute would be in six steps. At the first, advancing the left foot, and pivoting the body on the right heel as if wheeling right, the spontoon would be carried in front, holding it horizontally at the height of the shoulders, the left hand three pieds from the butt spike. At the second and third steps, successively advancing the right and left feet, the left hand would turn the spontoon, as previously described for salute at the halt, observing that the spontoon would be straight up when the right foot would reach its position, and that the blade would be close to the ground when the left foot reached its position. At the fourth and fifth steps, the movements made during the second and third steps would be reversed, making sure again that the spontoon would be straight up at the end of the step made with the right foot, and that it was horizontal once grabbed with the right hand, the left foot coming to the ground. At the sixth step, advancing the right foot, the spontoon would be put back on the right shoulder; then advancing the left foot, the officer would take off his hat and hold it alongside, until he had passed all those to whom he own honour: after he would put his hat back, and a few paces beyond, the spontoon would be taken off the shoulder, and carried on the left arm. While marching, the *capitaines* and *lieutenants* of each division formed a single rank to salute together.

Maréchal de Puységur observes that the various movements prescribed for the salute with the spontoon made this salute very complex, that if one looked for correctness in these movements, there was seldom any; that with regard to utility, there was none; and that thus the time employed in training for the salute with the spontoon, was wasted, or employed very uselessly. To rectify this salute and to make it easier and consequently more graceful and noble, this illustrious *maréchal* thought that it should be made similar to the old cavalry salute, which was in use in his time. For this purpose, he thought that, when the King, the princes, or the other persons whom the troops had to salute, would pass at the head of a battalion, the officers, spontoon in hands, should at first, without moving from their place, lower the blade of the spontoon in front of them with their right hand, until it was about half a *pied* from the ground; at the second step, return the spontoon to its initial position; and at the third, take off their hat with their left hand. This salute, he said, would be quite similar to that of the cavalry, and it would have all the nobleness of it.[36]

36 Jacques François de Chastenet Puységur, *Art de la guerre, par principes et par règles* (Paris: Jombert, 1749), p.68.

The Salute of Officers Carrying a Musket

The salute with the musket for fusilier officers, a weapon with which they were armed since the decree of 31 October 1758, had to be done in the same way as had been regulated for grenadier officers by that of 14 May 1754 and 6 May 1755. To distinguish the officer from the fusiliers, it is important to note that the officer carried the musket on the right shoulder while the fusiliers presented the musket on the left shoulder.

The salute with the musket at the halt was performed in four steps. the decree of 6 May 1755 described it in six steps but indicated that if they had to salute those with the spontoon, they had to synchronise their movement so that it was done simultaneously. At the first step, the musket being carried on the left arm as usual, wheeling right, the officer seized the musket firmly with the right hand behind the hammer, while removing his left hand, and it was transferred to the right, arm extended at shoulder height. At the second, the officer lowered the end of the musket to the ground, supporting it with the left hand which had been moved forward, and on which it would lean at two fingerbreadths from the trigger guard. At the third, the musket was placed back as it was at the end of the first step. At the fourth, the officer stood at ease by wheeling left, and joined the hand to the musket, after which he removed his hat with the right hand and put it back on as it has been described for the salute with the spontoon. Care had to be taken to begin these movements early enough so that the salute with the musket was done three paces ahead of the person being saluted, and if he was coming from the left, to precede them by a half-turn to the left.

The salute with the musket was done the same way while marching. At the first step, the left foot was moved forward, 10 paces before being opposite the person to be saluted. At the second, by taking two more steps, so that the end of the musket came close to the ground, at the same time as the left foot landed forward. At the third, by taking the fourth and fifth steps. At the fourth, moving the right foot forward.

The Salute of the Colours

To salute the colour, the *enseignes* had first to rest the butt spike of the lance on the right hip, holding it at a slight angle, and when they were to salute, they gently lowered the lance to the ground, lifting it up likewise, and then they took off their hat with their left hand.

The Salute of *Sergents* carrying a Halberd

To salute at the halt, *sergents* took off their hat with the left hand, while resting on their halberd.

6

Infantry Uniform, Arms and Equipment

Bibliographic References

From the beginning of the eighteenth century and as uniforms were renewed, the cut of them changed, evolving towards an increasingly military style, distinct from civilian clothing. The clothing of the troops was renewed every three years, the accoutrements and the knapsack were only renewed every six or seven years. Three clothing elements were reserved for the military, as the decree of 13 October 1782 reminds us, and civilians were prohibited from wearing them. These were the epaulette on the coat, the cockade on the hat and the sword-knot, all of which were considered distinctive marks of military status.

The distinctive marks of the various regiments of the French infantry of the Seven Years War were complex. They were the facing colours assigned to each regiment which were found on the cuffs, collar and lapels; as well as the shape of the pocket flaps which, by their arrangement and the number of buttons, allowed a wide variety of distinctive designs, and finally the golden or silver colour of the buttons and of the hat lace. The allocation of the facing colours was fixed by the decree of 1736: 'the waistcoat will be double-breasted, all in grey-white outside and inside, as well as the coat, without under any pretext whatsoever another colour could be used. Only the cuffs, will continue to have the colours assigned to each regiment.'[1] Despite this official text, coloured breeches and even more often coloured waistcoats persisted in many regiments. With fashion, the collar and the lapels appeared in the middle of the eighteenth century, they generally took the facing colour, they were formalised and generalised by the decree of December 1762.

The uniform, arms and equipment of the infantryman were regulated by the decrees of 10 March 1729, 20 April 1736, and those of 19 and 29 January 1747, and finally by that of 21 December 1762. Within a regiment, the *majors* were responsible for the application of and adherence to these decrees. For

1 Acte royal, 20 April 1736, *Ordonnance du Roi concernant l'habillement de l'infanterie française* (Paris: Imprimerie royale, 1736).

clothing, each regiment concluded a contract for the supply and manufacture of its uniforms, and they received cloth from the royal factories. It should be noted that each new decree was not a complete update of previous texts, so the articles of an old decree remained applicable as long as a new text did not specifically modify them. In 1757, references were still largely made to decrees dating from Louis XIV for the service of the infantry. With a lack of precision, most of these decrees allowed various interpretations. At the time, there was no comprehensive compilation of all the texts regulating military life; the works of Rochefort, Héricourt, Chennevières, and others were available but incomplete. Such a compilation was among the projects of the comte de Guibert, but it came to nothing.

From 1758 to 1762, the first official sources were the *États militaires*,[2] required reading for any officer of the Ancien Régime. The first edition contained errors as indicated by the authors in the disclaimer of the 1759 edition:

> Despite the precautions we had taken, a considerable number of mistakes had slipped into the military report that we gave last year. To obviate this this year, the Maréchal de Belle-Isle required that before printing anything, our manuscript be submitted to the examination of the war offices, relating to the different parts contained therein; and this order was punctually carried out.[3]

The significance of the *États militaires* is clear, both for promotions, and for the evolution of uniforms. It is important to refer back to the decree which defined the distinctive marks of the new uniforms of the reform of 1762; it shows that some regiments had already adopted the 1762 uniform during the Seven Years War. Similarly, the *Etats des troupes de France* of 1753, the *Seconde carte militaire* for the year 1754, the dictionaries of La Chesnaye of 1745, 1751, 1758, the military maps of France from 1733 to 1741 all give valuable information, particularly on the flags and standards which change little from the Régence, and on certain details such as buttons and collar.

The iconographic sources are also very valuable, even if they are not as exhaustive as the *États militaires*. What follows is a brief critical analysis.

The manuscript of the *Pavillons Anciens* produced around 1748 and kept in the library of Perpignan is of limited interest. Like the manuscript of Gudenus, created around 1735, it confirms the introduction of the collar in the regiments at that time. Concerning the colours (flags), the draftsman reproduced heraldically the texts of the decrees, leading to very frequent errors. In this area, this source is far too often faulted to make it a reliable vexillological iconographic base.

For the period of the Seven Years War, there are a few infantry plates of an anonymous series executed around 1755, three of which (Dauphin, Lyonnais, La Tour du Pin) are kept at the Anne S. K. Brown Military Collection, while

2 The *États Militaire de France* from 1758 to 1793 can be consulted on the Bibliothèque nationale de France website (Gallica BNF), <https://gallica.bnf.fr>.

3 Montandre Longchamp, *État militaire de France pour l'année 1759* (Paris: Guillyn, 1759), p.iii.

three others (Béarn, Cambis, Guyenne) are held by Parks Canada. These plates present little documentary interest. In particular, the illustration of the colour of Dauphin Infanterie is, as in the Perpignan manuscript, an attempt at pictorial representation of an incomplete heraldic description, leading to an erroneous graphical representation.

The Bouxwiller manuscript is an inventory of the collections of Landgrave Louis IX of Hesse Darmstadt–Buchsweiler Inventar der Uniformsammlung des Landgrafen Ludwig IX von Hessen-Darmstadt. It contains the descriptions of all the military artefacts appearing in the collection of the Castle of Bouxwiller-Pirmasen in Alsace. It mainly covers the regiments of the German states throughout the eighteenth century, but also German regiments in the service of France and some French regiments.

The manuscript in the Musée de l'armée entitled *Troupes du Roi, Infanterie française et étrangère, année 1757*, is remarkably precise, even if it contains a few errors, such as the colour of the Gardes suisses reproduced as the colour of the Régiment suisse de Planta. It is interesting to note that even though the author is not known, it is certain that he came from the studio of Charles Parrocel, the famous painter of battle scenes, who died in 1750. There are three famous engravings by Le Bas, executed after Parrocel's drawings; two of these engravings are titled: 'Halte des Gardes suisses' and the last one is titled: 'Halte des Gardes Françoises.' The similarities in the postures found in these three engravings and those represented in the series of the 1757 manuscript, as well as the studies by Parrocel kept at the National Gallery in London, leave no doubt about their provenance. In the 'Halte des Gardes Françoises', for example, we find a seated pipe smoker from the Régiment de Berry, card players from the Régiment de Jenner or the Régiment de Conti, a soldier seated on a drum from the Régiment de Rochefort, a lying soldier from the Régiment de Guyenne, a mirror view of a soldier with his hand in his waistcoat of the Régiment de Lorraine or the Régiment de Rouergue. The same is true for the other two engravings. These engravings were already available in 1736, so more than 20 years before the 1757 manuscript, but the latter also represents regiments and outfits that are later than 1736. What makes it possible to lift doubts about the dependability of this series of gouaches are the small modifications made to the original models of the 1736 engravings, such as the addition of a collar, a shoulder strap, or the tightening of the cuffs. Although the date 1757 appears in the title of the manuscript, the gouaches were probably produced over a longer period between 1736 and 1762; and by several draftsmen as demonstrated by the different styles. These plates were later assembled into a volume. Some of them may have been executed by Lenfant, a painter of battle scenes and a pupil of Charles Parrocel, who worked in his studio.

A plate entitled 'État nouveau des Trouppes de France mises sur pié comme elles se trouvent effectivement l'an 1758' published in Augsburg, indicates the colours of the uniforms and cuffs, using coloured triangles. It formed part of a series of a dozen plates representing practically all the European troops at war in 1758: Denmark, Sweden, Prussia, Austria, and Hanover. It is difficult to precisely date the information it contains. Thus, an infantry regiment is still named Joyeuse when it had become Vaubécourt in

July 1755, but it lists the new Régiment de Deux-Ponts raised in 1757 and ignores the Régiment de Bouillon raised the same year.

The *Teatro Militar de Europa* by Taccoli-Canacci, Alfonso, marchese de San Possidonio published in 1760, and kept at the Armería Real in Madrid,[4] is a remarkable series of plates because of the extent of the regiments represented, by its precision, and by the quality of conservation of its colours. By referring to the names of the *colonels* mentioned in this document, we can date the information to the second half of 1759. With the manuscript of 1757, it is the most complete iconographic document for this period. However, it should be noted that Taccoli used model templates, similar to those he had used for the representation of Spanish troops.

The printed work entitled *Recueil de toutes les troupes qui forment les armées françaises dessiné et illuminé d'après nature à Nuremberg chez Gabriel Nicolas Raspe en 1761* seems to be based on the texts of the *Etats militaires*. There is a second edition published in 1762 which is very interesting for the corrections made and the confirmation of certain modifications adopted in 1761 and described in the *Etats militaires*. Raspe makes a few systematic errors; thus, he ignores the rule which matches the colour of the hat lace with the colour of the buttons, and gives all the officers a gold laced hat and the fusiliers a white laced one. In the 1761 edition, he gives some of the infantry officers a command sash around the waist, and others a gorget; or again he gives soft black boots to officers and black gaiters to fusiliers. Finally, due to their alteration over time, the colours are not always interpretable; blue has often turned purple and sometimes green. The 1768 edition is more precise, especially on the design of the pockets, for example. The 1762 edition is undoubtedly the most interesting for the information it allows to cross-check and confirm.

There is also a series of gouaches by Johann Christian Becher, entitled *Wahrhaftige Nachricht derer Begebenheiten, so sich in dem Herzogthum Weimar by dem gewaltigen Kriege Friedrichs II., Königs von Preußen, mit der Königin von Ungarn, Marien Theresen, samt ihren Bundesgenossen zugetragen*, produced between 1757 and 1763 and whose original is kept in the Herzogin Anna Amalia Bibliothek.[5] This is a very beautiful series with outfits drawn on the spot, which gives it great documentary value despite some erroneous attributions.

The series of small drawings from the manuscript of Johann Gottfried Schultz, *Abbildung Preußischer Kayser und Französischer Soldaten aus dem siebenjährigen Kriege* of around 1757–1760 is kept at the Grafisches Kabinett of the Kulturhistorischen Museums in Görlitz. It also constitutes a contemporaneous source drawn on the spot, which is very interesting. There are about 10 representations of French soldiers, including French infantry officers in city clothes, an engineer, a Chasseur de Fischer, and others. Like

4 The Taccolli Manuscript from the Real Biblioteca del Palacio Real de Madrid (RB) <https://rbdigital.realbiblioteca.es/s/realbiblioteca/item/11818>, accessed 10 May 2024.

5 The Becher manuscript from the Herzogin Anna Amalia Bibliothek (HAAB), <https://haab-digital.klassik-stiftung.de/viewer/image/1373196092/31/LOG_0011/>, accessed 10 May 2024.

the Becher manuscript, its interest lies in the representation of outfits directly observed by the author.

For the colours (flags), we use the *Carte Générale de la Monarchie Française 1730–1733* by Lemau de la Jaisse as a base,[6] along with its sequels, the *Cartes du militaire de France* from 1733 to 1741. Anna Beek's and Spofforth's engravings from the War of the Spanish Succession are also always useful to consult. For this same period, the manuscript of Du Vivier in 1715 mostly gives us representations of colours of regiments which had been disbanded by the time of the Seven Years War, which limits its interest for this period. The gouaches of Delaistre and Hermand produced during the Regency also constitute a precious source.

The aforementioned manuscript *Troupes du Roi, Infanterie française et étrangère, année 1757* gives many details on the colours and patterns of the flags, it is one of the main sources for this period. The *Tableau militaire des drapeaux, étendarts et guidons des troupes au service de la France... pour l'année 1771* by Chaligny kept by the Department of Yvelines, as well as Montigny's booklet of 1772, *Uniformes militaires, où se trouvent gravés en taille-douce les uniformes de la Maison du Roy, de tous les régiments de France, les drapeaux, étendards et guidons, avec la date de leur création et les différentes figures de l'exercice, tant de la cavalerie que de l'infanterie*[7] are two works that give us a very complete overview of the colours, guidons and standards of that time, however, upon analysis they cannot be primary sources. There are also rare examples of colours kept in collections such as the Musée de l'armée, the Armeria Réal in Turin, and the cantonal archives of Schwitz in Switzerland.

Finally, all the paintings, drawings, red chalk drawings, and engravings of contemporaneous artists such as Eisen, Charles Parrocel, Lenfant, Carmontelle, Le Paon, Le Bas, Joseph Vernet, and Blarenberghe constitute good sources; without forgetting modern authors like Henri Boisselier, Roger Forthoffer, Lucien Rousselot, Michel Pétard, Eugène Leliepvre, and Dugué McCarthy.

The Soldiers' Uniform

The Hat and its Cockade

The hat was made of black wool; those worn by *sergents* were of good Berry lambswool or other equivalent quality and those worn by soldiers of ordinary lambswool. The decree of the Council of State of 10 August 1700 required that a mark be branded on the lace, bearing the first letter of the name and the surname of the manufacturer, followed by the letter T for troops. The three-cornered hat had a four pouces (10.8cm) high crown with nine more lignes (2.25cm) for the turned-up brim. The hats respectively weighed 10,

6 La Carte générale du militaire de France de 1733 par Lémau de la Jaisse, <https://bibnum.institutdefrance.fr/medias/54/1b/45/8c/541b458c-1e6e-4725-bba0-97659f1e6cfb/attachedfiles/bib_mazarine_2_8072_Res_HR.pdf>, accessed 10 May 2024.

7 Montigny, <https://gallica.bnf.fr/ark:/12148/bpt6k15213965?rk=21459;2>, accessed 10 May 2024.

11 and 12 ounces, for the three sizes: small, medium and large. They were manufactured in accordance with the decree of 26 January 1746.

For troops, the hat was edged with a lace of fake gold or silver, straddling the rim of the hat. The width of this lace was different depending on the rank; for the fusilier it was 16 lignes (3.6cm) wide, including 12 lignes on the outer rim, while for the *maréchal des logis* it was 20 lignes (4.5cm), with 16 lignes on the outer rim. Following the Prussian fashion, the three sides of the brim were turned up, in particular that of the front. The hat was worn with the front point slightly turned to the left. The silver and gold-coloured threads of the hat lace were made with a copper thread which was then simply silvered or silvered and then gold plated depending on the desired metal colour. The hats of *sergents* were edged with a real silver thread.

The cockade was an exclusive attribute of the military, it was forbidden for civilians to put it on their hats. It was made of cloth or paper ribbon and was held in place on the edge of the left point of the hat by a black silk strap fixed by a small button. During the eighteenth century, white or black cockades were used, black could be a mark of mourning. However, it is impossible nowadays to know what determined the choice of one or the other colour for a specific regiment. In March 1764, in the decree concerning the funds destined to the maintenance of the troops and in the patterns annexed to it, mention was made of cockades of white cotton canvas for both horsemen and infantrymen or light troops, but it was the regulation of 25 April 1767 which definitively determined that the cockades of the infantry would be white. One might think that this was not a major distinguishing attribute; authors like Père Daniel did not even mention the cockade, even in the *États militaires* from 1758 to 1769 it was never described either for the infantry, the cavalry, or the dragoons. It was only described for the regiments of the Gardes françaises and Gardes suisses who had black cockade at that time, or for the Gendarmerie de France for which it was initially black and became white in the *États militaires* of 1769. The Gardes du Corps companies also wore white cockades mixed with the colour of each specific company with the exception of the first company which wore a black cockade. In a portrait of Louis XV painted by Van Loo, we see a Garde du Corps of the first company in the background, his cockade is not visible, but a black *plumetis* (feather) borders the silver hat lace. The *Manuel de l'homme du monde* of 1761 states about the companies of Gendarmes and Chevaux légers of the Garde du Roi: 'The difference in the clothing of the Gendarmes and Chevaux légers of the Garde du Roi is that the Gendarmes have golden buttonholes, black cockades and the Chevaux légers have silver buttonholes and the white cockade.'[8]

However, this apparent lack of interest is contradicted by a passage in the *Histoire de la dernière guerre en Bohème*, describing the War of the Austrian Succession where one can read:

> After the total retreat of the French troops, all was quiet in Prague, except those who had seemed attached to the Emperor. A tribunal was established against

8 Pons-Augustin Alletz, *Manuel de l'homme du monde* (Paris: Guillyn, 1761), p.251.

Charles Eisen, 'Exercice de la Garde du Roi' (Exercise of the King's Guard). (Anne S.K. Brown Military Collection)

> those of that party which was soon dissolved; the main ones having first been kidnapped and sent to Hungary. It was forbidden to have any commerce either with the French or with the Imperials. The young Prince de Mansfeld, for having come to the Grand Burgrave with a white cockade, experienced the cruellest treatment on the part of a lieutenant of hussars, who apologized for having taken him for a French officer. although this prince had told him his name.[9]

Similarly, for the period of the Seven Years War in the *Gazette de Vienne* of September 1757:

> If we are to believe the reports of deserters who come to us from these camps [Bernstadt and Schöne], the King of Prussia has thought of a new expedient to nurture the courage of the soldier, and give him hope of a happy future. Several officers who speak French go through the Prussian regiments, they wear the uniform of France and the white cockade, and helped by this ruse, they make the troops believe that there is a treaty of friendship concluded between the courts of Versailles and Berlin: to which they add that they have little patience to have, that circumstances are about to change, and that they will have excellent winter-quarters.[10]

Thus, we can see that, in the middle of the eighteenth century the colour of the cockade, which was an attribute specific to the military, clearly indicated belonging to a nation or a coalition, and the white cockade was the colour of the French nation.

If we refer to iconographic sources contemporaneous to the Seven Years War, such as the anonymous manuscript of 1757, the hats of the majority of the regiments represented do not carry a cockade and when they have a cockade like the Grenadiers royaux or the Fusiliers de Montagne, it is white. The fusiliers of Taccoli's manuscript of 1760 all wear a white cockade, as do the troops of the Maison du Roi, while many other documents, pictures or *États militaires* indicate that it was predominantly black in the Maison du Roi during this period. Raspe's publications in 1761 give white cockades to all infantry, cavalry, and dragoons. Finally, Becher's gouaches, which have the advantage of representing soldiers drawn on the spot, give white cockades to the fusiliers except that of the Régiment de Bresse (probably) which has a round white cockade with a red centre. He also illustrates a round red cockade for a drummer wrongly associated with the Régiment de Piémont, but who belonged to a Swiss regiment, while the fusilier of the same Régiment de Piémont has a white cockade. La Porterie, in his *Institutions militaires* published in 1754, writes that for the cavalry and the dragoons the cockade was of coarse-grained black silk, but he says nothing about that of the infantry. Chereau in 1756, attributes black cockades to the Maison du Roi, except for the Chevaux Légers, the Mousquetaires and the Gendarmerie, which wore a white feather plume and a white cockade. Finally, Pajol, without citing his

9 Eléazar Mauvillon, *Histoire de la dernière guerre en Bohème* (Francfort: Paul Lenclume, 1745), vol.2, p.222.

10 *Supplément à la Gazette de Vienne*, N°54 du 3 septembre 1757.

source, indicates that in 1757, the army of the coalition under the command of the Duke of Sachsen-Hildburghausen which included contingents of Austrian, Imperial and French troops, wore a white and green cockade. Here is a little piece of cloth that raises many questions.

Grenadiers' Bearskin Caps

Around 1745, bearskin caps were introduced for the grenadiers, probably in imitation of that of the horse grenadiers of the Maison du Roi, which recruited among the grenadier companies of the infantry. Here again, it was a fashion that began without regulatory text. The bearskin cap was officially described for the Grenadiers royaux in 1762 then for the grenadiers of the light troops in 1763, but it was not officially generalised to regular troops until 1767. However, as early as 1748, Puységur complained about it: 'it would also be necessary for the grenadiers to abandon the bearskin caps that some regiments make them wear.'[11] Theoretically, they were not abolished until 1776. What is remarkable is that given the price of this equipment, it was not possible for the *colonels*, with the exception of a few wealthy ones, to afford this expense, so it was with the endorsement of the war commissaries, without any official text, that this equipment was paid for by the King from the funds assigned to clothing.

This bearskin cap could be dark brown or black and measured about 30cm high, it was adorned with a double braid and a tassel. The fur flow ran upwards. The circular patch was embellished with a flame of the facing colour bordered with a white or yellow braid depending on the colour of the buttons; this is how it appears in the drawings of Taccoli or Becher. The front of the cap could be adorned with a sewn brass plate, decorated with an embossed grenade. The anonymous series of 1757 from the Musée de l'Armée only represents fusiliers wearing hats, only the gouache depicting a Grenadier de France shows a black bearskin cap in the shape of a pinecone or a mitre without plate. The representations of grenadiers by Taccoli in 1760 show no plate except for the grenadier of the Légion Royale who has a bearskin cap with a front plate decorated with a silver grenade. In Becher's series of plates, the grenadier of Régiment Lorraine Infanterie has no plate, but a yellow tassel can be seen on the left side. The grenadier of the German Régiment Royal Deux-Ponts has a grey plate, probably made of metal, without any visible decoration. The grenadier of the Swiss Régiment de Diesbach has a blue plate with a white border, decorated with a white grenade, it is probably an embroidered pattern as existed at this period. Finally, a gouache by Blarenberghe, painted around 1790, representing the King's entry into Mons in 1747 shows us a company of grenadiers with a brown bearskin cap, with a red circular patch, white braid and tuft, a brass plate sewn to the front; and on another painting representing the siege of Oudenarde in 1745, a company of grenadiers takes position in a trench for an attack, they are dressed in a white coat, with blue facings and waistcoat, the black bearskin cap with a blue circular patch and a white tuft.

11 Puységur, *Art de la guerre*, p.107.

The grenadier, in addition to the bearskin cap, also had a hat identical to that of the fusilier. During marches, the bearskin caps were often left in the sutlers' carts. In 1758, a grenadier of the Régiment du Comte de La Marche reported this incident:

> This departure was not favourable for me; for two wretched sutlers who had all my equipment on a cart, having drunk themselves like jays, did not follow the line of the baggage, and were looted by hussars: these rascals also caused the loss of the bearskin caps of our grenadiers and the rich costume of our tambour major that we had entrusted to them.[12]

It is not easy to determine with certainty the shape of the bearskin cap of this period. There are no known artefacts, there is no regulatory text, and the representations are rare, often summary, and are most often limited to front views. What is certain is that it was different from the bearskin cap worn at that time by certain cavalry regiments, which was entirely made of fur and had the shape of a sugar loaf. The bearskin cap of the infantry was in imitation of that of the horse grenadiers, it was made of a fur band surrounding the head with a rising front part. There was a skullcap behind the fur part with a falling flame ending in a pompom. Since this was not regulated equipment, there were probably many variations depending on the supplier. Becher's gouaches and the 1757 manuscript show a pinecone shape for the rising frontal part, whereas the shape is rounder on Taccoli's representations in 1760. Some gouaches by Blarenberghe or Le Paon give us a rear view of this type of bearskin cap. If we add to it certain plates by Taccoli such as those representing Anhalt, Royal Marine or Vermandois or even Raspe in 1761, we find a form of bearskin cap with a high frontal part in fur and at the back a lower skullcap over a fur headband. When we proportion the measurement of the soldier's face to the bearskin cap in the different representations, we obtain a maximum height between 30 and 32 centimetres at the front.

There does not seem to be any fur colour selection. The contemporaneous illustrations show both brown and black bearskin caps. It is brown in the 1757 manuscript and in Becher; in Taccoli it is clearly brown for the Gardes françaises and the Gardes suisses as well as for the grenadier of the Légion Royale and it is black or sometimes dark brown for the other regiments represented by a grenadier.

Note that it is unlikely that the grenadier companies sent to Canada or the Indies wore bearskin caps. This is what can be deduced from the many lists of equipment sent, received, or distributed, in which there is never any mention of a bearskin cap. But such caps were probably made locally, especially in Canada where the fur was readily available.

One more surprising fact, Taccoli on plate 70, figures 68 and 69 depicts bearskin caps for the Régiment Royal Artillerie, and for the companies of sappers (guastatori) and miners (minatori); a regiment and companies which, to the current author's knowledge, did not wear bearskin caps. But

12 Anon., *Mémoires d'un militaire, depuis l'année 1735 jusqu'au quartier–d'hyver de 1758* (Wesel et partout: publisher unknown, 1759), p.209.

we know from Michel Pétard's study of a 1755 painting by Joseph Vernet that the bombardiers of the navy wore bearskin caps. It should be noted, however, that in this series, Taccoli breaks down plate after plate the movements for throwing a grenade, so has he put a bearskin cap on miners and sappers so as not to interrupt the series? It is possible.

Fatigue Caps

Infantrymen also wore a fatigue cap à la dragonne. This cap was cut from old uniforms recovered during their renewal. This cap was not yet regulated and there are relatively few contemporaneous iconographic representations of it. On one of the plates of the 1757 manuscript at the Musée de l'armée, we see three soldiers of the Swiss Régiment de Jenner playing cards, one of them wears a fatigue cap; it is in cloth of the colour of the blue waistcoat, the point falling on the side and ending with a white tuft, it is bordered with a wide turned up blue band, there is a simple white edging around the head at the bottom of the cap, its front is not decorated with any pattern.

Blarenberghe's paintings and miniatures show us a greater variety of fatigue caps. On the vellum illustrating the march to the trench at Oudenarde in 1745, we see two fusilier companies receiving their shovels and pickaxes, they are in waistcoats and wear their fatigue caps, their regimental identification is not possible, but it allows us to see these fatigue caps from every angle. A first company wears red waistcoats, ochre breeches, and the fatigue cap is white background, the point falling back and ending with a white tuft. It is bordered by a red headband higher in front and rear, the headband is edged in white, the front is decorated with three white fleurs-de-lis. A second company wears white waistcoats and breeches, and their fatigue cap is of the same cut as that previously described. It is white with a white tuft, the headband is blue with a white edging, also decorated with three white fleurs-de-lis. In a corner of the painting, we can see a group of fusiliers carrying gabions, they have white waistcoats and blue breeches, their fatigue caps are red with a white headband, no additional details can be seen. On the gouache depicting Tournay in 1745, artillerymen are unloading a caisson of cannonballs, and they wear fatigue caps. Since the artillery was part of the infantry, where it ranked 47th, it dressed like the infantry. The artillerymen are in red waistcoats and breeches, they have blue fatigue caps, with a red headband edged in white, no decoration can be seen on the front of the headband.

From the regulations of 1767, the cap changed shape and took the name of 'pokalem' with a front flap which could be lowered as a visor. However, as we will see a little later, this type of cap was already distributed among the troops for winters during the Seven Years War.

Hairstyles

During campaigns, hair was worn naturally. It was cut short around the face and left long at the back and plaited in a lovelock, that is to say that it was gathered in a braid with a comb, bound with a ribbon, and then put in a taffeta net or worn in queue. From 1767, the braid was rolled up under the hat. On the temples the hair was rolled on a piece of cardboard or on a lead blade. The *sergent* had to make sure that the soldiers did not leave their quarters without having their hair in a queue or in a lovelock, with their face and hands washed. Hair was powdered only for reviews.

The engravings of Le Bas, made around 1750, show us hair tied at the back with a ribbon forming a very long fake queue. These hair ribbons were listed among the equipment transported aboard ships in 1755 for the troops sent to Canada.

In *L'art du perruquier* published in 1766, we can read:

> For some time, it has been imagined for the soldiers of the Régiment des Gardes françaises and suisses, in order to preserve their crimps against all kinds of weather, use a method that is not quite the same for both, but which has roughly the same effect. The manner of the Gardes françaises is to use a blade of lead, thin and narrow, about three pouces long. After removing the curlers from the side hair, they take the mass in their fingers, slip a part of the lead blade under it at half-length, and bend it back over it, roll the hair over this first fold, and hold this loop in place by pressing on it with a second bend, the rest of the blade. The surplus of the mass of hair above this last fold, moves outwards, falls and hides it, which forms two parallel curls. The Swiss do nothing but roll the curl around a circular card, and fix it to the card with a pin.[13]

The first text regulating the haircut appeared in the decree of 25 April 1767: 'the hair of the soldiers will be rolled up in a lovelock under the hat, the sides will be rolled on a blade of lead or a piece of cardboard.'[14] This regulation only confirmed a fashion that had appeared around 1755.

The *sergent* also had to make sure that the soldiers were shaved once a week by the 'frater' who was a surgeon's assistant; which allows us to imagine the faces of the soldiers in the field. Theoretically, only grenadiers wore moustaches, but if this was the rule, there were many exceptions, as André Corvisier noted when studying muster rolls. Grenadiers, as well as cavalrymen, whether they had black, brown, or blond hair, had to grease their moustaches with boot polish to blacken them. Bohan complains about it: 'I infinitely blame the uniformity that we wanted to give to the moustaches. By which oddity do we want that one, who has blonde hair and eyebrows, has black moustaches? … We have nonetheless tyrannized the grenadiers and cavalrymen to give satisfaction on this article…'[15]

The Coat

Just like in the cavalry, three uniform sizes were cut for the infantrymen. On this topic, in the instruction of 29 January 1747 on the style and the making of a coat, it is mentioned: '…that we take the measurements of three men of

13 François de Garsault, *Description des arts et métiers, Art du Perruquier* (Paris: Saillant et Nyons, 1767), p.5.

14 Acte royal, 25 April 1767, *Règlement arrêté par le roi pour l'habillement et l'équipement de ses troupes* (Paris: Imprimerie royale, 1767).

15 François-Philippe Loubat baron de Bohan, *Examen critique du militaire françois* (Genève: publisher unknown, 1781), vol.1, p.94.

different sizes and heights; so that by means of five aunes a quarter of cloth, and three-six aune for the cuffs, the three soldiers are equally dressed.'[16]

The cloth manufactures were Lodève and Bédarieux in Languedoc, of Elbeuf in Normandy, the cadis or knitting factories of Canourgue in Gévaudan. The factories making cadis (a kind of coarse twill also known as tricot) were Canourgue in Gévaudan, and the workshops of twill weaving of Aumale in Picardie had since Colbert and Louvois a status of Royal Manufacture – imposing manufacturing standards on them and guaranteeing, for a large part of their production, a monopoly for the supply of fabrics necessary for the uniforms of the troops. The pieces of twill serge were commonly called tricots or serges de Tricot from the name of a large town in the province of Picardy where strong twills were also manufactured to make breeches and waistcoats for the troops. When they were intended for the clothing of the troops, the pieces of fabric were tagged with a lead marker bearing on one side 'Troupes du Roy' and on the other, the name of the city where the fabric had been controlled. Pieces of fabric measured one aune wide by 15 to 16 aunes long. A piece Aumale twill, which was thinner, was used to make the linings, the pieces of fabric had a width of 5/8 aune (0.74m). All units of measurement used in the royal decrees were those of Paris and for pieces of fabric the aune measured 3 pieds 7 pouces 8 lignes (1.188m). Here is an indication of the cost of the different cloths of Lodève in 1778: the grey-white cloth for the infantry from 6 livres 10 sols to 7 livres 10 sols per aune, the standard blue cloth for the cavalry at 10 livres per aune, grey cloth for cavalry greatcoats at 7 livres per aune, standard green cloth for dragoons at 10 livres per aune, standard chamois cloth for waistcoats from 7 livres 10 sols to 8 livres per aune. The coat of each *caporal*, *anspessade* or soldier was made up of one and three-quarter aune of cloth from Lodève or Bédarieux, of identical quality and width, and a half to a third of the same cloth for the cuffs of the sleeves and for the collar.

The colour of the uniform of the French regiments was grey-white. The choice of this shade was due to several factors. Dyed fabric cost more than a white fabric; and the mordant of the dyes altered the quality of the cloth and reduced its durability. Furthermore, it was easier to cheat on the quality of a dyed fabric. On the other hand, dirt showed more easily on a grey-white fabric. Uniforms were only washed a few times a year and only during warm periods; spring or summer. On a daily basis, maintenance to remove stains was done with mixture made of miller's bran and white clay. The coat was only renewed every three years, and not for the entire regiment, but by thirds or quarters. The soldier had only one coat and, even if many activities were done in the waistcoat, he worked, walked in all weathers, went to battle and slept always with the same outfit. Clothing was severely put to the test, so, within the same regiment or in an army, there would have been a very wide variety of grey-white shades depending on the original factory, wear and cleanliness of the outfits. At the beginning of the eighteenth century when the supply of uniforms was still the responsibility of the *capitaines*, some of

16 Acte royal, 29 January 1747, *Instruction sur la façon et traitement d'un justaucorps de soldat* (Paris: Imprimerie royale, 1747), p.1.

Pierre Lenfant, 'Le testament de la tulipe' (The tulip will) (1758). (Anne S.K. Brown Military Collection)

them, as a cost-saving measure, left their companies in rags most of the time and dressed them properly only for reviews or exercises. The reform of 1762 eliminated this type of abuse by transferring the cost of the uniform to the expense of the King.

At the time, there was also concern about the waterproofing of uniforms. Before the uniform pattern was cut, the pieces of fabric were brushed with thistle heads. This variety of thistles, grown especially for this work, was called chardon à bonnetier (hosiery thistle). The treatment was applied to both sides of the fabric to create a slightly looped and woolly surface that trapped air, thus making the fabric temporarily water repellent rather than truly waterproof.

Coats and waistcoats were lined with twill of Aumale or cadis of Canourgue. The lining of the coat had to be white according to the decree of 20 April 1736, but already at that time some French regiments such as the Régiment du Roi, or the Régiment Royal des Vaisseaux had the privilege of having coloured linings, which gave coloured turnbacks. This distinctive element was generalised by the reform of 1762.

The skirts of the coat had to be one pouce (27mm) from the ground when the soldier was kneeling; and the waist had to be low, so that the belt marked the waist and covered the side buttons. The pieces of the coat overlapped at the back, as for an overcoat, to close better and to protect against the cold, and the pleats were not topstitched. Below the belt, the coat took on a loose and rounded shape. The instruction of 29 January 1747 indicated 'the four skirts of the coat must have at the bottom, each half the width of the piece of cloth and a gusset three or four pouces longer.'[17] To flare the skirts of the coat, additional triangular pieces of fabric called the gussets were sewn, point up, between the skirts, then from the two buttons fixed under the belt, in the small of the back, four pleats were formed to give this flared and rounded shape to the bottom of the coat.

After the reform of 1762, skirts were systematically turned back, but during the Seven Years War this was not yet a constant rule. The 1757 manuscript shows the regiments either with unfolded or turned back skirts, but we know that some drawings were copies of 1736 originals, a period when the bottom of the coat was unfolded, not turned back. The uniforms of the manuscript of Taccoli in 1760 all have turned back skirts. On Vernet's paintings made around 1756, the uniforms have turnbacks and all infantrymen in Becher's manuscript also have turnbacks. Thus, during the Seven Years War, following an established fashion, most regiments wore the skirts of the coat turned back and fastened with a clasp. This clasp was sometimes adorned with a fleur-de-lis, a heart, or a coloured grenade, as illustrated by contemporaneous illustrations such as Eisen, or Becher.

In some regiments the coat was embellished with lapels on the chest, such as the Régiments Royal, Limousin, Cambis or Montmorin. These lapels stopped at the level of the navel leaving two, three or four buttons below. These distinctive lapels, also called bavaroises, were generalised to all regiments by

17 *Acte royal*, 1 January 1747, p.1.

the decree of 1762. During the war, a certain number of regiments, without waiting for the reform of 1762, adopted lapels as a new distinctive element of the uniform, as confirmed by the *États militaires* or Raspe's publication in its edition of 1762.

The decrees did not yet fix the number of buttons on the front of the infantryman's coat, they only regulated the number of buttons on the pockets which were one of the distinctive elements. The front of the coat was fastened with nine to 12 large buttons down to the level of the pockets. There were also two large buttons in the small of the back which marked the junction of the pleats of the coat, and served to support the belt. There were usually three large buttons on each cuff and sometimes a small one underneath. A small button on the left shoulder near the collar was used to fasten the shoulder strap. The colour of buttons was the same as that of the hat lace and constituted one of the distinctive elements of the regiments.

The buttons were made of an embossed sheet of metal and mounted on a wood or bone core. It could be made of copper or tin. They were flat or domed and sometimes adorned with a motif. The 1762 decree describes the buttons of the Régiment de La Marine as follows: 'the white buttons, glued and puttied on boxwood, flat shaped with the number 6.'[18] The embossing was done in two steps, a first step with an iron form in a concave mould, then a second step with a sheet of lead placed between the iron form and the metal sheet, with a concave mould or a design in hollow of the motif or number to be reproduced on the button. Malleable and soft lead made it possible to model and to emboss the sheet of metal in the hollow of the mould. This gave the visible part of the button called the shell. The back of the button, generally made of walnut or boxwood, sometimes bone, was called a mould. It was formed on a lathe and was flat on one side and slightly domed on the other side, the latter side being placed inside the button. The back of the button was pierced with four holes where a cord was passed, this cord was used to sew the button on. To preserve the shape of the button and prevent it from deforming too easily, the shell of the button was filled with a wax-based mastic, then the cord was fixed on the wooden core and to finish the edges of the shell were folded over the wooden core.

Metal shank buttons were available from this time, but they were more expensive to produce. Once the shell was completed, a second metal sheet was lightly stamped, onto which a metal ring was welded, this piece was placed over the wooden core. The shell and back plate were then soldered together at the edges with a tin alloy. The instruction of 29 January 1747 specified that it was necessary 'to mention to the tailors to open and make eyelets with punches, to attach the shank buttons, and to pass strips of canvas through them, and to put interfacings of coarse cloth under the buttons and on the side of the buttonholes.'[19] Finally, solid metal shank buttons were gradually introduced. They were cast in a mould and the protrusion at the back was then pierced with a hole. This last type of button became the regulatory model with the decree of 1767.

18 Acte royal, 10 December 1762, *Ordonnance du Roi concernant l'infanterie française* (Paris: Imprimerie veuve C.M. Cramé, 1762), p.39.

19 *Acte royal*, 1 January 1747, p.1.

Aquitaine Regiment, officer (1761). (Artwork by Sergey Shamenkov © Helion & Company)

Dauphin Regiment, standard bearer (1757). (Artwork by Sergey Shamenkov © Helion & Company)

Saint Chamond Regiment, grenadier (1757). (Artwork by Sergey Shamenkov © Helion & Company)

Royal des vaisseaux Regiment, *sergent* with hallebard (1757). (Artwork by Sergey Shamenkov © Helion & Company)

La Reine Regiment, drummer, queen's livery (1757). (Artwork by Sergey Shamenkov © Helion & Company)

Royal Roussillon Regiment, fusilier (1757). (Artwork by Sergey Shamenkov © Helion & Company)

Berry Regiment, fusilier (1757). (Artwork by Sergey Shamenkov © Helion & Company)

Guyenne Regiment, drummer King's small livery (1757). (Artwork by Sergey Shamenkov © Helion & Company)

Note that in some descriptions the colour was designated by the type of metal used: brass buttons for yellow and tin buttons for white. The Régiment de Cambis and Régiment de Flandre had the particularity of having alternately yellow and white buttons with a hat lace alternately gold and silver.

Buttons could be flat or domed, only the *États militaires* prior to those of 1758 indicated the form of the button for certain regiments, such as Brissac which had large buttons; Penthièvre, flat buttons, and Saintonge domed buttons. Exceptionally, buttons were 'façonnés', that is to say embroidered with gold or silver threads drawing a motif. In this case, it was not the button makers, but the braid makers who produced them. The Régiment de la Reine and the Régiment de Diesbach had such buttons, but the motif is unknown. If we are to believe the *États militaires* of 1754 or the *Étrennes militaires* of 1756, the Grenadiers de France once had buttons covered with blue fabric.

The coat had false pockets, the shape, arrangement, and number of buttons of which constituted an important distinctive mark of each infantry regiment. They were arranged lengthwise (vertically) or crosswise (horizontally), and shaped in escutcheon, half-escutcheon, or double pockets with single or crow's feet buttons. The designation 'ordinary pockets' found in *États militaires* meant, crosswise pockets with three buttons.

The real pockets were placed on each side in the folds of the coat between the cloth and the lining of the sides of the front skirts, so that the top of the pockets was well sewn on the interfacing at the waist. They were made of the same ecru canvas as the breeches.

The sleeve was said to be 'en botte à l'ordinaire' when the cuff of the sleeve was folded back as the upper part of a boot. The cuff was worn with the buttonholes open so that it could be folded down, which made it possible to cover the hand in case of bad weather or cold. The cuffs of the sleeves were of the facing colour, according to the usage of each regiment.

For many of the infantry regiments of the Seven Years War, the cuffs remained wide and folded back, but following the evolution of fashion from the beginning of the century, the size of the cuffs was gradually reduced, so uniforms with narrower cuffs appeared which could no longer be folded down without being slit and were kept turned up, buttoned on the outer seam. With, as always during this period, multiple variations both in the texts of the *États militaires* and in the contemporaneous illustrations where slitted and unslitted wide cuffs coexisted with narrower slitted or unslitted cuffs. Eisen's red chalk drawing around 1755–1758 show us the exercise carried out by fusiliers of the Gardes françaises with wide slitted cuffs, then on a charcoal drawing of 1755, Eisen illustrates an infantry fusilier with much narrower, unslitted cuffs. We find the same varieties of cuffs on the plates of the 1757 manuscript where for most regiments, when the upper part of the cuff is visible, it is wide and unslitted, but for regiments like Alsace, Bergh, Royal Écossais, or Royal Pologne cuffs are narrow and slitted, and for Bentheim, they are slitted and fastened with two small buttons below. In Becher's series, cuffs are narrow.

Most commonly there were three buttons on the cuff, arranged on the top and outer part of the cuff and a small one underneath.

There was no mention of collars in the decree of 1746, but we know they were already worn in many regiments. This new fashion did not spread to all regiments, but the collar was definitively imposed by the decree of 10 December 1762. In the manuscripts of Gudenus around 1735 or that of the *Pavillons anciens* preserved in the library of Perpignan, produced around 1748, we see that it was a long collar, sewn at the level of the neck and placed on the shoulders like a small stole. A painting by Chardin, kept at the National Gallery in London, entitled 'Le château de cartes', painted around 1737, gives us an excellent representation of this type of collar with unbuttoned points.

At the beginning of the Seven Years War, the collar changed shape, it was now sewn all along the neckline of the coat and was worn folded back. In some cases, the collar could be kept closed and raised by two small buttons placed on the right side and two buttonholes at the left point of the collar as shown in a study of a soldier by Blarenberghe.

Let us consider a few more examples. The Régiment de Piémont is shown with a black collar in the 1757 manuscript and in Becher's gouache, but there is none in Taccoli in 1760 or Raspe in 1761, neither in the *États militaires* of 1758 in 1762 which do not mention a collar; it does not appear officially until the reform of 1762. The Régiment de La Tour du Pin has no collar in the 1757 manuscript, but Taccoli and Raspe illustrate a very peculiar white collar with red edging, and the *États militaires* from 1758 to 1762 describe that the collar was white with a red lining, which explains the presence of a red edging in Taccoli's and Raspe's illustrations. After the reform of 1762, the collar became scarlet red. And finally, the Régiment de Périgord, which sported two distinctive colours with blue cuffs and a red collar. As we can see, according to contemporaneous sources, for the same regiment there were descriptions or illustrations with or without collar, and it is therefore difficult to generalise. We will come back to the collar in more detail with the description of the distinctive features of the uniform of each regiment. In the establishment tables of the troops sent to Canada in April 1755 – La Reine, Artois, Bourgogne, Languedoc, Guyenne, Béarn – we note in theory the absence of collars for these regiments, but certain authentic contemporaneous Canadian documents show that these uniforms had a collar.

On the left shoulder, there was a shoulder strap in the colour of the coat, fastened with a small button, it was used to hold the belt of the cartridge box.

In theory, only the cavalry, the dragoons and the Grenadiers de France wore epaulettes at that time, but a response from the Minister of War, made to provide details on the decree of 27 February 1760 concerning the artillery, reveals interesting information. By this decree, soldiers and officers of the Corps de royal de l'artillerie were provided with two epaulettes and we learn that 'this epaulette is only a kind of distinction to the uniform of the corps as for all other royal unit of infantry.'[20] Here it is Raspe, in his 1762 edition, who confirms this provision for the royal regiments, but not exclusively,

20 'Uniforme des officiers et des régiments du corps Royal de l'artillerie (1759-1792)', *Carnet de la Sabretache, revue militaire rétrospective*, 1896, vol.4, p.457.

and the epaulette takes on the distinctive colour. At that time, the various regiments of the Grenadiers Royaux drawn from the militias were already distinguished by an epaulette on the right shoulder, of a different colour for each regiment.

Waistcoats

The waistcoat was cut in a three-quarter aune of tricot or cadis, being half an aune and one-twelfth wide. The fabric of the waistcoat came from different factories in the provinces of Picardy or Languedoc. Waistcoats were double breasted and shorter than the coat by approximately eight to nine pouces (21–24 cm) and the crosswise pocket flap had to be without buttons. The waistcoat was closed in front by 10 to 12 small buttons in one or two rows down to the level of the pockets. Here again the text of the decree was not respected, in particular the crosswise pocket flaps were generally closed with three small buttons. For some regiments the waistcoat was embellished with laced buttonholes or frogs.

The waistcoat was one of the distinctive elements of each regiment, it could take the facing colour, or be of a different colour. They were blue, red, or simply white. The decree indicates that only the outer layer of the waistcoat could be dyed, and that the twill lining had to be white. The sleeves of the waistcoat were slit at their ends and closed with one or two small buttons; this cut was said to be 'à la marinière'.

Finally, it is necessary to note the peculiarities of the Régiment de Rohan-Rochefort and of the Régiment de Normandie, which had on their white waistcoat, small red lapels for the first and black one for the second.

Breeches

The fly-front breeches stopped below the knee. There was slit on the outer seams at the level of the knee where it closed with four or five bone or wooden buttons covered with fabric, and a little buckled garter kept it below the knee. To adapt to different sizes and to more easily tighten them at the waist, the breeches were slit in the back and closed by lacing passing through eyelets.

Here is La Noue du Vair's description of the soldier with fly-front breeches in his *Réflexions sur la constitution militaire*, where he advocates fall-front breeches: '...nothing has so bad grace for the soldiers, as breeches open in front, which they rarely take care to button, they reveal a disgusting shirt and all around the opening a grime which highlights all the filthiness of the soldier.'[21] But, in a memoir concerning armaments for Canada kept at the National Archives of Canada, there is a very interesting mention concerning the supplies to Quebec to be delivered to the troops as needed. It concerns cloth from England for fly-front breeches with this precision: 'Sieur Michel was asked to send from Holland to Brest 1,000 to 1,200 aunes of cloth specific for the use in question. The braguet or brayet is a strip of canvas falling in front along the legs under the panties "to cover what must not be seen".'

21 Stanislas Louis de comte de La Noue de Vair, *Nouvelles Constitutions militaires* (Francfort sur le Mayn ; Knoch et Eslinger, 1760), vol.1, p.87.

Charles Eisen, 'Exercice de la Garde du Roi' (Exercise of the King's Guard). (Anne S.K. Brown Military Collection)

Each pair of breeches, with their pockets and interfacings without lining, required one aune of tricot or cadis. The interfacing was a band of strong canvas, one or two pouces wide, sewn to the reverse of the fabric to reinforce it, particularly at the level of the waistband of the breeches. Coloured breeches were theoretically prohibited for the soldiers since the decree of 20 April 1736. They were made of white tricot for the soldiers and grey-white cloth for the *sergents*. When they derogated from the decrees, the breeches were of the facing colour as in a painting by Le Paon kept at the Château de Chantilly, which shows an episode of the Seven Years War where a regiment with red facings is wears red breeches.

The fall-front breeches worn by cavalrymen and dragoons was probably already in use in the infantry, but it was not made official before the instruction on the clothing of the troops of April 1767. Each *sergent*, *caporal*, *anspessade*, soldier and drummer were provided with canvas breeches when they received their clothing, to be used as a lining; it was the soldier's underwear.

Stockings, Gaiters and Shoes

The decree stated of 1736, 'instead of stockings which are issued to *sergents*, a pair of gaiters is issued to each *caporal*, *anspessade*, soldier and drummer.'[22] The *sergents* wore coloured stockings, it was an element which, among other things, made it possible to identify them from afar and to distinguish him from the rest of the company in gaiters. During the cold season, soldiers wore unbleached woollen stockings under their gaiters to protect themselves from the cold; the stockings went up to the thighs. The stockings could cover the whole foot but there were also open-toed stockings which covered only the heel and part of the foot. They were held at the calf with a small cord garter.

Gaiters were made of strong unbleached canvas, closed on the outside by small bone buttons covered with canvas, and tightened below the knee by a canvas garter with a brass buckle. The upper part was fixed to the buttons of the breeches, and the lower part held in place by a small, buckled leather strap passing under the shoe. The gaiters had to go high enough above the knee so as not to slip and, at the bottom, they had to cover the buckle of the shoe. In summer they were made of white canvas. For winter, the King had black wool gaiters distributed. Monro in his *Traité de médecine d'armée*, when dealing with the dress of the soldiers, tells us that: 'Most of the French troops wore, during the last campaigns [of the Seven Years War], greased black gaiters, and kept the white gaiters only for parade days.'[23]

Shoes were made of blackened leather with buckles and wooden heels. They were at the soldier's expense, but he received in return a gratuity withheld by the *capitaine* for their supply. In peacetime, a soldier needed two pairs a year with several resolings. The shoes were maintained with a shoe polish made of wax, tallow, and lampblack. It was the intendancy

22 Acte royal, 20 April 1736, *Ordonnance du Roi concernant l'habillement de l'infanterie française* (Paris: Imprimerie royale, 1736), p.6.

23 Donald Monro, *Médecine d'armée* (Paris: Didot le jeune,1769), p.xxiii.

service that ensured supply and negotiated the necessary contracts. There was no differentiation between the right foot and the left foot, in practice it was the mobile or fixed part of the buckle of the shoe which determined the right or left foot. The custom at the time, for both civilians and soldiers, was to alternate shoes on each foot. As for sizes, we can suppose that, as for uniforms or hats, shoemakers had several standard sizes made, probably three, to adapt to all feet. The shape and dimensions of the shoe buckle were not regulated. Museums have a few rare copies; the buckle was of variable shape and size according to the times, the fashion, and the suppliers. In 1772, M. Poissonnier in a *Mémoire sur l'habillement des troupe* wrote about shoe buckles: 'Who knows how many varieties shoe buckles have undergone, even in the past few years. Sometimes round, sometimes square, sometimes oval, sometimes simple and plain, sometimes laden with ornaments, at first very small, then imperceptibly increased to a size whose excess could only be stopped by the size of the foot.'[24]

Shirts and Neckcloths

Nothing was said about shirts in the decrees. They were the soldier's undergarment and made of unbleached linen. They were very long and went down to the knee. We learn from La Porterie that unlike that of the cavalrymen or dragoons, those of the infantrymen did not have cuffs.[25] The soldier usually had at least two shirts.

The *caporaux*, *anspessades*, soldiers and drummers were obliged to have a neckcloth made of black crepe or cheesecloth, which was tied around the neck. La Porterie mentions that cheesecloth was used because it was the fabric that lasted the longest and was the most comfortable, because it could be washed and cleaned. Cheesecloth is a delicate, very light cloth.

Infantrymen, unlike cavalrymen and dragoons, did not have greatcoats. A company only had one hooded greatcoat to protect soldiers on guard duty during winter or rainy weather.

For the winter season, soldiers were given twill vests and woollen gloves or mittens, just like those sent to troops serving in Canada. This equipment was mentioned in the instruction of 1767 and became official by the provisional instruction of 1778 for the infantry on campaign. At that time distributing greatcoats to the troops who would campaign in cold countries was considered. However, this piece of equipment clearly already existed during the Seven Years War. In 1758 *maréchal* de Belle-Isle wrote to Monsieur Foulon, war commissary and intendant of the army of the Prince de Soubise, asking him to make sure that vests, pokalenes and greatcoats were retrieved at the end of winter.[26] The pokalene was a fatigue cap whose flaps covered

24 Antoine Poissonnier des Perrieres, *Mémoire sur l'habillement des troupes, Nouveaux mémoires de l'Académie de Dijon* (Dijon: Causse, 1772), vol.2, p.433.

25 François de La Porterie, *Institutions militaires pour la cavalerie et les dragons* (Paris: Guillyn, 1754).

26 Archives de l'Etat du Valais, <https://scopequery.vs.ch/detail.aspx?ID=126710>, accessed 10 May 2024.

part of the face to protect it from the rigours of winter, it became the pokalem and was officially introduced as a service cap in 1767.

There was also the problem of winter with the light shoes in use. Yet soldiers had to go about their daily business – guards and chores – and sometimes marched in the cold, the snow, the frost. We can imagine that they wrapped their feet and shoes in canvas and pelts to insulate themselves from the cold and that they wore several layers of stockings, if they had any. They were already being given wool gaiters such as those prescribed by the 1775 decree. As for troops sent to Canada, they had very quickly adopted for the winter the moccasins and mittens of the local militias.

An instruction from M. Guibert, *major général de l'infanterie*, addressed to the *majors* of the regiments present at the army in 1761, makes it possible to know the contents of a knapsack of a soldier in the field. This comte de Guibert was the father of the famous military theorist. The latter, who was only 13 in 1756, accompanied his father as an aide-de-camp, then as *capitaine* in the Régiment d'Auvergne where his father had served as *major*.

> Care will be taken that it is [the knapsack] only of the size necessary for what it must contain, which must be reduced exactly, not including what the soldier has on his body, to two shirts, a pair of tricot or canvas breeches, a pair of white or black gaiters, a pair of knee pads, a comb and two brushes, and bread for four days. The effects that have just been detailed, together with those that the soldier has on him, are sufficient for him. Officers and *sergents* must watch with the greatest care that he carries nothing more and be responsible for it. As it is necessary for him to have a bag in which he wraps himself to sleep, he will roll it up and tie it, after having tightened it well so that it takes up less space, between the body of the knapsack and the lid, which closes it, so that it is covered by it.[27]

From this text, we learn that the infantryman had a canvas 'sleeping bag' as well as a pair of knee pads.

Other Equipment

The intendancy service distributed a tin spoon to the soldiers to eat and to renew them, when the soldiers lost them, there were moulds for spoons and tin ingots in the stocks of the intendancy to cast them. The soup plate or mess kit was made of wood or clay in the navy and metal (tinplate) or earthenware in the army, according to Bardin. It could be a common bowl for three, five or seven soldiers of a tent, or an individual mess kit.

The canteen, a small essential accessory, was not yet provided by the intendancy. The canteen was made of wood or of a specific variety of squash and held by a small leather band. It was sometimes sculpted with motifs by the soldiers, as shown by the rare examples that have been preserved.

27 Victor François de Broglie, *Correspondance inédite de Victor François, duc de Broglie, maréchal de France, avec le prince Xavier de Saxe, comte de Lusace, lieutenant-général, pour servir à l'histoire de la guerre de Sept Ans (campagnes de 1759 à 1761) Juin-Déc. 1761* (Paris: Albin Michel, 1903), vol.4, p.657.

The soldier also needed to light fires. It required three items: a 'briquet de fer', a flint, and some amadou (also known as amadou tinder). The briquet, or steel, made of iron or steel was also called a fusil, its use dated back to the Iron Age. It was usually in the shape of an oval handle which was knocked against a flint flake; the torn pieces of steel formed incandescent sparks that ignited the amadou. Amadou was derived from a very common parasitic fungus that could be found on hardwood trees (fomes fomentarius). Thin strips of the fibrous inner part were harvested and boiled in water to eliminate their soluble parts, then dried and struck with a mallet to loosen the texture. Finally, it was soaked in a solution of potassium nitrate (saltpetre), dried one last time, and kept in a small airtight box away from humidity. If all soldiers knew how to strike a steel, it is likely that there was only one for several soldiers or for the whole barrack room.

For the tobacco distributed to each soldier, he needed a tobacco box and the equally indispensable pipe to smoke it. Care was taken to have spare pipes readily available to provide to the soldiers in case they broke or lost them.

For illumination, an oil lamp made of terracotta or metal was necessary. The intendancy provided oil and cotton wicks. It was most often navette oil, taken from a plant close to rapeseed which gave an inexpensive oil. There must have been several lamps per tent or room.

During winter quarters, the intendancy provided a blanket for each two or three soldiers.

Fusilier's Accoutrements

Each soldier was provided with a half-pouch, in cowhide dyed red or black. A perforated wooden block that could hold 30 cartridges was fixed inside the pouch. The decree specified that the wooden block was nerved – a way to strengthen a piece of wood. In the eighteenth century, the term nerve was also given to tendons. These tendons, mainly those of cattle, were crushed to make very resistant and flexible fibres which were then glued to reinforce a wooden object such as cavalry saddles. In the case of the wooden block for cartridges, it was reinforced with bonded tendon fibres then covered with canvas.

We sometimes find identical pieces of equipment designated with different names depending on the era or the authors. Thus, the pouch carrying grenades was alternately called grenadière, gibecière or giberne. 'Cartouche' designated the perforated wooden block containing the cartridges, which was slipped into the pouch, as well as the pouch itself, and the cartridge consisting of powder and a ball wrapped in paper. This wooden block could also be called cartouchier and a few years earlier, when only the powder was wrapped in paper, the empty cartridge was called a gargousse and the wooden block, a gargoussier.

The grenadier's pouch contained 30 cartridges while the fusilier's half-pouch could hold from 16 to 20 cartridges, but even when the latter was enlarged to hold 30 cartridges it continued for some time to be called a half-pouch in the texts. It was around 1750 that the capacity of the half-pouch was increased to 30 rounds, the same as the grenadier pouch. This was a necessity, as there were no ammunition-wagons permanently attached to the infantry regiments. There were such wagons under the custody of the artillery, and it was the *général* who decided on their distribution.

The 1757 manuscript essentially shows red pouches. With Taccoli, they do not appear on the majority of gouaches or are simply line drawn or in grey, only the plate of the grenadier of Planta shows a brown pouch, as on the representations of grenadiers with a reddish-brown ventral pouch, made of Russian leather, attached to the waist belt and ornamented with a grenade. Finally, with Becher, the pouch is black or brown.

In contemporaneous texts, red leather was often referred to as Russian leather. However, it did not come from Russia, it was cowhide which received a special treatment, including a so-called Russian oil, the formula of which came from Russia where it had remained secret for a long time. This birch (or willow) oil gave the leather greater rigidity, very good impermeability and resistance to humidity, and its characteristic empyreumatic odour of birch bark smoke. The dark red colour was given by a dye made from the wood of the Brazilian Pernambouc tree, but there were also Russian leathers dyed black.

Black leather, on the other hand, was obtained by soaking the leather in an iron gall dye made with scrap metal (iron salts) and crushed gall nuts (a swelling growth of oak due to the bite of a parasite) which constituted the tannic part. They were mixed in sour beer and then heated to form the dye bath. The leathers of the belts were never greased.

The wooden block was held in place in the half-pouch by tightening it like a purse with a small leather cord. The pouch closed with two flaps, the first of fine and supple leather which covered the holes of the wooden block; the second, wider and thicker, was the visible part which gave the shape and the external appearance of the cartridge pouch. It was on this external tab that the grenade-shaped metal motif of the grenadier pouch was fixed. The brass motifs decorating the cartridge pouches of fusiliers only appeared after 1765. A gouache by Le Paon, kept in Grasse, shows us a grenadier of the Régiment de Bentheim during the Seven Years War with a pouch decorated with five brass grenades, one placed in the centre and the other four at the corners, but this painting is later.

The cartridge pouch had a small pocket called bourse de giberne; here is how Bardin describes it:

> A sort of purse or rather a small leather pocket intended to contain the musket cloth and the spare flints. The purse is in glossy black sheepskin, and sewn with the grain outside against the middle of the outer face of the front of the cartridge box. On each side, the purse forms 20 mm deep bellows, so as to be flat when empty; it is 180 mm in development; its apparent height is 90 mm; its length from seam to seam, fold not included, is 120 mm; its upper part closes with a button and a buttonhole.[28]

28 Etienne Alexandre Bardin, *Dictionnaire de l'armée de terre* (Paris: Perrotin, 1841), vol.2, p.830.

This small pocket contained an essuie-pierre which is a piece of linen cloth made for cleaning flints, a spare flint, three rounds of balls and powder, a musket cloth, which was a piece of serge or leather heavily impregnated with grease based on olive oil and tallow for the maintenance of the metal parts of the musket, and a wooden flint for exercises. There was also a leather pad for the musket pan with its chain, which allowed it to be hung on the trigger guard. This leather pad was essential, indeed during military campaigns, the soldier moved with a loaded musket, the hammer uncocked and the pan covered with this leather pad which made it possible to avoid the production of a spark from a shock, which in turn could fire the shot. The pocket also contained a pin which was a small needle of iron or copper, with a point at one end and a ring at the other. It was used to clean the touch hole of the musket; it was attached by a brass chain to one of the buttonholes of the coat or to the trigger guard.

There were also a few pieces of equipment shared within a squad, such as a small oil vial or a small grease box and a screwdriver, a worm, which was a small spiral hook that could be screwed to the end of the ramrod when it was necessary to unload the musket. Finally, a spring-hook to disassemble the lock plate for its maintenance.

The 1747 decree specified 'two cords attached to the bottom of the cartouche [pouch], to carry a wooden powder-flask.'[29] Under the half-pouch, a reserve of powder was suspended by two leather cords. But the increase in the capacity of the half-pouch around 1750 and, above all, the greater use of the cartridge led to the disappearance of the powder-flask, which was a large reserve of powder, the soldier only keeping a pulvérin which is a small flask with very fine priming powder. The pulvérin was useful for example in case of strong winds to put priming powder back into the pan after a march. It was most often carried across the shoulder with a small leather cord.

The shoulder belt carrying the half-pouch was made of white buffle, well sewn, without studs or stitching. It measured five to six pieds (162–195cm) long by two and a half pouces (6.7cm) wide. It was placed on the shoulder, from left to right. 'Quite frequently we come across an inconvenience which results in further discomfort and fatigue for the soldier, that must be avoided: it is to suffer him to carry the pouch low and tossing about his thigh. The rule is that it should be pulled up until it touches the corner button of the coat.'[30] A strip of leather called a traverse was sewn above the pouch to stabilize it. The term buffle indicated cowhide or oxhide that has undergone a special treatment with lime, it was also said to be chamois skin. This hide was then bleached.

The waist belt of the 1746 model had a single strap, with a bayonet scabbard above the sword, also without studs or stitching, closed by a copper buckle with a buckle tongue. The coat had no belt loops and the waist belt rested in front on the last button at the bottom of the coat and on the two buttons located in the small of the back where the folds of the coat converged. On the gouaches of the 1757 manuscript in the Musée de l'Armée, the detail of the

29 Acte royal, 19 January 1747, *Ordonnance du roi portant règlement pour l'habillement de l'infanterie françoise* (Paris: Imprimerie royale, 1747), p.5.

30 Broglie, *Correspondance*, vol.4, p.656.

waist belt cannot be distinguished except for the Régiment de Mailly where it had a single strap, and we only rarely see a bayonet as for the Régiment de Picardie.

Most of the time the waist belt was worn over the buttoned and turned back coat, but during hot weather it was permitted to wear it over the waistcoat under the unbuttoned coat. On marches during campaigns the waist belt could be worn slung over the right shoulder; this is how all the infantrymen appearing in the series of gouaches by Becher are represented. However, when soldiers took up arms or were on guard duty, the waist belt had to be worn over their coat, as mentioned in the Instruction drawn up by the war council for the *sergents* published in the *Code militaire* of 1761.[31] According to the decree, only the *sergents*' waist belts were stitched, but all fusiliers represented in the 1757 manuscript wear stitched belting. The maintenance of the belts had to be carried out without grease so as not to stain the uniforms. Powder of white pipe clay, a clay that turned white after heating, was used. Ground into a fine powder, it was mixed with soapy water to maintain and whiten the belting.

At the start of the Seven Years War, this model of waist belt was being changed as explained in the article on the evolutions of the infantry taken from the *Encyclopédie* published in 1756.

> The expression 'close ranks to the point of the sword' is beginning to fall out of general use in the troops. It is replaced by that of 'close ranks to the front.' The reason for this change is that the King having ordered to renew the waist belts of the infantry (which must be completed within the space of three years), the new waist belts will be made in such a way that the soldier will carry the sword on the side along the thigh, in much the same way hunting knives are carried. Now, when all the infantry will wear the sword in this way, the expression 'close ranks to the point of the sword' will no longer be exact, because the soldiers of each rank will no longer be able to touch the tips of the swords of the soldiers of the rank preceding them. However, as this expression is old, and it would not be impossible for it to prevail over the new one, we will continue to use it, but not giving it the same meaning as that of 'close ranks to the front', by which is meant that they must be squeezed together as much as possible, without hindering the march of the soldier.[32]

Finally, the manuscript of Taccoli in 1760 shows us all the fusiliers without swords and with a waist belt with a simple vertical bayonet scabbard, like that of a hunting knife. But Taccoli uses model templates, similar to those he used to represent the Spanish troops, who have already adopted this type of waist belt. This model of waist belt was already worn by the fusiliers of the provincial militias who no longer carried swords and it officially appeared for the regular infantry in 1767. Yet this usage was not new, in his *Essai sur la castramétation*, published in 1748 at the end of the War of the Austrian

31 Pierre Briquet, *Code militaire ou compilation des ordonnances des Rois en France, concernant les gens de guerre* (Paris: Durand, 1761), vol.4, p.359.

32 Le Blond, *Elemens de tactique*, p.7.

Succession, Le Blond writes: 'In some regiments, the use of swords has recently been replaced by that of a kind of hunting knife, which is worn along the thigh. This way the ranks can be drawn together at a distance of less than three pieds.'[33]

So, the evidence would suggest that several different models of waist belts were worn during the Seven Years War. The 1746 model, with a single or more rarely two straps with an oblique sword and a bayonet which was parallel to it. A model reproduced in the gouache of the 1757 manuscript for the Régiment de Mailly or on those of Becher. Then the model described in the 1756 *Encyclopédie* with the sword placed almost vertically which became the regulatory model of waist belt 1767, but this last decree directed it exclusively to grenadiers, *fourriers, sergents* and musicians. It is this model that we see on some of Eisen's chalk drawings. And finally, the waist belt of the militias or of Taccoli and Le Blond which was a simple bayonet scabbard like that of a hunting knife. It is this model that was included in the regulations of 25 April 1767, where it was intended for fusiliers who no longer carried a sword.

The current author has not found any original models kept in public collections. Also, to get an idea of the different angle of the sword when carried on the waist belt of the 1746 model and that of 1756, measurements were taken from two drawings by Eisen, who knows his subject perfectly and who gives us representations of these models, horizontal . First of all, a bayonet worn as a hunting knife, vertical along the leg, hangs at 270° (with vertical being 0°) as on Taccoli's plates. For the 1746 model, worn by a Garde suisse in Chereau's series engraved after a drawing by Eisen, the sword is inclined at 332°; and for the waist belt described in the *Encyclopédie* of 1757, the measurement taken on a sanguine by Eisen gives an inclination of 296.5°, so, a gain of 35.5° and the tip of the sword hardly protrudes behind the soldier allowing the ranks to close even more. These are only two comparative and empirical measurements, but they give us an idea of the space that had been reduced between the soldiers and of the differences between these two models of waist belt.

The knapsack was still made of canvas, it was also called a bissac and was worn across the shoulder. It often had only one shoulder strap. There was no official description, but the numerous sketches by Watteau, the engravings by Le Bas and a drawing taken from the work of La Porterie give us a fairly good idea of it, with the illustration of the latter having two shoulder straps. At that time, only foreign regiments had leather knapsacks which were worn with two shoulder straps. This type of knapsack was introduced during the Seven Years War and was only generalised by the infantry regulations of 1767 and then by those of 1778. Here is what was said about it in a letter that *maréchal* de Brogiie had sent by M. de Guibert, *major général de l'armée*, to the *majors* of the infantry regiments in 1761.

> Experience has shown that the way of loading the knapsack, called en bretelle [the model with two shoulder straps], is infinitely preferable to that of carrying it on

33 Guillaume Le Blond, *Essai sur la castramétation* (Paris: Jombert, 1748), vol.2, p.16.

Two drawings by Charles Eisen showing sword-belts. (Private collection)

> one shoulder, the strap which supports it crossing over the chest. For the first, the load bears equally on both shoulders, opening them up and holding them back: by the old method, on the contrary, all the weight bearing on the chest, presses and tightens it to the point of inconveniencing much over time. You will therefore want to compel all the soldiers of the regiment that you command, to have their knapsack en bretelle on the marches. It is also to be observed that the shorter it is attached, the less he will fatigue: it is a principle of theory as well as of experience that the effort of a weight against its fulcrum decreases as it approaches it.[34]

The canvas knapsack did not protect the items contained therein from bad weather, the rain penetrated the knapsack and could soak those items, increasing their weight, and wearing them out much faster. When the soldier arrived at the camp, he had nothing to change into to dry off, and his bread was wet, like everything else. The leather knapsack, already in use in foreign regiments, remedied these drawbacks. In this regard Guibert writes:

34 Broglie, *Correspondance*, vol.4, p.656.

> I therefore beg you, Sir, to establish as far as possible the use of leather knapsacks in the regiment you command, and M. le Maréchal instructs me to particularly recommend this object to you as important to the well-being and to the preservation of the soldier, for the reasons that I have just detailed for you. It is not intended, however, that you make a general purchase of it; he only wishes that no others be given to your recruits, and that whenever there is a new knapsack to buy, either for an old soldier or for a recruit, it is of leather in preference to any other, by means of which the use will be established imperceptibly and without it costing you any extraordinary expense. It is necessary that you notify the officers in charge of recruits' equipment at the assembly quarters of the regiment you command.[35]

We therefore learn that foreign regiments already wore a leather knapsack with two shoulder straps, without further details. We have to wait until 1764 and the state of expenses for the fusiliers which mentions knapsack of canvas or calfskin lined with canvas. A gouache by Le Paon, preserved in Grasse townhall, shows us a grenadier of the Régiment de Bentheim loaded with this type of knapsack with shoulder straps, the skin on the outside. It has a rounded shape and does not yet have the rectangular shape of that of the soldiers of the Empire.

During battles, the knapsack and anything that could encumber the soldier were left at the camp, this was no longer the case during the Revolutionary and Napoleonic Wars. During marches, it was either carried by the soldier or loaded on the wagon attached to each battalion. It was only around 1778 that soldiers began to carry their knapsack on a permanent basis, according to the *Journal Historique et Littéraire* of October 1778. At that time, *maréchal* de Broglie commanded an instruction camp in Normandy:

> Maréchal de Broglio must make known and test in part in this camp the regulations made for the infantry in the field. As everything is essential for this service, they go into the greatest details, from the dressing of the horses intended to carry tents and pots to the funeral honours to be paid to the soldiers, from the Maréchal de France to the private who will die at the army. From now on soldiers will be trained from time to time to march several leagues with their knapsack, their weapons and equipment of all kinds, so that they grow accustomed to wearing them during the campaign without being tired. Copper pots being subject to verdigris, there will only be wrought iron.[36]

Fusiliers' Arms

The Regulation Musket

The soldier of the Seven Years War was equipped with a 1746 model musket or the newer 1754 model. For lack of financial means, the manufacture of

35 Broglie, *Correspondance*, vol.4, p.658.

36 *Journal historique et littéraire, 1er octobre 1778* (Luxembourg: Chevalier, 1778), vol.107, p.221.

muskets was only resumed in 1754 because of the threat of war. At the start of the war in 1756, the 1754 model had not yet completely replaced the 1746 model. According to J. Boudriot, between 1754 and 1763, 208,000 muskets were manufactured.[37] The troops sent to Canada in 1755, like the new levies of the Compagnies Franches de la Marine, were equipped with 1746 model muskets, taken from the arsenals of the navy and often in poor condition, which Dieskau deplored, who wanted to be provided with weapons of the new model. *Major général* baron de Dieskau was sent to Canada in February 1755 as commander of the French troops to conduct the campaign against the British.

The model which was used as a basis for the 1746 and 1754 model muskets of the was that of 1728–1729. The modifications were only additions to the regulation of 1729, without any great technical evolution.

The 1746 model had a barrel of 44 pouces (119cm) and was eight spans long at the breech-end. The lock plate ended in a point. The feather spring between the foot of the pan cover and the pan was removed, this was the only major modification compared to the 1729 model. From 1741, the ramrod was made of iron with a nail-head butt. There was not yet a ramrod spring to block it. Three bands secured the barrel to the wooden stock from front to back: the nose band, the centre band, and the lower band. The centre band and the lower band were held by compression on the stock. The stock had no collars for the loops. The lock plate was square with an iron pan, with a swan-necked cock. The nose band was short, and all screw heads were round. The socket bayonet had two L-shaped slots to attach it the barrel and a hollowed blade.

The 1754 model had the same barrel. The feather spring of the pan was reintroduced. The rings for the musket sling hitherto placed on the side of the side-plate of the musket were relocated below the stock; in front of the trigger guard and under the centre band. The rings that were circular on the 1746 model became flat in the shape of a basket handle. The rings were fixed, one to the centre band, the other to the trigger guard, by a pivot. The nose band was lengthened by a third, then measuring approximately seven centimetres and improving the stability of the bayonet. The centre band and the lower band were affixed to the stock with a pivot spring, but this spring was not used to hold the ramrod. The 1754 model musket measured 160cm, including 119cm for the barrel and weighed approximately 4.2 kilograms. The cock, always swan-neck shaped, was slightly thicker, but remained fragile, the head of the jaw screw was slit for a flat blade screwdriver. The lock plate measured approximately 16.5cm long and the screw head of the hammer had a diameter of 1.5cm, the pan was still made of iron but was deeper than on the 1746 model. The side-plate had the shape of an elongated S and measured 10cm. The butt plate was shortened.

Visually, the two models could be easily identified; on the 1746 model, the musket sling was placed on the left side of the musket and held by a round ring at the level of the centre band and on the side-plate, while on the

37 Jean Boudriot, *Armes à Feu Françaises, Modèles réglementaires* (Paris: L'Émancipatrice, 1979), vol.1.

Two studies of soldiers by Antoine Watteau. (From *Figures de différents caractères, de paysages, d'études dessinées d'après nature par Antoine Watteau…*)

1754 model the sling was placed under the barrel of the musket and passed through flat or round rings. They were further distinguished by the shape of the stock of the 1746 model which presented a gentler rounding of the pied de vache formed by the small of the stock where it joined the butt.

The Manufacture of Regulation Muskets

It is instructive to dwell for a moment on a few major stages in the manufacture of a musket to better understand the problems encountered by the soldier on the battlefield, problems which are explored in the chapter concerning infantry tactics. We will examine the manufacture of the three main parts: the barrel, the lock plate, and the wooden stock.

Muskets were manufactured under the supervision of commissioners of the Corps royal de l'artillerie in the factories of Charleville, Maubeuge and Saint-Étienne. The creation of the Manufactures Royales dated back to the time of Colbert. The Manufacture Royale status ensured them a monopoly for the production of weapons in France and imposed manufacturing standards on them, such as the single calibre of barrels produced, both for military and civilian uses. The office of the Secretary of State for War concluded a contract with one or more contractors, who in turn subcontracted the work to small specialised local craftsmen. There were not yet large arms factories that brought all the necessary craftsmen together in the same workshop. The workshops were scattered throughout the city and the surrounding villages. These workshops could bring together more than a dozen workers like the cannon makers or be as small as a master and one or two apprentices, like at a gun lock maker. In Saint-Étienne, the establishment of a factory, bringing together contractors and workers in the same place, dated from 1764–1765. The arms factory of Tulle was under the control of the Secretary of State for the Navy and did not become a Manufacture Royale until 1777. It was water power that drove the powerful hammers of the forges, this explains why, during periods of drought, some manufacturing sites were moved from one valley to another. There were a multitude of specialised trades doing only part of the work, it was only semi-industrialised process. The smith manufactured the iron bars to make the barrel, the blacksmith gunner was specialized in the shaping of the barrels, the semeur checked and corrected the straightness of the barrel, the grinder gave it its final external shape, and the garnisseur adjusted the breech.

The quality of the iron was fundamental, and workers could only use that which was provided to them by the state after controls. The iron of the musket barrels was drawn from the forges of Berry and Franche-Comté. To get a two-pound barrel, up to 12 pounds of iron were necessary.

The barrel was forged from an iron bar called a pattern. It was a flat wrought iron bar, reinforced and thickened at the level of the breech-end. This bar was then rolled into a U-shape then into a tube on a spindle, and with a hammer on the anvil the lips of the tube were slightly overlapped. Then it was forged, that is to say welded all along the tube; a heated core was slipped inside the barrel and the lips were forged. The barrel was then calibrated and progressively drilled with drill bits of increasing size. As the barrel tended to deform during this stage, it was regularly straightened. To ensure the regularity of the bore, a brass wire was stretched like a cord in the tube, which was inspected by rotating it in front of a light source, the areas where the barrel did not fit perfectly were marked on the outside, the barrel was then put on the anvil and the metal was pushed back inwards with the hammer, the barrel was drilled once more and checked until the bore was regular and no light could be seen when the brass wire was inserted into the barrel; this operation was called setting the barrel.

The barrel was then given its final external shape with a sandstone wheel and then with a file, while maintaining a regular thickness of metal, with an extra thickness at the level of the breech-end.

The forging technique to make a round barrel began with a square shaped iron bar, gradually transformed into an octagonal shaped bar and then into an a 16-sided bar to finally obtain a cylindrical barrel, while taking care to keep a regular and sufficient thickness of metal throughout the barrel. At the level of the breech-end, the octagonal shape was preserved. A calliper was used regularly to check the work of the grinder, marking the place where metal still had to be removed. Finally, with nearly 20 successive taps, the barrel was drilled at the level of the breech-end to form the screw pitch where the breech would be screwed.

It now remained to manufacture the breech, a screw that closed the rear of the barrel at the level of the breech-end. The breech consisted of three

Charles Eisen, 'Garde royale musketiers' (Royal Musketeer guard) (1758). (Anne S.K. Brown Military Collection)

parts: the threaded plug screwed into the breech-end; the neck that entered the stock above the handle of the musket, which was pierced to allow passage for the large screw of the lock plate; and the breech-pin pierced in the middle to allow passage for a vertical breech-screw securing the barrel to the butt of the musket. Finally, the lugs of the bayonet and the foresight were brazed onto the barrel, the latter was placed 20 lignes (4.5cm) from the muzzle. Finally, the touch hole of the barrel was pierced with a small drill.

This simplified description of the manufacturing process of a musket barrel shows the complexity of obtaining large series of reliable muskets to equip the army. The barrels were then tested by inspectors of the Royal Artillerie. This test consisted of two successive shots: the first shot with an ounce of powder and a ball of the appropriate calibre, and a second with a half-ounce of powder and the same type of ball. During the test, the musket barrel rested on a horizontal easel and its breech pressed 'against a beam reinforced with iron bars' so as to prevent its recoil, thus 'the test was stronger.'[38] The barrels which passed the test were paid for and marked at the level of the breech, and the others were destroyed and their metal given back to the blacksmiths.

The regulation calibre was 7¾ lignes (17.44mm, or 0.69 pouces), which meant that 18 balls could be produced per pound of lead. The outer diameter of the barrel at the level of the breech was 16 lignes (36mm), the outer diameter at the muzzle was 8½ lignes (19.1mm). The total length of the barrel was 3 pieds 8 pouces (119cm).

D'Espagnac, in the *Essai sur la science de la guerre* published in 1751, specifies that certain regiments had their muskets treated against rust. Considering the additional cost of this treatment, it was probably reserved to some prestigious units such as the Gardes françaises, the Gardes suisses or the Régiment Du Roi. This was also the case with the muskets given to infantry officers in 1758.

The flintlock would equip the muskets of the French army until 1840 when the army moved to percussion locks.

The cocking-hammer held a piece of flint between its jaws, it was activated by a spring which was released by the trigger; the movement of the cocking-hammer brought down the flint on the lock plate. With the brutal shock of the flint against the lock plate, the latter opened completely under the action of a spring, exposing the pan filled with powder, the shock of the flint against the lock plate produced sparks which in turn ignited the powder and, through the touch hole, communicated the ignition to the powder in the barrel.

The lock consisted of about 20 parts; its manufacture was less technical than that of the barrel. It measured 16.5cm long. Here again there was already a certain industrialisation amongst the different trades: forgers, founders, tappers, grinders, and filers, right up to the locksmith who assembled and completed it. This artisanal manufacturing method meant that the wooden stock was adapted to each lock, parts were not interchangeable. If parts had to be transferred from one lock to another, it was necessary to file and adjust.

38 Pierre Surirey de Saint Remy, *Mémoires d'artillerie* (Paris: Jombert, 1745), p.397.

Attempts were made to manufacture identical locks based on mechanical processes where the locksmith roughly forged the lock, then when he had forged a certain number, he heated them to redness and placed them in a stamping die and with a powerful strike of a hammer gave the preformed lock the shape of the mould. These were then filed, and placed in new moulds which gave a unique and regular template for drilling the holes. However, this rather unsuccessful method was abandoned.

In a report made after the camp of instruction in Le Havre in 1756, the duc d'Harcourt deplored the poor quality of the weapons: 'The big flaw I found is that most of the weapons are very bad; the barrels are good, but locks in general are defective; and most of those issued this year are of very bad iron'[39]. The cocking-hammers broke like glass or the pans had way too much play resulting in nearly one misfire in three. As one of the consequences of these failures, at the Dunkerque camp of that same year, a grenadier from the Régiment de la Marine had his wrist shattered by his musket, which burst in his hands, because there were several cartridges in the barrel. The swan-necked cocking-hammer disappeared from the 1763 model for a less fragile model, similarly the head of the jaw screw was no longer slit but pierced with a hole.

Knot-free walnut was used for the musket stocks. They were supplied preformed. The quality of the wood was also checked. Despite standardization efforts, each lock being unique, the stock was adjusted to a specific lock. At the level of the butt, the slope of the spur was a slightly softer on the 1746 model. The curvature of the butt, called the pied de vache, was a little more marked on the 1754 model than on the 1746 model. The butt of the stock was reinforced with a plate.

The flints came from blond flint cutting shops in Berry. The *caillouteurs* were the workers who cut flints. The stones were then sorted according to their size. The flint mounted on the musket was held between the jaws of the cocking-hammer by a small piece of leather, cloth or by a small lead sheet. The bevel of the flint was placed upward so that when it struck, the largest surface of the flint hit the pan.

Officially, there was not yet a pan cover to protect the lock from the elements and shocks, it only appeared tardily in the decree of 1 March 1768. However, La Porterie in 1754 gives us the drawing of a leather pan cover, demonstrating that it existed before 1768. Failing that, soldiers wrapped the lock of their musket in canvas. When troops were bivouacked, in the presence of the enemy, the soldiers lay down with their loaded weapons in their arms, as Jacques de Mercoyrol de Beaulieu describes in his memoirs:

> …the two brigades [Picardie and Navarre] were soon standing with their arms, each having rested holding them in their arms and covering them to protect them from the dampness of the night, as each particular officer had recommended to his troop, the capitaines made an immediate inspection to see if the primers were well dried and to remedy those which, neglected, would not be, which was carried out.[40]

---

39 *Revue d'histoire rédigée à l'État-major de l'armée, Section historique*, n°27 mars 1903, p.512

40 Mercoyrol de Beaulieu, *Campagnes*, p.131.

Loading was done with a ball cartridge. The cartridge was made of a wrapping of parchment or paper which contained the powder with the ball placed on top. The calibre was the same as that of the cavalry carbine, the dragoon musket, or the pistol, for a ball of 18 to the pound. The cartridge had a powder charge of half the weight of the ball. As muskets fouled rapidly, there were also smaller balls (21 to the pound) to be able to continue loading and firing.

Major progress was made with the replacement of the wooden ramrod with an iron one. On 13 June 1741, the regulation about the infantry musket ramrod required an iron ramrod with a nail-head, 3 pieds 7 pouces 8 lignes (118mm) long. The trial of a steel ramrod was abandoned due to the poor quality of the steel produced at that time, which were deemed too brittle. The end of the ramrod was tapped to receive the screw thread of a worm.

The bayonet measured from 17 to 18 pouces long (48cm), including the socket, the blade measured 14 pouces (37.8cm) and the socket three pouces (8.1cm). The bayonet weighed 9½ onces (290g). It was made of two welded parts: the blade and the socket to fix it to the barrel. The bayonet locking ferrule only appeared on the Model 1763 musket, and the hitherto L-shaped mortise became Z-shaped. The musket mounted with its bayonet measured 6 pieds 2 pouces (2m) and many authors wished it to be longer, in particular to cope with cavalry charges. The fusilier most often abandoning his sword, it was the musket prolonged by its bayonet which constituted his edged weapon in hand-to-hand combat. Finally, according to the instructions, from 1750 the soldiers always had to fix bayonets for all manoeuvres and for firing exercises. Bayonets were manufactured in the Manufacture Royale of Klingenthal in Alsace.

The Vincennes Musket 1758–1760

Although not followed up, it seems interesting to mention an attempt, carried out in 1757, to design a breech-loading musket for the infantry; it is still known as the 'fusil de Vincennes.' It was original in its design compared to earlier attempts at a 'fusil à dé' such as the musket of M. de Chaumette in 1704 or that of the Rêveries du *Maréchal* de Saxe and his regiment of dragoons. All things considered, because at that time the technical mastery of steel and cartridges was still lacking, it was a bit like the idea of Dreyse's rotating breech. In the 'fusil de Vincennes', the unlocking tail was placed on the left and it was not the breech block which moved back, but the barrel which moved forward.

The Château de Vincennes was one of the residences of the young Louis XV. Then under the Regency, a royal porcelain factory moved there in 1740, before being transferred to Sèvres. In 1752, the construction of the École Militaire, dear to Duverney, was progressing slowly on the Champ de Mars, due to lack of funding. D'Argenson resolved, while waiting for the completion of the work, to temporarily install the school in the King's residence at Vincennes, where it remained until 1756. In 1757, Duverney decided to set up an arms factory there. This marked the beginnings of the Manufacture d'armes de Vincennes.

Paris Duverney, who was the patron of this factory, was working to initiate the production of a musket, and the inventor, M. Bourdier, was promising much. Here is what Duverney wrote to M. de Crémille in March 1758:

> A year ago, an establishment was begun at Vincennes for the new arms which are known to you; but the obstacles that you know of in this country have suspended its execution. Six weeks ago I involved myself in this important business… Finally, I believe that nothing can revive soldiers or make an impression on our enemies like this new weapon![41]

The arms factory was run by Sieur Bourdier, a gunsmith who had developed this breech-loading musket. It was a musket whose barrel and breech-end were joined by a conical screw, the breech-end which contained the screw, could turn on the button of the breech. It unscrewed with a simple half-turn. Thus unlocked, the barrel could slide forward on the wooden stock and release the chamber where the cartridge was placed. Slightly larger in diameter than the barrel, the cartridge was gently forced into the barrel when locking it. The lock was slightly modified, but the sequence afterwards was similar to that practised for the regulatory musket:

> 13th command: Open the barrel
> 1st step: turning the lock slightly outwards, put the left hand on the crank; in this closed position, the crank which serves as a handle is placed underneath, the thumb pressing on the iron and the four fingers covering the handle of the said crank and, at the same time, by an effort of the two hands will turn it, the left hand coming to body and the right turning the trigger-guard outwards; the crank causes the barrel to make a half-turn, which is released and is slid forward on the barrel, this translation is guided and limited. At the end of this manoeuvre, the crank is then in a vertical position above the barrel.
>
> 2nd step: the left hand grabbing the barrel immediately above the mount, the right hand pulling the butt of the stock down, will leave it to place itself on the cartridge holder…[42]

Without needing a ramrod or ramming, it was possible to have a longer musket and bayonet. The total length of a copy kept at the Musée de l'armée is 168cm long with a bayonet that measures 94cm, including 70cm of blade and a hilt guard similar to a dagger. It is a weapon with a short wooden stock.

One of the reasons for the failure of this weapon was related to the poor quality of the powder, the saltpetre still contained a lot of residue which very quickly clogged all the moving parts of the musket. In March 1766, Gribeauval distributed some of these muskets, then kept at the Arsenal, to the miners. This last test was not followed-up.

41 'Le fusil à manivelle 1758', *Carnet de la Sabretache*, 1895, vol.3, p.234.
42 'Le fusil à manivelle 1758', p.236.

Rifled Carbines

D'Espagnac in his *Essai sur la science de la guerre* published in 1751 mentions that there were a few rifled carbines in the infantry, and that it was the oldest in service and experience who were armed with them. However, no mention is made of carabiniers in the muster rolls and establishment tables of the infantry, as was already the case for the cavalry. It is difficult to know if there were any carabiniers in the infantry regiments of the Seven Years War. These few chosen soldiers were the forerunners of the future chasseurs of 1760, and then of the chasseurs carabiniers of the light infantry companies at the end of the Ancien Régime (1788). One could wonder why the infantry did not adopt this more accurate rifled weapon quicker. Here are several reasons for this: first of all, the carbine was much shorter than the musket, and in three very close ranks accidents were already frequent with muskets. Then the loading of the rifled carbine took much longer and required special training and target practice. The calepin (a type of greased paper cartridge), which replaced the standard cartridge, contained the charge of powder and the ball, the soldier tore the paper of the cartridge with his teeth and emptied the charge of powder in the chamber then slid the remainder of the cartridge into it. The ball then had to be forced into the rifled barrel with a small mallet and then with the ramrod, finally the lock had to be primed using a powder horn. In theory, the range of rifled carbines was longer than smoothbore muskets, but to maintain accuracy, a lower powder charge was used, so the range remained close to that of the musket. Furthermore, there was an extra cost to engraving the rifling inside the barrel. For all these reasons, the smoothbore musket was preferable for poorly trained troops. It was not until 1837, and the adoption of the Delvigne-Pontcharra rifled carbine, and the creation of the Chasseurs de Vincennes that line infantry adopted the rifled carbine.

The Sword

'Every soldier shall have a sword 26 pouces of blade (70.4 cm), with a two-pouces shoulder; the rest of the blade with two edges up to the point, which was reinforced with a central ridge.'[43] That was all the decrees said about the fusilier's sword, fortunately many examples have survived. At the beginning of the eighteenth century, its hilt was said to be à la mousquetaire with a pas d'âne ring allowing the index finger to slide in it to ensure a better grip of the sword. Around 1740, a simplified hilt with a single guard appeared, similar to that of the cavalry. It is this model that we find on the representations of the time.

The increase in firepower by the adoption of the cartridge and especially the socket bayonet made the sword unnecessary and inconvenient: 'swords are so cumbersome in war and so rarely useful that most soldiers throw them away or sell them during the campaign' writes Héricourt.[44]

---

43 Acte royal, 19 January 1747, *Ordonnance du roy portant règlement pour l'habillement de l'infanterie françoise* (Paris: Imprimerie royale, 1747), p.5.

44 Héricourt Nicolas d', *Elemens de l'art militaire*, (Paris: Gissey David, 1756), vol.1, p.240.

Rochefort worried that the swords were the responsibility of the *capitaines* who were required to renew them at the start of each campaign, but the soldiers soon threw them away. So that, according to the *Encyclopédie Méthodique* of 1787, the sword disappeared during the Seven Years War: 'It is only since the beginning of the last war that we have neglected to wear them and that they have gradually been suppressed.'[45] This suppression only became official by the decree of 25 January 1767. At that time, supporters of the deep order, shock, and hand-to-hand combat vainly demanded its reintroduction. Swords were inconvenient, as proof here is what Puységur describes in his *Art de la guerre* as he demanded their abandonment: 'Even a single man cannot go a little fast, without putting his hand to the hilt of his sword, lest it runs between his legs and knocks him down; all the more so in combat, especially in the woods, hedgerows or entrenchments, the soldiers to shoot being obliged to hold their musket with both hands.'[46]

Grenadier's Belts and Arms

Originally the role of the grenadier, from which he took his name, was the throwing of grenades. But fairly quickly, around 1678, the grenadier was given a musket and he became an elite soldier, the throwing of grenades taking on less and less importance.

The Pouch

Was the grenadière or pouch, in which were kept hand grenades, still worn during the Seven Years War? The answer is yes, if we are to believe the manuscript of Taccoli in 1760, which shows us grenadiers with, fixed on the belt, a ventral pouch decorated with a grenade motif, and with the indispensable wick to light the grenades inserted in the shoulder belt at the level of the thorax. Taccoli in his series of plates depicting grenadiers, also illustrates the various steps to throw a grenade. Girard in 1740 and Bottée in 1741, are the last two authors of the eighteenth century to describe the instructions for grenade throwing, which disappeared from the decrees. The grenadière was, for these two authors, carried on a shoulder belt which passed over the left shoulder, with the grenadière hanging on the right side. For the *Encyclopédie* in 1757, depending on the circumstances, the pouch carried either cartridges or grenades: 'The pouch is used to carry a provision of cartridges, or grenades when service requires it.'[47] The perforated wooden block containing cartridges was then taken and replaced by grenades. The 1757 manuscript shows us a very fine Russian leather cartridge pouch, the flap edged with a silver braid and decorated with a silver grenade surmounted by a crown.

---

45 *Encyclopédie Méthodique, Art militaire* (Liège: Panckouke, 1785), vol.2, p.283.

46 Jacques François de Chastenet Puységur, *L'art de la guerre par principes et par règles* (Paris: Jombert, 1749), vol.1, p.219.

47 *L'Encyclopédie Encyclopédie ou Dictionnaire raisonné des sciences, des arts et des métiers* (Paris: Briasson, David, Le Bretond, Durand, 1757), vol.7, p.658.

Hand grenades were about the size of a four-pound cannonball, or about 65mm in diameter, they weighed only two pounds, and they contained about four to five ounces of powder (120–150g). Grenades were mainly used in sieges and when attacking entrenchments: 'The grenadiers use them to throw by hand during attacks of a covered way, an entrenchment, or in the middle of troops, where they kill, cripple, and cause much disorder.'[48] Grenades could be thrown 13–16 toises (25–30m) away. During the Seven Years War, they were listed among the supplies intended for the troops in Canada or Germany, no doubt for attacks on forts and redoubts, and for the few sieges of this war. Finally, there are examples of hand howitzer or grenade launchers from this period in the collections of the Musée de l'armée, but there is nothing to indicate that they were used during the Seven Years War.

The grenadier's belts were special. First of all, there was the cartridge pouch of black leather or red Russian leather, whose wooden block contained 30 rounds. The shoulder belt that carried the pouch was adjustable by a buckle, it was made of cowhide and measured one and a half pouces wide (4.06cm). Just above the pouch, a strip of leather called a traverse was sewn horizontally on the shoulder belt, to carry an axe. Grenadiers were equipped with a hatchet with a hammer on the back side, which was carried in a loop sewn on the traverse above the pouch. A plate from the work of Surirey de Saint Remy as well as the painting made by Joseph Vernet around 1756 at the port of Antibes show us how this hatchet was fixed. Puységur in 1749 is not convinced of the utility of this small axe, he writes: '...their small axes are of no use to them ... they are made to carry small axes to use in attacks on the covered way, or the like, to cut palisades and break down doors ... it would take them a long time to cut a palisade.'[49]

On some models, the traverse was used to attach both the axe and the bayonet. Michel Pétard in his series of works *Équipements militaires de 1600 à 1870* gives us the drawing of a very nice model preserved in the Historical Museum of Zurich. The pulvérin (a small flask containing priming powder) hangs from two small straps sewn to the inside of the shoulder belt, just above the leather traverse, which is used to carry an axe and bayonet, where a small leather purse, containing the musket cloth and spare flints, is also attached.

> The cartridge pouch used by officers of the grenadier companies will differ from that of the officers of the fusilier companies, only in that it will be garnished with a grenade embroidered in gold or silver, instead of fleurs de lys; and the cartridge pouch of the grenadier sergent will only be garnished with a grenade imprinted in gold or silver.[50]

From the decree of 19 January 1747, there were 10 axe-bearing soldiers in each grenadier company, who carried a larger, long-handled axe. These axe-

48 Bardet de Villeneuve, *Traité de l'artillerie* (La Haye: Van Duren, 1741), vol.7, p.71.

49 Puységur, *L'art de la* guerre, vol.1, p.222.

50 Acte Royal, 12 September 1758, *Ordonnance du roi concernant l'armement et l'équipement des compagnies de fusiliers de ses troupes* (Paris: Imprimerie royale, 1758).

bearers became carpenter soldiers in 1766, then disappeared in 1771, before being reintroduced in 1778 under the name of sappers.

The Musket

The musket and the bayonet of the grenadier were similar to those of the fusilier.

The Grenadier's Sabre

The grenadier was armed with a sabre with a curved blade, the blade was 31 pouces (84cm) or 5 pouces longer than the blade of the fusilier's sword. The hilt had double branches that connected to a knuckle-bow. There are many copies in public or private collections.

Ranks Distinctions of Non-Commissioned Officers

The Sergent

It was the regulation of 19 January 1747 which determined the distinctions of the various ranks of non-commissioned officers.

The *sergent*, who had an important role as a company's instructor, received special attention in all the decrees of the seventeenth and eighteenth centuries. An entire chapter was devoted to them in the decree of 1746, where their uniform differed in the better quality of the fabric, and in the possibility of wearing coloured stockings. They wore grey-white cloth breeches whereas they were made of white cloth for soldiers. Their cuffs were decorated either with three trimmings or with a wide edging of gold or fine silver.

A small object also undoubtedly distinguished the *sergent* – a watch. It was an essential measuring instrument for adjusting the rhythm of guard duties, changing of the guard, and roll calls, for which he was responsible whether in garrison or during campaigns. These were not the precious gold watches, costing 180 to 300 livres, but ordinary watches with cheaper mechanisms which came from Neuchâtel or Geneva.

The *sergents* were also armed with a partisan or halberd 6½ pieds long (2.10m) a little shorter than the spontoon of the officers. The halberd was an old thrusting weapon whose head was of various shapes, often a spike with, at the base, an axe blade and on the other side a hook. According to Bottée, halted, the *sergents* held their halberd with their right hand near the hook behind the axe blade. Unlike the officer with his spontoon, the *sergents* did not salute with the halberd, but only with the hat. When marching, *sergents* 'carry the halberd half-dragging like the spontoon, but this has no grace, because the pole is too short to give balance, so it must be carried with the head and butt spikes levelled, where even the head a little lower like the Italians.'[51]

The regulation of 9 December 1758 replaced the halberd with a musket. The *sergent* was also given a cartridge pouch: 'The cartouche or half-pouch

51 *Capitaine* Bottée, *Etudes militaires contenant l'exercice de l'infanterie* (Paris: Le Clerc, 1750), vol.1, p.70.

of the sergents will be pierced with twelve holes, it will be covered with a flap of red or black cowhide, and decorated in the middle with a fleur-de-lis imprinted in gold or silver.'[52]

The Caporal

The cuffs of the *caporaux* were edged with a wool braid of the colour of the buttons and decorated with three wool laces. These laces were placed either parallel or more often perpendicular to the edge of the cuff.

The Anspessade

The cuffs of the *anspessades* were edged with a yellow or white wool braid depending on the colour of the buttons. Let us recall that the *anspessade* was not a non-commissioned officer.

Company and Squad Equipment

The squad was equipped with a tent with the poles, crossbar and wooden pegs necessary for its assembly. There were five tents per 40-man company and six tents per 45-man grenadier company.

Each squad was equipped with a pot and its lid, a mess tin and a barrel or tin can with a capacity of 12 quarts, or about 11 litres. Most cooking pots were still made of tinned copper, they had three small legs to be stable. Despite the tinning, poisoning with verdigris remained frequent and from that time many articles were published on this danger. It was also from this period that they were replaced with cast iron pots, which had the disadvantage of being heavier, or tin pans, but the latter had the disadvantage of having weak welds. Tinplate was made of sheet metal covered with tin. From the instruction of 1778 on the service of the infantry, the pots were all made of wrought iron.

There was one bell of arms per company and one more per battalion for the picquet.

Each fusilier company had 10 tools: three shovels, three pickaxes, two axes, and two billhooks. These tools were carried in turn by the soldiers by means of holsters of un-blackened cowhide so as not to dirty the uniforms. Each of these holsters closed with two buckles and was attached to a two-pouces-wide strap. The 1753 decree was excessively precise on the dimensions of these tools, but hereafter, their measurements are expressed only in centimetres. The shovel was rectangular, the handle measured 65cm, the blade was 19.8cm high, 18.2cm wide in its upper part and 14.8cm at the cutting edge, and the socket was 9.4cm long. The pickaxe had a sharp pointed end and flat 'axe' blade; the handle was 74cm long, the iron head was 25.7cm long and the 'axe' blade was 6.7cm wide at the cutting edge. The billhook had a 12.8 cm long handle, the iron of the blade ended in a hook and was 23.2cm high by 8.1cm wide at the tip by 5.8cm at the level of the handle. The big axe

52 Acte Royal, 9 December 1758, *Ordonnance du roi concernant l'armement des officiers et des sergens des compagnies de fusiliers de ses troupes, et des cartouches ou demi-gibernes dont ils doivent être pourvus du 9 Décembre 1758* (Paris: Imprimerie royale, 1758).

had 59.6cm long handle, the blade of the axe was 19.4cm long and its cutting edge had a height of 10.4cm.

On camp, these tools were used to clear the ground, prepare latrines, and dig ditches, but they were also used during service in the field as shown by the memoirs of Jacques de Mercoyrol de Beaulieu, *capitaine* in the Régiment de Picardie:

> Suddenly, the fog left the heights and seemed to thicken on the plain. M. de Chevert marched the brigade frontally to seize the hedges which were seven or eight hundred paces from the edge of the wood against which we stood, about halfway to the enemy. The regiment in line arrived at these hedges. M. de Chevert, whose plan was to march frontally against the height held by the enemies in order to attack them, continuing to think that this was only a rearguard of their army, ordered that all the soldiers who had axes or billhooks were to be used to cut the hedges and the soldiers began to work.[53]

The equipment of the guards consisted of a shovel, a hooded canvas greatcoat to protect them in winter, and a torch or a tin lantern.

Usually, a regiment or a battalion would have had a motley appearance with various shades of grey-white uniforms depending on the newness or cleanliness of them. Coats could be with or without collars, have various shaped cuffs, and skirts free or turned back. The belts could be one of three types and the knapsacks of canvas or leather, with one or two shoulder straps.

Here is how a French officer was described in a letter from a pastor in the town of Celle, published shortly after the war, and dated August 1757:

> This detachment having stopped at my door, I thought it my duty to speak to the person leading it, to inform myself of his views. He was a little enseigne, badly groomed, filthy, without a shirt, I believe, having only to cover two very dirty paws [hands], cuffs which I took to be of paper attached to his waistcoat. He deigned to assure me with an air of well-taken protection, snubbing his nose, raising his eyebrows, stretching out his hand and assuming the tone of a Maréchal de France, that he had given the strictest orders to his troops not to commit any disorder… If we wanted to judge French troops by the samples we have seen so far, we would have a pretty sad idea of them?[54]

Drummers and Fifers Uniforms

Livery Dress

From the decree of 18 January 1683, there was only one drummer per company: for a total of 17 drummers per battalion and only one fifer per infantry regiment. The latter was attached to the *colonel*'s company. Each regiment also had a *tambour major*. The *tambours majors* were of very old creation, they were found under different titles, such as *maître tambour* or

53 Mercoyrol de Beaulieu, *Campagnes*, p.121.

54 Anon., *Lettres écrites à un ami* (Maestricht: Jen Edme Dufour, 1765), p.7.

tambour colonel, they officially took the name of *tambour major* from 1651. From then on, a *tambour major* was assigned to the first company of the regiment, he was responsible for teaching the drum beats to the drummers of his regiment. The function of this non-commissioned officer continued to exist in all the regiments of the Ancien Régime, although it did not appear systematically in the regulatory texts. The decree of 1762 gave him the rank of *sergent*.

The uniform of musicians was regulated by the decree of 20 April 1736: 'the same quantities and qualities of wool cloth, fabric and buttons will be used for the clothing of the drummers as for that of soldiers, with the small livery with frogs down to the pocket only, both in His Majesty's regiments and in the regiments which wear those of the colonels.'[55]

Described here is only the royal livery, which was worn by the majority of the regiments like the royal regiments, the provincial regiments and the Régiment du Dauphin. The livery of the gentlemen's regiments, when it is known, is described with the other distinctive attributes of each of regiment. The blue field of the King's livery came from the azure blue of the royal coat of arms. Blue was reserved for people of the Household of the King and the Dauphin, as recalled by His Majesty's decree of 6 February 1753, where it was forbidden for anyone to have their servants wear the King's livery unless they had the right to do so by special authorisation. It was also forbidden for all officers to have this livery worn without having obtained the written permission of the Grand Ecuyer de France. A second decree of the same day, stated that it was forbidden for any person of any quality and condition whatsoever, to have their servant wear a blue livery, even if the braid was different from that of the His Majesty's livery.

The braid was the second element characterising a livery. A first model of braid was worn under Louis XIII and until the beginning of the reign of Louis XIV. Beneton de Morange de Peyrins in his *Traité des marques nationales* describes it as follows: 'the braid of the royal livery which was fashionable at the time of the marriage of Louis XIV, was in a chequerboard pattern with white, red and blue squares, opposed to each other… it is only since this marriage that this braid has been changed.'[56] Van de Meulen gives us a very nice representation of it in a painting kept at the Château de Versailles entitled 'Louis XIV in the trench at the siege of Tournai, 2 June 1667'.

A new type of royal livery braid was adopted around 1670, it would be kept until the end of the monarchy: 'a wide red velvet [braid] on which is embroidered a double white cord, which by crossing in a necklace, forms large circles. In what is called the small livery, the braid is simple and for the grand livery it is doubled with between the two a smaller white braid decorated with red triangles opposed two by two by their point…'[57] Lucotte in the *Encyclopédie*, in the article devoted to passementerie, gives us a plate

55 Acte royal, 20 April 1736, *Ordonnance du Roi concernant l'habillement de l'infanterie française* (Paris: Imprimerie royale, 1736), p.10.

56 Etienne Claude Beneton de Morange de Peyrins, *Traité des marques nationales* (Paris: Le Mercier, 1739), p.303.

57 Beneton de Morange de Peyrins, *Traité des marques nationales*, p.303.

showing the way in which the three white cords of the braid of the royal livery were woven and the precise design they formed.[58]

The braid, which was placed along the edges of the coat or between the two braids of the grand livery, was a narrow braid, approximately 1.4–1.5cm wide. It had a white field decorated with the same pattern of white cords as the grand livery with, in the centre of the loops formed by these cords, an embroidered motif of red opposed triangles. There are few indications on the width of the livery braids of the drummers of the Ancien Régime, only the decree of 1786 indicates a livery braid of 9 lignes (2.4cm). Similarly, the liveries of the Maison civile du Roi from the years 1775–1780, preserved in the collections, have a livery braid of approximately 2.9cm with a border approximately 1.4cm wide.

Foreign regiments were authorised to have their drummers wear a blue livery as was the case for the Swiss Régiment de Boccard and Régiment de Diesbach, but with their own livery braids.

As can be seen in eighteenth century depictions, there was no uniformity in the arrangement of livery braids. For economic reasons, the trend was to reduce the quantity of braids. At the beginning of the eighteenth century, they could cover the coat almost entirely, as on the plates of Delaistre in 1721 or the engravings of Le Bas in 1736. Whereas at the end of the Ancien Régime, they were limited to the seams of the coat, the sleeves, where they were arranged in chevrons or armlets, and to the buttonholes.

In general, drummers wore the King's small livery on which the braid was simple, placed on all the seams of the coat at the level of the back, the sleeves, the armholes, on the edge of the coat at the front. and at the back at the level of the skirts, on the edge of the cuffs, at the buttonholes of the coat and of the pockets and it edged the lapels if the uniform had any. It was on the sleeves that there were the greatest variations: either braid in longitudinal bands on the seams of the sleeves, or in armlets, or, more frequently between 1767 and 1770, in chevrons.

There are relatively few depictions of drummers from this period. We can consult the engravings of Le Bas executed after drawings by Parrocel around 1736. On certain miniatures by Blarenberghe executed around 1750 or those by Becher during the Seven Years War, the braid edging the buttonholes, also called frogs, is pleated to form a rounded shape. The Bouxwiller manuscript describes a drummer's uniform for the Grenadiers de France for the period 1749–1762. The livery braid is placed on all seams: sleeves, armholes, and back yoke, on the edge of the coat and the lapels, on the collar, cuffs and pocket flaps. The braid also edged the buttonholes of the coat, pockets and cuffs. Finally, Becher, for the period of the Seven Years War, gives us three representations of musicians: a fifer and a drummer erroneously attributed to the Régiment de Piémont but the colour of the liveries and braids, as well as the presence of swallow nests on the shoulders indicate that they belonged to two Swiss regiments, and finally a drummer from the Régiment Royal Lorraine in the livery of King Stanislas Leczinski.

58 *Encyclopédie ou dictionnaire raisonné des sciences, arts et métiers, Tome 1 des planches* (Paris: Panckoucke, Stoupe et Brunet, 1777-1779), vol.1, plate XI fig.1.

The Régiment Du Roi was an exception to the rule about the small livery and wore a grand livery dress; that is to say two braids separated by an inner border. In a memoir, written around 1755, on the quantity of fabric required to dress the Régiment Du Roi, it is indicated with regard to the drummers: coat in blue cloth, 2¼ aunes each, lined with 3¼ aunes of red twill of Aumale red.[59] Cuffs in half-scarlet (one aune of Aumale). 29½ aunes of grand livery braid for each coat (nearly 33m of livery braid), with 19 and five-eighths aunes of passementerie (23.3m) and 6¼ aunes (7.4m) of edging for each waistcoat. Two crosses on each coat. The quantity of braids as well as the presence of edging clearly indicate a grand livery dress for this very particular regiment, which depended only on the royal will. This is confirmed by the somewhat earlier painting by Parrocel, preserved at Versailles and entitled 'Camp of Régiment du Roy' where we see a drummer wearing a grand livery with the braids arranged in armlets on the sleeves.

It was not until the decree of April 1767 that the uniform of the *tambour major* was officially distinguished from that of other drummers by a double edging of livery braid, on the cuffs and the collar. But such a distinction already existed before, as evidenced by the account of a grenadier of the Régiment de La Marche Prince who mentioned in 1758 the richness of the dress of their *tambour major*. The *tambour major* probably adopted the ceremonial mace at the end of the seventeenth century, but it was not until 1791 that a regulation officialised it and fixed the movements and signals.

The Musical Instruments

The dimensions of the drums of this period were not yet fixed by a regulation. The wooden shell of a drum of the Régiment de Hainaut infanterie, dated 1747, kept at the Musée de l'armée, measures 34cm in diameter by 44.8cm in height.

De La Borde describes its construction in his *Essai sur la musique ancienne et moderne*. The drum shell was made from a plank of oak or walnut two lignes thick (5mm) and 13 to 14 pouces (35 to 38 cm) wide, it was formed into a cylindrical shape. Inside were placed two one-pouce (2.7cm) wide wooden rings called counter-forces. The heads were made of calfskin or goatskin. The batter head was thicker than the bottom one, which was called the snare head. They were wetted before being stretched over two small rings six lignes (1.6cm) wide. These skins were fastened to the shell by two large wooden rims 18 to 19 lignes high (4cm), each pierced with 12 holes through which a six toises long (11.70m) hemp rope was passed. This rope was used to stretch or loosen the heads by means of tension straps, which were made of pieces of leather through which passed the rope. To make the sound more pleasant, two small holes were drilled in the large snare ring through which a gut string was passed. This string was held in place on the shell by a button at the bottom and by a tension rod at the top, which could be turned to tighten or release the snare. When the drum was carried on a shoulder strap by the drummer, this tension key for the snare was placed near his left hand.

59 Général Vanson, 'Le Régiment du roi', *Carnet de la Sabretache, revue militaire*, 1897, p.676.

The snare was stretched so that the drum gave only one vibration with each stroke of the drumstick. The drum had to be carried so as not to hinder the march and to leave the left arm free to beat, it was carried at a slight angle against the left side and the top rim reaching 2 pouces (6cm) above the belt.

The drumsticks measure approximately 1½ pieds (48cm). The proper way to beat the drum was to hold the right stick tight with the whole hand, the left was held with the thumb and the first two fingers. The tips of the drumsticks had to strike the middle of the batter head.

Here again there was no regulation fixing the colour or design of the motif painted on the shells. The shell was sometimes left unpainted, but more generally it was painted in the facing colour of the coat, the rims could be unpainted or painted blue, red or in a two-tone pattern of alternating red and white or blue and white bands. The rare examples that have come down to us, such as those from Royal Roussillon or Hainaut, kept in the collections of the Musée de l'armée, have fairly similar designs. This design consisted of a central oval escutcheon charged, for royal and provincial regiments, with the arms of France; or charged with the arms of the prince of the blood or the gentleman owner of the regiment, surmounted by a heraldic crown corresponding to his title. Behind the escutcheon, crossed in saltire, are painted flags in the colours of the regiment; generally, three on each side, the *colonel*'s white flag placed above and behind. All the drum shells represented in the 1757 manuscript are natural, without any decoration. The Régiment de Royal Lorraine represented by Becher carries a drum with alternately blue, yellow, and black opposed triangles with blue, white, and black rims.

The shells of the drums of the foreign regiments had their own specific decorations, which unfortunately are often unknown. Some copies are in foreign museums, such as the drum of the Swiss Régiment de Courten, preserved in the museum of Valère in Sion in Switzerland. It is of the same model as that of the French infantry, namely: a central escutcheon with the arms of Courten surmounted by a helmet and a lambrequin. The Musée Condé has a drum of a Swiss regiment with a blue background, sown with fleur-de-lis and, in the centre, the arms of France and Navarre in a cartouche supported by two angels, surmounted by a royal crown, behind a bundle of four flags on either side; in the centre a white *colonel*'s flag and three ordonnance flags, on the last flag we clearly distinguish the first quarter, it carries 13 flames alternately: black, yellow, red, black, yellow, black, red in the middle at the pole, black, yellow, black, red, yellow, black, with the black flames slightly narrower. This could be a drum of the Gardes suisses in the colours of the livery of Choiseul from 1762. Becher's manuscript shows us a drum of a Swiss regiment with red flames pointing upwards and blue flames pointing downwards. The Museum Kloster Michaelstein in Blankenburg keeps a drum of the Régiment de La Marck, which has on its front the arms of the House of La Marck.

Copper drum shells could already be found during the Seven Years War, like the repoussé copper shell of a drum of the Régiment des Grenadiers de France, which is in a private collection. They were officially introduced by the decree of 25 April 1767. In 1783, Turpin Crissé in 1783 denounced this expensive choice:

> Since a few years, the old usage [of wooden drum shells] has been changed; and part of the infantry regiments today have copper drum shells. I do not know what the reason for this change may have been; I see no other than the frenzy that the Frenchman has had for 30 to 35 years to imitate all his neighbours.[60]

The decorations were embossed on the copper plate. There are still rare copies from this period in collections, they have embossed patterns similar to those on wooden drums.

The shoulder strap of the drum was made of bleached buffle and it could be covered with a livery braid. At Fontainebleau there is a painting by Jeaurat de Berty dated to 1757, which represents a drum, a fife case, a shoulder strap, and belt of a musician; probably from a soldier of the Maison du Roi like the Gardes françaises. The case of the fife is a wooden case closed at the top and bottom by a brass stopper, it is carried by a cord of mixed white and red, finished with a pompom and a white and red tassel. The shoulder strap is made of three braids of the royal livery side-by-side and lined in white, adjustable by a brass buckle. Similarly, the sword belt is trimmed with a livery braid. In Becher's plate, the shoulder straps are covered with a livery braid.

The decrees specified that there should not be more than one fifer per infantry regiment. The instrument was played with the same embouchure as a transverse flute, it had six holes and its range extended over two octaves from low D to double octave D. It measured about 50cm. De La Borde in 1780 in his *Essai sur la musique* wrote: 'For some time now, in regimental music, the small flute has been substituted for the fife, because the latter is much more out of tune than the small flute, having no key like it.'[61] Gradually, from the beginning of the eighteenth century fifers disappear from the French regiments, but remained present in the Swiss or German regiments. Here is what Warnery thought of fifes:

> In several armies, the infantry has only drums and little fifes; the latter have for them only their little cost; it is an acquisition we made from the Swiss, which does not give a great idea of their old music; the way in which they play it, proves its antiquity, is more apt to grate the ears and make people cry, than to animate in combat.[62]

Some regiments already had oboists; they were then at the expense of the *colonel* of the regiment. The creation of regimental bands, made up of real musicians, officially dates from 1763, but it is likely that some regiments already had them. Thus, in the diary of the camp of Valence in 1755 one can read: 'During its duration [of the mass], a detachment of the musicians of the concert of Grenoble, which had been joined by the symphony of the Régiment de Bretagne, executed several pieces of music and sang a motet

60 Lancelot Turpin de Crissé, *Commentaires sur les institutions militaires de Végèce* (Paris: Nyons, 1788), vol.2, p.4.

61 Jean Benjamin De La Borde, *Essai sur la musique* (Paris: Pierres, 1780), vol.1, p.257.

62 Charles Warnery, *Remarques sur l'essai général de tactique de Guibert* (Varsovie: publisher unknown, 1782), p.79.

and the Exaudiat.' It is not known which instruments or how many musicians composed this 'symphony'.[63]

Officers Uniforms

Colonel, lieutenant colonel, major, capitaines and lieutenants

From 1737, officers were required to equip themselves at their own expense and to wear the uniform when they were with their regiment, it was 'the most decent and the most suitable to make them known and to make them respected by the soldiers.' These uniforms had to be similar to that of the rank and file according to the decree of 10 April 1737, 'with the sole difference that their coat will be of Elbeuf cloth or other similar manufactures, which are finer cloths of better quality than those of the troops.'[64] The officer most often wore stockings and shoes and some contemporary sources say that infantry officers should not present themselves to general officers during a campaign without wearing gaiters.

The Gorget

The gorget was the chief distinguishing feature of an infantry officer on duty. It was found in most armies of this period, whether British, Hanoverian, Prussian or French. The crescent-shaped gorget was of gilt metal for French infantry officers, of silver for Swiss infantry officers and of steel for German officers. It was at that time mostly undecorated, and only rarely decorated with a grenade or stamped with the King's arms or those of a prince. It was especially under Louis XVI that the addition of decoration on gorgets became widespread. La Chesnaye tells us that 'foreigners' gorgets are larger than those of the French.'[65] It was tied around the neck with two cords of the facing colour of the regiment. *Colonels*, *capitaines*, *lieutenants*, *sous lieutenants* and *enseignes* wore the gorget. After the introduction of lapels, which became widespread in 1762, officers secured the gorget to the topmost buttons on the lapels with a small braid of coloured silk. The gorget denoted that the officer was on duty. They had to wear it, for example, when they travelled with their company, were on guard duty or took part in a court martial.

In the infantry, *majors* and *aide majors* did not wear the gorget. Instead, they were distinguished by their cane and, as we will see in the section dealing with the transmission of orders in Volume 3 of this work, this cane could have a head. In 1759, *majors* wore a cuirass over their coats during battle: 'With regard to the infantry, His Majesty wills that the brigadiers and major officers of the regiments, including the aides majors, whose functions require that they are on horseback on the days of combat, wear cuirasses,

63 Bibliothèque Nationale de France, Camp de Valence 1755, commandé par Monsieur le marquis de Voyer, maréchal de camps des armées du roi.

64 Acte royal, 10 April 1747, *Ordonnance du roy qui enjoint aux officiers des troupes d'infanterie, cavalerie et dragons de porter l'habit uniforme pendant le temps qu'ils seront aux corps* (Paris: imprimerie royale, 1747), p.2.

65 François-Alexandre Aubert de la Chesnaye Des Bois, *Dictionnaire militaire, portatif* (Dresde: George Conrad Walther, 1751), vol.2, p.22.

as well as the officers of the cavalry.'[66] *Majors* wore the full cuirass, it was in polished black steel.

Epaulettes

Epaulettes were introduced in the French army in the years 1748–1750. Initially to distinguish, by their colours, the various regiments of Grenadiers royaux, they were then mentioned in the decree for the dragoons of 1750: 'an epaulette on the left shoulder of the colour of the border of the saddle cloth.'[67] In 1757, they appeared on the service dress of the Chevaux légers de la Garde du Roi, who from then wore a gold epaulette with silver fringe on the right shoulder. But the epaulette was not yet a grade distinction.

On 12 January 1759, under the ministry of *maréchal* de Belle-Isle, an instruction introduced epaulettes as a distinctive mark of rank for officers of the infantry, cavalry and dragoon regiments. It was not before the decree of 10 December 1762 that the distinctive details according to the rank became known. For this reason, this major innovation in the silhouette of officers is often wrongly attributed to Choiseul, when in fact we owe it to Belle-Isle. Raspe's collection in its 1762 edition, which corresponds to the outfits worn in 1761, already shows officers with epaulettes, thus confirming the application of Belle-Isle's instruction. Similarly, the decree of March 1762 concerning the creation of the Régiment de volontaires étrangers de Dunkerque already distinguished the rank of *capitaines* and *lieutenants* by epaulettes, nearly nine months before the decree of Choiseul.

The *colonels* had two gold or silver epaulettes according to the colour of the buttons, with rich bullion fringes. The *lieutenant colonels* wore a gold or silver epaulette according to the colour of the button, with bullion or campaign fringes on the left shoulder, and a counter-epaulette without fringe on the right shoulder. The *majors* had two gold or silver epaulettes with thread fringes and without bullion or campaign fringes. The *capitaines* and the *aide majors* had an epaulette with thread fringes on the left shoulder and a counter-epaulette on the right. The *lieutenants* could not wear the full epaulette in gold or silver; the top of their epaulette was decorated with yellow or white silken rhombuses, so that, if the button was yellow, the epaulette had a golden background with white silken rhombuses; if, on the contrary, the button was white, the background of the epaulette was silver with yellow silken rhombuses; the silken fringe was mixed with gold or silver threads depending on the colour of the button. The *sous lieutenants* or *cornettes* wore an epaulette with a yellow or white silken background according to the colour of the button with gold or silver squares of the opposite colour. The *porte drapeau*, a new grade appearing after 1762 wore an epaulette with a yellow or white silken background edged in gold or silver, according to the colour of the button.

The epaulettes changed very little until the end of the Ancien Régime, they were similarly described in the ordinances of April 1767 and February

66 'Vieille tactique', *Carnet de la Sabretache, revue militaire rétrospective*, 1895, p.45.

67 Acte royal, 1 May 1750, *Ordonnance du Roy, concernant l'habillement, l'équipement & l'armement de ses régimens de dragons* (Paris: Imprimerie royale, 1750), p.4.

1779. In particular, at that time, the epaulette denoting rank was always worn on the right shoulder. It was only with the multiplication of functions in the rank that epaulette and counter-epaulette began to alternate on the left or the right shoulder depending on the function. General officers had to wait until 1775 to wear the epaulette.

It is difficult to have a precise idea of the appearance of these epaulettes, each officer dressing at his own expense and buying from his tailor and trimmer. As contemporary paintings show, the tab of the epaulette was made of soft fabric and ended in a single row of fringes falling on the shoulder. It did not have the stiff bearing and firmness, with a wide crescent, of the epaulettes of the end of the Ancien Régime or the Empire. For example, a painting representing a *major* of the Irish Régiment de Clare shows a wide shoulder strap at the end of which hang fringes in the extension of the strap. While the portrait of the marquis de Poyanne, as a *colonel* of the Carabiniers, shows us a complex silver epaulette with fringes and flower-patterned knots. The Dauphin Louis of France, represented in a portrait in 1765 in the uniform of *colonel général* of the dragoons also wears this type of epaulette.

Epaulettes from this period are rarely preserved in museums or private collections, and there are few contemporary iconographic documents, so a small glossary of passementerie can be useful here to understand the terms. What differentiates thread fringes from a bullion or campaign fringes, is the diameter of the fringe. However, whatever the precise name of each fringe type, the passementerie techniques to make these different types of fringes and increase their diameter all involved twisting metallic threads on a spinning wheel. That is why most often the floating end of the fringes ends in a loop, this loop is fixed on a hook of the spinning wheel during the twisting of the threads. The metal thread used in passementerie is called purl, a more or less coarse length of stretched gold or silver wire, which has been spun around a long iron needle by means of a spinning wheel. When the purl is flat and shiny, having been flattened between two steel wheels, it is called bullion.

Officers' Equipment and Arms

The Sword

Each officer went to a private retailer for the making of his sword and of his equipment, which again made for a wide variety of models and a richness that depended on the wealth of the officer. The fusilier officer's sword was similar to the soldier's sword in general, but it was lighter with a finer hilt. While the soldier's sword evolved towards a simple knuckle bow model, that of the officer sometimes remained of the so-called à la mousquetaire model with a 'pas d'âne' ring. The grip was finely twisted or fluted as was the button and other parts.

For the grenadiers, the grenadier officers' sabres that have been preserved show a guard with several branches, sometimes with a fleur-de-lis between the branches. Officers of foreign regiments sometimes obtained their sword from their country of origin. Thus, the officers of the Scottish regiments kept their famous basket-hilted sword, and the sabres of the grenadier officers of the German Régiment de Nassau had a basket hilt decorated with the arms of Nassau.

The sword knot was made of gold or silver threads according on the colour of the buttons. They were, interwoven with threads of the facing colour of the regiment. Likewise, the belt was made of embroidered or embossed leather.

The Spontoon

The spontoon was one of the distinctive marks of the officers of many European armies of the seventeenth and eighteenth centuries. Along with the gorget, they were two vestiges of feudal armies, and were marks of command.

The spontoon was a pike 7½ to 8 pieds long (2.43m to 2.59m), including the blade. The pole was made of ash, 1 pouce in diameter (2.7cm), and it was left unpainted. The willow-leaf shaped blade measured 8 pouces (21.6cm); it was reinforced along the pole by two 18-pouces(48cm) iron bands riveted to the pole by six nails.

The handling of the spontoon was codified: 'In line, placed in front of their regiments, the officers, sword in hand, face, a foot and a half or thereabouts between his two heels, the wrist a little inward at eye level; the left arm extended carelessly on the side of the sword, or the hand along the left side.' On the march, 'the officer marching at the head of a unit, the spontoon in the hand, carries it half-dragging, the blade forward. To do this gracefully, he must start with the left foot; on the second step, lower his spontoon, and bring it forward; so that on the third step, which is taken with the right foot, the spontoon goes back; and continuing to walk with the left foot, give a small movement from the right hand (the wrist of which is turned in) so that when the right foot is forward, the right arm is behind. Lacking these slight observations, one sees very good-looking officers, who have no grace at the head of a unit.[68]

Officers' Muskets

The Seven Years War was the occasion for a new attempt to arm infantry officers with a musket. Discussions on the armament of officers were not new, they had really gained momentum since the War of the Spanish Succession during which some officers were seen carrying the regulation spontoon and others the musket. Also, by the decree of 1 December 1710, the King agreed that for the good of the service, the armament of officers should be uniform, he decided that the *colonel*, the *lieutenant colonel* and the *capitaines* would retain the spontoon in accordance with the 1690 decree and that all junior officers, such as *lieutenants* of grenadiers or fusiliers, would be equipped with muskets with the exception of the Gardes françaises and Gardes suisses. The century progressed and theses clashed; for Puységur, each company was deprived of five firearms, and there was no good reason to arm officers differently from soldiers; while other authors, such as *maréchal* de Saxe or Belle-Isle, were not in favour of it. In May 1754, a decree regulated the new dimensions of the spontoon, reducing it to seven pieds, and the officers of

---

68 Bottée, *Etudes militaires*, vol.1, p.70.

grenadiers were equipped with a musket instead of the spontoon. During the Seven Years War, as had already happened at the beginning of the century, officers of all ranks carried the spontoon or the musket, and Belle-Isle, visibly reluctantly, admitted the necessity:

> You will agree, Sir, that it is very unfortunate that we have to part with what we have deemed good and useful because it is inconvenient and disagreeable to our officers and that, as good Frenchmen, they do not want to obey. I will not undertake to deal with this subject again and since we already have so many other objects to correct and that it is wiser to avoid repeating an order which will not be executed, I therefore think of derogating from what the decree prescribes for the spontoon, it is appropriate that the Comte de Clermont, who is informed that almost all the officers no longer have spontoons because of the extraordinary fatigue that the troops have suffered for a year, and of the loss of the baggage, and knowing the impossibility of making spontoons in the quarters occupied by the troops, allows that, without consequences, the officers of infantry will be armed with muskets for this campaign, observing that they should be similar if possible, that the barrels should be blued because they are easier to maintain than the others and that it would be disagreeable for the officer to set a bad example about the cleanliness of the arms.[69]

A few months later, two decrees appeared determining which officers were allowed to carry the musket instead of the spontoon. First of all, the decree of 31 October 1758, concerning officers and *sergents* of the fusilier companies stated:

> His Majesty having deemed it necessary for the good of his service that the officers and sergents of the fusilier companies of his infantry troops should henceforth be armed, as well as those of the grenadier companies, with muskets with their bayonets. He ordered and orders the following:
>
> Officers of fusilier companies; both French and foreign, will be required to obtain muskets without delay from the firearms factories established in Saint-Étienne, Charleville and Maubeuge, and bayonets which have been manufactured at the bladed weapons factory in Alsace. No musket will be admitted which does not absolutely conform to the model which has been sent to these factories for the officers of the grenadier companies; this musket will have a calibre of 16, to receive the ball of 18, and of the same construction as that of the soldier, with this difference that it will be only four pieds in length, that its wooden stock will be of walnut wood, that it will be finer and lighter, and that the fittings will be of polished iron, arranged relatively to the length. The bayonet shall have a blade of eight and a half pouces, fluted, three-quarters and sharp at its extremity. This officer's musket will weigh, armed with its bayonet, seven pounds at the most. The sergent's musket will be similar to that of the soldier, and will be supplied for the first time only from the King's stores at the expense of His Majesty.[70]

69 Joseph Margerand, *Armement et équipement de l'infanterie française du 17e au 20e siècle* (Paris: Éditions militaires illustrées, 1945), p.92.

70 Acte Royal, 31 October 1758, *Ordonnance du roi concernant l'armement des officiers et des sergents des compagnies de fusiliers* (Paris: Imprimerie royale, 1758).

Then the decree of 9 December 1758, gave more details on the equipment of infantry officers and non-commissioned officers.

> The armament of the officers and sergents of the fusilier companies of His troops and the cartouche or half-pouch with which they must be provided… The cartouche or half-pouch for the use of the officers, will be pierced with eight holes, of the diameter and depth suitable to receive cartridges with balls; this cartouche will be covered with a red or black morocco flap, it will be adorned with a fleur-de-lis embroidered in gold or silver in its middle, according to the uniform of each corps, and lined and bordered with a white leather. The strap which will carry this cartouche with its traverse [a strip of leather] will be of stitched white buffle; it will be a pouce and a half wide, and will have a buckle. The cartouche for the use of grenadier officers of grenadier companies shall not differ from that of the officer of fusilier companies, except in that it shall be adorned with a grenade embroidered in gold or silver, instead of a fleur-de-lis.[71]

Let us summarize the evolution of the equipment and armament of officers and *sergents* on the battlefields of the Seven Years War.

At the outbreak of the war, officers of the general staff: the *colonel* and the *lieutenant colonel* are on foot, wore a gorget and carried the spontoon, while the *majors* (including *aide majors*) carried the cane as their distinctive attribute with which they transmitted orders. They were mounted and wore a cuirass and boots.

In each of fusilier company, the *capitaine* carried a spontoon, but the *lieutenant* and the two *sergents* respectively carried the spontoon and the halberd until 1758 and then, from the campaign of 1759, they adopted the musket; this represented an addition of 48 muskets per battalion. And for the grenadier company, the *capitaine* carried a spontoon and, since 1710, the *lieutenant*, the *sous lieutenant*, and the two *sergents* were armed with muskets, this did not change.

This increase in the firepower of a battalion must be put into perspective, in fact the officers' half-pouch contained only eight cartridges and they only used them for the defence of their person as we can read in a letter from December 1759, written by M. de Cornillon *major général* of the infantry addressed to *maréchal* de Belle-Isle: 'The fire of the officers and that of the sergents must therefore be reserved for unforeseen cases, and for the preservation of their person, as has always been practised by grenadier officers.'[72] Finally, if we are to believe the chevalier de Meyrin, *capitaine* in the Régiment de Soissonais, who wrote in a memoir after the training camp at Dunkerque in 1778: 'We saw during the last war in Germany that the officers left their muskets in the baggage, this proves that they are more inconvenient than useful. Indeed, this weapon having to be used only for their personal defence, they rarely find themselves in the case of needing it.'[73]

---

71 Acte Royal, 9 December 1758, *Ordonnance du roi concernant l'armement et l'équipement des compagnies de fusiliers de ses troupes* (Paris: Imprimerie royale, 1758).

72 'Vieille tactique', *Carnet de la Sabretache*, 1895, p.46.

73 Margerand, *Armement et équipement de l'infanterie*, p.97.

There would be no instruction on musket handling for officers before the decree of January 1766. This decree, as well as the series of plates engraved by Gravelot to illustrate its text, gives us a very interesting detail allowing us to quickly distinguish the soldier from the officer; the soldier carries his musket on the left shoulder, the officer carries his musket on the right shoulder. Blarenberghe's gouaches confirm this detail. It is likely, as was often the case, that the prescription confirmed prior usage.

The allocation of a cartridge pouch to officers brought a small change to his uniform, by the addition of a shoulder strap in the colour of the coat to hold in place the shoulder belt of the pouch. The adoption of the epaulette a few months later solved this small problem of maintaining the shoulder belt.

It should be noted that, as early as May 1750, the officers of the dragoons were all equipped with a musket and a pouch containing six cartridges.

The officer's musket was a lightened version of the Model 1754 measuring 4.5 pieds (1.46m, including one metre for the barrel) and weighing only 2.75kg. It had a walnut wooden stock, polished iron fittings, a finer Model 1754 lock plate than that of the standard model, and a 21.6cm long bayonet. Officers carried the bayonet attached to the traverse sewn above the pouch in the same way as the axe of the grenadiers.

Public and private collections preserve officer's cartridge pouches that do not comply with the regulations, richly decorated with a leather flap sometimes covered in velvet, bearing the arms of the *colonel* of the regiment. This is the case with an officer's cartridge pouch from the Régiment de Penthièvre and with another from the Régiment de Navarre, or even the German Régiment de Lowendhal that M. Pétard reproduces in his series of studies on military accoutrements. No doubt they belonged to officers of the regimental staff: *colonel*, *lieutenant colonel* or *major*.

The royal decree of 20 March 1764 to regulate the drill of the infantry temporarily reintroduced the spontoon and the halberd.

> The colonel and the lieutenant colonel will be armed with spontoons; the major, aide majors, sous aide majors and the quartier-maître will only be so with their sword, which they will hold in their hand whenever they are on foot or on horseback at the head of a unit. All other officers, except those of the grenadiers, will be armed with spontoons and swords, in conformity with the models which will be sent to each regiment. All sergents and fourriers of the fusilier companies will be armed with halberds and swords, the models of which will be sent.[74]

Equipment of Mounted Officers

These were the infantry officers of the regimental staff. At this time, there was no official text regulating the equipment of mounted officers. We must try to get an idea of it from the few iconographic documents of the time. Like the painting by Vernet entitled 'Le port d'Antibes' dated 1756 kept at the Musée de la Marine, which shows two mounted officers of the Régiment Royal Comtois. The saddlery was à la royale and resembled that

74 Acte Royal, 20 March 1764, *Ordonnance du pour régler l'exercice de l'infanterie* (Paris: Imprimerie royale, 1764).

of the dragoons. One of the officers has blue saddle cloth and housings, bordered with a wide gold braid, the other has a saddle cloth with a red background bordered with a gold braid (the Régiment Royal Comtois had yellow buttons). The braid was probably silver for regiments with white buttons as depicted on a painting by Blarenberghe, with an infantry officer whose horse has a blue saddle cloth edged in silver. Here again the horses and their equipment were the responsibility of the officer and they could have several horses.

Fodder being, after provisions for the soldiers, the major concern of the intendancy services, it seems interesting to give an estimate of the number of horses which followed an infantry regiment during the Seven Years War for officers, regimental artillery, sutlers, and others. This calculation is taken from that of Drummond de Melfort on the details of the composition of an army. The author of the *Traité de la cavalerie* used as a reference the composition of an army after the reform of December 1762 which saw the battalions reduced from 17 to nine companies, but he still counted the train of the regimental artillery introduced by the decree of 1757; which allows us to date this text to the beginning of the year 1763. Here is the estimate made for a regiment of two battalions of 17 companies each.

For the regimental staff: the *colonel* had 15 horses in his suite; the *lieutenant colonel*, eight; the *major*, eight; and for each battalion, an *aide major* with four horses and a *sous aide major* with three. The chaplain and the *chirurgien major* of the regiment each had one horse, to which the four horses of the cart that they shared had to be added. For each battalion, each of the 17 *capitaines* had four horses; each of the 17 *lieutenants*, three horses; and each of the 17 *sous lieutenants*, three horses.

For the two artillery pieces, there were six horses; and for the cart of the sutler of the battalion, four horses. This represented 44 horses for the staff and 180 horses per battalion, making a total of 411 horses for a regiment of two battalions, which seems to be a minimum. To which must undoubtedly be added the pack horses, called platoon horses which *maréchal* de Broglie quoted in his instructions of 1759 and which totalled 17 horses. And this excludes the horses of the provostship when a regiment had such a privilege.

The Uniform of the Prévôt and the Archers

Thirty-four infantry regiments had the privilege of ensuring their own military justice. The *prévôt* and the *archers* wore the uniform of the corps of the Connétablie (Constabulary). For the *prévôt*: a blue coat with red lining, scarlet waistcoat and breeches, the coat and the waistcoat adorned with silver braids and silver buttonholes on both sides arranged two by two down to the pockets; four buttonholes on each cuff; four on each pocket; and four in the small of the back on each side; a silver aiguillette; a buff-coloured waistcoat with silver braids and silver edging; blue saddle cloth and housings bordered with a silver braid; and a black hat laced silver. The uniform of the *archers* was similar without braids or buttonholes, with white buttons, white laced hat; blue saddle cloth and housings bordered with a white braid.

The auditor and the registrar wore civilian clothes.

Aumôniers' Attire

Chaplains wore the uniforms of their respective religious orders. The Recollects wore the brown homespun robe of the Franciscans, as can be seen in a painting by Van der Meulen depicting the capture of Salin in 1674. Circa 1757, Becher depicts 'Ein Französischer feld pater' in a black cassock and black hat on a white mule. As for the pastors, they wore the black pulpit robe with white facings over a black coat and black breeches.

The Chirurgien's Uniform

It was by the decree of 15 July 1757, and at the request of M. de la Martinière and M. Desport, that the first uniform for army surgeons was created.

> The cloth will be thorn grey in colour. The coats will be made as an overcoat with small folded back red cuffs, vertical pockets, red waistcoat and breeches. The buttons will be of gold threads in a limace [spiral] pattern. That of the chirurgiens majors of the armies will have a gold or embroidered braid of their choice. That of the aide majors will have six gold buttonholes on each side in front, namely, one on each side below the collar, two below, and three at the level of the pocket, three on each cuff and three on each side in the small of the back. That of the [surgeon] boys will only have gold buttons...[75]

75 'Premier uniforme des chirurgiens militaires', *Carnet de la Sabretache, revue militaire rétrospective*, 1893, p.426.

7

Colours and Pennants

Colours

Colours were made of taffeta, a silk fabric. They were created by assembling different pieces of coloured fabric, such as the cantons, and borders. For example, the white cross was made of three pieces: one large and two small, sewn onto the field cloth. The complex motifs such as the coat of arms of the Régiment du Dauphin, the ship of Royal des vaisseaux, mottos or the fleur-de-lis were often painted with a shadow effect. Not being embroidered like those of the cavalry, they were more fragile. There were no regulations as to their size, although, over the centuries, they became smaller. By the middle of the eighteenth century, they were usually 5 pieds 6 pouces (180cm) square with a cross of 30–36cm, but they could be slightly rectangular as some surviving examples show.

The pike had an iron butt spike to be stuck in the ground, it was usually terminated by a single golden point, 6 pouces long (16cm). The butt spike could have the shape of a fleur-de-lis as for the Gardes suisses. The pike measured from 9 to 10 pieds (2.92–3.24m). There were no regulations dictating the colour of the pike; we know from the *Encyclopédie* that the pike of Royal Artillerie was blue adorned with painted golden fleur-de-lis,[1] but that is about all.

The majority of the colours of the French regiments were distinguished by their white cross with coloured cantons and a white streamer. The addition of golden fleurs-de-lis on the cross or in the cantons was often granted by the King in recognition of a fine military action. But there were some exceptions to these white crosses, such as the Régiment de Bourgogne, whose *colonel*'s colour had a white Cross of Burgundy, or the Régiment de Bretagne, which had its cross adorned with ermines instead of fleurs-de-lis.

The streamer was made of white taffeta, about 20cm wide by 70–80cm long. The streamer was tied to the pike with a cord of white silk threads for the *colonel*'s colour and mixed colours of the cantons for the ordonnance colours. Until the Régence (1715–1723), the colours changed almost

1 *Encyclopédie ou Dictionnaire raisonné des sciences, des arts et des métiers* (Geneve: Pellet, 1777), vol.3, p.576.

every time a new *colonel* took charge of a regiment, at least for gentlemen regiments. In particular, the colours of the reign of Louis XIV very often borrowed motifs from heraldry – gironné, taillé, bendy and chevrons.

The decree of 10 February 1749 fixed the number of colours of the French regiments at two per battalion, including one white one in the *colonel*'s company. This decree did not change during the Seven Years War, thus the instruction of 9 June 1753 clearly indicated 'the two colours of each battalion.'[2]

The Swiss carried one colour per company, each regiment comprised two battalions of six companies, for a total of 12 colours per regiment, including a *colonel*'s colour. From 1753, German infantry regiments had two colours per battalion. The Scots, Irish, Italians and Liégeois had two colours per battalions, like the French regiments.

The correspondence of the marquis de Marcieu informs us about the supply of colours to the infantry regiments and shows us that it could take some time. The chevalier de Marcieu was *colonel* of the Régiment Royal Vaisseaux from 1719 to 1734, it was under his command and no doubt on his initiative that the colour was modified by the addition of a painted vessel on the cross, at any rate it was he who proposed to the King different designs. On 20 March 1723, the duc de Chartres, *colonel général* of the infantry, wrote to the *colonel* of the Régiment Royal Vaisseaux: 'The various designs you sent for the colours of the regiment were presented to His Majesty: his choice fell on the one whose cross is decorated with a vessel in the middle. We will be careful to comply with his decision when we give new colours.'[3]

On 4 November 1725, two and a half years later, the marquis de Marcieu wrote to M. de Breteuil:

> As we are working on the general clothing of the Régiment Royal Vaisseaux in Lyon and we have to deliver it at the beginning of its winter quarters, you would like me to beg you to give your orders so that we send it the new colours that it has been promised for two years, having an absolute need of them. I was even assured 15 months ago that it would receive them as soon as the Régiment Du Roy would have been supplied. M. Peron and Malo can show you the way His Majesty has ordered them to be in the future.

On 19 November 1725, Breteuil replied:

> As these supplies were in great arrears, we have not yet been able to recover on this part… You can count on me employing the Régiment des Vaisseaux in the first state that I will sign for the supply of the six colours that the King is providing it with and you can have them towards the beginning of next spring.

---

2 Acte royal, 17 February 1753, *Ordonnance du roi portant reglement sur le service de l'infanterie en campagne* (Paris: Imprimerie royale, 1753), p.7.

3 Guy Joseph Hély Emé, marquis de Marcieu, *Deux lieutenants généraux des armées du roy: commandant en Dauphiné au XVIIIe siècle* (Grenoble: Allier, 1928), vol. 1, p.63. The later letters are also from this source.

Spring came, followed by several others, but still no colours arrived, and M. de Rochas, First War Commissioner wrote from Fontainebleau on 29 June 1731:

> The work on your colours has been somewhat delayed in that the painter, having come to Versailles on the letter I had written to him, gave me to understand that the vessel you requested was very different from that carried by the regulations and the design that I have in the book. The latter is actually only with her masting without sail, the one you want must have all its sail deployed, the painter tells me that he had a design for it taken from the book of the late M. Le Blanc, but that we had forbidden him its execution. I saw this design again when I was in Paris to come here, and having had it presented to me then, I found that, as the painter had told me, there was much more work to do. So I wanted to know what it would cost more to the King, he gave me to understand that it would be ten écus per colour, on which I dared not pass without reporting it, what I could only do here only eight days ago. M. d'Angervilliers always willing to do anything that can give you pleasure, even though it costs 20 pistoles more, [made sure] that your vessel would navigate at full sail. I immediately placed the order for signature and sent it to the painter with great recommendation to work on it without delay and to take care that the work would be so well executed that you would not reproach for which I would have enough means to make him bear the trouble. I will press him and I will take care that your colours would reach Metz at the beginning of August.'

If we are to believe the text appearing on the selected design, it was in January 1721 that it had been approved by the King, but in June 1731 the colours were still not made. These were the colours of a Royal regiment, whose upkeep was the responsibility of the King and whose design was particularly complex.

There was also a type of fabric used for certain colours and whose representation is not easy: it is the shot silk fabric. It was a silk fabric, woven with threads of two different colours. The warp yarn, arranged lengthwise, was of one colour while the weft yarn, arranged perpendicular to it, was of another colour. This gave the fabric changing colours and iridescence depending on its folds, on the light, or on the position from which it was seen. This type of fabric is described for the colours of the Régiment Royal Artillerie or Régiment de Vivarais from 1684 to 1749, or for that of Périgord. If we take the example of the colour of the Régiment de Périgord in the 1757 manuscript, the top triangle at the hoist is of shot silk woven with red and yellow threads while the second triangle along the cross is made of red and green threads. It is quite difficult to render this effect on an illustration, in the case for example of red and yellow threads, according to the fold and the angle under which it is seen, the fabric is red is some places and yellow in others with a brief iridescent transition, but by no means an orangey colour.

In line of battle, the regulations of 1753 prescribed that the colours should be placed in the centre of the battalion and guarded by the *sergents*. In camp, they were placed five to 10 paces (5–10m) according to the various authors, in front of the first tents, vis-à-vis the central street.

> The officers who carry the colours, plant them, on arriving in the camp, in the middle of the space at the front of the camp with the piles of arms, the colonel's colour between the two companies of the centre, another between the colonel's and the lieutenant colonel's companies, and the third between the last two companies; they must not leave until the caporal of the picquet has posted sentries there.[4]

And for the night 'once the retreat is beaten, a sergent and a caporal of the picquet will fold the colours, and will lay them down together on four small trestles which will be placed for this purpose near that of the arms of the picquet of each battalion, between the front of the camp and the pile of arms.'[5] Upon arrival in quarters or in a garrison, the colours were deposited with the corps commander.

The decree of 1762 saw the abolition of *enseignes* and the creation of the post of *porte drapeau*, usually chosen among the former *sergent majors*.

The details of the colours of each regiment will be given when describing their distinctive characteristics. By convention, for the representation of the colours, the heraldic description of the quarters of a shield are used: the pike being placed to the left of the person looking at the colour; the first quarter is located top hoist; the second, top fly; the third, bottom hoist; and the fourth, bottom fly.

Regimental Pennants

The pennants were small flags used to indicate the location of the camp and baggage of the various regiments. During this period there were at least two types of pennants.

The camp pennants were described in the 1753 decrees for the infantry and in the 1755 instruction for the cavalry. They were used for the alignment of the tents of the companies. The *Cavalry Instruction* of 1755 states that 'the pennant field shall be one pied square and of woollen fabric of the colours assigned to the regiment, the name of which shall be written upon it.'[6] The pennants were attached to two white pegs, 7 pieds (2.3m) high with an iron butt spike. Even though the 1753 decree for the infantry merely specified that the name of the regiment should be written on this pennant, it was also presumably of the facing colour of the regiment.

The baggage pennant is described by La Chesnaye as 'carried at the head of the baggage by an infantry or cavalry valet, it is made of serge in the colours of the brigadier's livery or that of the corps commander.'[7]

4 Acte royal, 1753, *Instruction sur le service de campagne* (Metz, Veuve Brice Antoine, 1753).

5 Acte royal, 17 February 1753, *Ordonnance du roi portant reglement sur le service de l'infanterie en campagne* (Paris: Imprimerie royale, 1753). p.28.

6 Acte royal, 22 June 1755, *Instruction sur le service que les régiments de cavalerie devront faire dans les camps qui s'assembleront pendant la présente année 1755* (paris: Imprimerie royale 1755), p.50.

7 François-Alexandre Aubert de la Chesnaye Des Bois, *Dictionnaire militaire* (Dresde: George Conrad Walther, 1751), vol.1, p.1017.

Héricourt tells us that there was also a pennant per brigade for small baggage, it was:

> A pennant in the shape of a flag on which the name of the brigade is written: the major général chooses in each infantry brigade, a wise valet to carry it; the maréchal des logis of the cavalry similarly chooses from each cavalry brigade; these valets have twenty sols for each day's march. The junior officer leading the pennant picks up all the valets of the baggage of his brigade; he leads them in such a way that they do not fall into the march of the troops or the baggage nor march before the guards. The valets are forbidden to leave the pennant, on penalty of flogging. With the exception, however, of those who walk with their masters in the divisions.[8]

8 Nicolas d'Héricourt, *Elémens de l'art militaire* (Paris: Gissey, 1756), vol.1, p.121.

8

Provincial Militias

> Militia is a collective term which formerly designated the totality of men of war. The inhabitants of a city, of a country, armed themselves, assembled and marched to war, this is what was called the French Militias; but since our Kings have maintained in their pay regular and always available troops, the word militia in France has no longer expressed anything but a corps of infantry, composed of the inhabitants of towns and countryside, which are forcefully enlisted to march against the enemies of the state when necessity requires it, that is to say when regular troops are insufficient.[1]

Provincial Militias

During the seventeenth century, the repetition of conflicts which decimated the regular army, forced Louis XIV to find new recruits, also by the decree of 24 November 1688, a new complementary recruitment system was created, relying on the general population and which represented a first form of conscription. These militias, raised by drawing lots, when the army needed additional troops had a temporary status until 1726, but the frequency of conflicts made them practically permanent during certain periods, but it was only with the decree of 25 February 1726 that they actually became permanent. They were suppressed in March 1791.

Recruitment of the Provincial Militias

The general principles of the recruitment and organisation of the provincial militias can be summarised as follows:

> The militiaman during the peace is not quite a soldier, he has only contracted the obligation to present himself as such, when summoned; he is therefore related to the military administration for only one point, which is to give it knowledge of his

1 François Philippe Loubat, Baron de Bohan, *Examen critique du militaire françois* (Genève: Publisher unknown, 1781), vol.1, p.44.

> existence and his residence: this duty once fulfilled, all his relations with it cease; he is an ordinary citizen.[2]

Although the 1726 decree extended levies to most of the Kingdom, not all regions contributed equally. Some provinces, which had rallied to Protestantism and were not considered as trustworthy by the government, as well as the recently acquired provinces had little or no contribution to the militias, except if necessary.

Since 1736, the designation of new militiamen was made by drawing lots each year, to renew one sixth of the establishment. In peacetime, the militiamen drawn by lot continued to go about their business; militia battalions assembled regularly for eight to 10 days a year to teach recruits the basics of manoeuvres and the handling of weapons, to review soldiers and equipment, and to appoint junior officers. These training camps were better organised for the companies of grenadiers, which constituted the elite of the militias. The grenadiers were gathered every year for a period of one month, chosen outside the harvest periods. In wartime, militia regiments were permanently assembled. They were mainly used to replace regular regiments in the garrisons of the places of the northern and eastern frontier, but also to reinforce the coastguard militias in Bretagne, Normandie, Languedoc or Provence; for example, the Marmande and Fontenay militia battalions who were engaged during the Saint-Cast affair in 1758. They were also used as labour to maintain and build certain fortifications.

The unfairness of the ballot system was one of the reasons for its eventual rejection. Each parish had to, according to its population, provide a certain number of soldiers. The ballot was made primarily among single men or men who had been married for less than a year, but local particularisms remained the rule, creating great disparities. Similarly, the rules of the ballot sometimes changed from year to year. Furthermore, the number of men levied in each province was not proportionate to their population. All eligible men did not participate in the ballot, they were first presented by the trustees of the militia to the sub-delegate of the province, who retained those who would participate in the ballot, based on their size and their appearance. Many trades were exempt from this charge, including craftsmen or servants. These exemptions especially benefited townspeople, and so the peasantry contributed the bulk of these battalions. But depriving the countryside of its labourers worried the government, and in 1758 Belle-Isle, reinstating the decree of 30 October 1742, wrote to the intendants of the provinces: 'The levy … will be made preferably in the cities and alternatively in the parishes of the flat country so that the inhabitants of the countryside contribute to the said levy only for what the cities will not have absolutely provided.'[3] Tiller-men who owned a plough, either on their own or on a lease, were exempt, as was one of their sons over 16, but they had to maintain four horses. At the end

2 Jean-Christophe Sandrier dit chevalier des Pommelles, *Mémoire sur les milices, leur création, leur vicissitude et leur état actuel* (Paris: publisher unknown, 1789), p.19.

3 Acte royal, 10 July 1743, *Ordonnance du roy, portant augmentation de trente-six mille hommes de milice du 10 juillet 1743* (Paris, Imprimerie Royale, 1744).

of the War of the Spanish Succession, due to the financial difficulties of the state, it had allowed parishes to be exempted from participating in the ballot in exchange for a contribution. If somebody did not show up without a valid reason for a ballot, he was declared a fugitive and, if he was caught, he had to serve for 10 years.[4] The decree of November 1733 had been much more severe, condemning them 'to serve their lives in the militia.' Replacements via financial contributions varied over the century, its prohibition was not constant. They were mostly tolerated; although such a replacement paid by the family of the militiaman competed with the recruitment of the *capitaines* of the companies of regular units. 'The main purpose of the prohibition of these replacements was to leave to the officers the means of adding to the recruits raised in the parishes, those which they could make elsewhere' said Bourgelat in his *Réflexions sur la milice* in 1760.[5] A decree of 2 August 1743 reminded *capitaines* of infantry, cavalry and dragoons that they were prohibited from having a militiaman sign an engagement 'before he has finished his service in the militia.'[6]

Fugitives from the militia were those men who having been warned to go on the day indicated before the commissary in charge of raising the militia, to draw lots there, and who had neglected or refused to be there, were declared a fugitive by the minutes of the ballot of the militia, on the denunciation of the trustee or of the men of the community.

Militia officers were in theory chosen from officers who had already served, been discharged, or retired in the provinces. If they were appointed by the King, it was the intendant who established the list, thus in certain provinces these officers included many bourgeois who had never served in the army. The venality of the charges was prohibited in the militia, a remarkable thing for the time, thus the career of the *colonels* of the Grenadiers de France was an exception, because it was merit which presided over their promotion.

Border provinces by their geographical locations, their traditions, and their privileges – for example, the provinces of Boulonnais, Béarn and Roussillon – resorted to a poll tax and had their own organisations. Militia regiments were designated by the name of their *colonel* joined to that of their généralité (administrative division).

Sometimes, militia battalions directly took part in military campaigns, but more generally militiamen were used to fill the ranks of regular regiments which dwindled during campaigns. They served as recruit battalions. Desertion was frequent. Militiamen were promised a limited commitment, but their service was most often prolonged as long as the war lasted. And even at the end of the war, they were often not given any leave and remained forcefully enlisted until the end of their engagement. They were then incorporated into the infantry, artillery, cavalry or dragoons, to the great satisfaction of the *capitaines* thus relieved of part of their work as recruiters.

4 Acte royal, 6 August 1748, *Ordonnance du roy concernant les milices* (Paris: Prault, 1750).

5 Claude Bourgelat, *Réflexions sur la milice* (Lyon: publisher unknown, 1760), p.40.

6 Pierre Briquet, *Code militaire ou compilation des ordonnances des Rois en France, concernant les gens de guerre* (Paris : Veuve Gandouin, 1747), vol.3, p.385.

The Organisation of the Provincial Militias

Throughout the Seven Years War, the organisation of the provincial militias regularly underwent changes. Levies by lot only took place during the first three years of the war: 1756, 1757 and 1758, but no militiamen were released before the end of the war. On 1 January 1755, a decree was issued to release the oldest of the militia classes and to make a new levy, but fear of a British incursion on the coasts delayed this measure for the coastal provinces; it was postponed to the autumn of 1755.

At the beginning of the war in 1756, the militia comprised 107 battalions from the 29 généralités of France, each of the battalions had eight fusilier companies and two grenadier companies, and each of these companies had 50 men. According to the decree of 1 January 1756, fusilier companies and those of grenadiers postiches increased from 50 to 60 men and the grenadier companies remained at 50 men, or 590 militiamen per battalion. Then by the decree of 5 December 1756, only fusilier company was increased to 65 men, or 630 men per battalion. The provincial militias then had a total strength of 63,130 men and 2,354 officers. In March 1757, the two militia battalions of Mirecourt, levied in the Duchy of Lorraine, formed the Régiment Royal Barrois and the Régiment Royal Lorraine. There were then only 105 militia battalions. During the war, these two regiments would continue to be funded by the communities of Lorraine, like the militias. It was decided to assemble in field battalions a certain number of soldiers drawn from the militia, to have them follow the Army of Germany, and to use them to complete the infantry regiments.

In May 1757, the war had barely begun, and regular units were already not at full strength; the means to replenish the ranks of the infantry were the subject of many communications between the minister and the general officers. Of course, they were careful not to tell the militiamen the purpose of their formations. By the decree of 25 May 1757, 12 battalions, each 10 companies of 65 fusiliers, were formed by detaching 120 companies from the militia battalions. By the end of 1756, they were quartered in Neuss, Düsseldorf, Kleve, Wesel, Lippstadt and Münster. These battalions then took the name of the *colonels* who commanded them. In October 1757, the measure was repeated by forming nine new field battalions, involving 45 other militia battalions, from which 90 companies were extracted. These nine battalions were assembled between Strasbourg, Landau, Wissembourg and Haguenau. Overall, the 21 field battalions thus brought together totalled 13,650 men. As a result, the 105 battalions that remained assigned to guard of various places in France were each reduced to six fusilier companies of 65 men.

By the decree of 1 November 1757, a new levy of militia was made in the provinces, to replace the fusilier companies which had been detached. Each of the six fusilier companies of a battalion was increased by 20 men so that these companies now had 85 men, with an increase in the number of *sergents*. The theoretical strength of a militia battalion became 510 men.

With the decree of 20 March 1758, all the soldiers of the detached militia field battalions which had been sent to Germany were incorporated into the regular units of the Army of Germany, with the exception of officers, non-commissioned officers, and drummers, who returned to France. This measure, which had already been used during previous wars, nevertheless contravened the decrees regulating the formation of the militia. This measure was only applied once during the Seven Years War, it partly explained many desertions and all the efforts that the men made to escape the ballot.

In 1758, the army of the comte de Clermont transferred 15 regular battalions to the army corps under the command of the Prince de Soubise. To compensate, 15 additional militia battalions were taken from the 105 militia battalions of France. But this time, complete battalions were targeted and they kept their names, taken from the généralité from which they came: the battalions of Amiens, Châlons, Lons-le-Saunier, and more. They were not incorporated into regular regiments, they essentially performed garrison duty in certain places in Germany, and some were attached to the Artillery Park or to the headquarters of the army. In theory less exposed than regular troops, they still sometimes suffered significant losses, if only through illness. Thus, some of these battalions having suffered too much during these campaigns in Germany were relieved and replaced by new battalions from France during the years 1761 and 1762.

By another decree of 1 April 1758, the militia battalions were again increased to eight fusilier companies. However, 57 battalions were increased to 528 men divided into eight companies of 66 men plus two officers, while each of the remaining 48 battalions had a total strength of 428 men in eight companies of 56 men plus two officers.

The decree of 25 August 1758 once again reorganised the militia battalions, which were all increased to 720 men. Each militia battalion had a staff composed of a *colonel* without a company and an *aide major*. Each of the eight fusilier companies consisted of: two *sergents*, three *caporaux*, three *anspessades*, 81 fusiliers and a drummer, commanded by a *capitaine* with a *lieutenant*. Each grenadier company consisted of two *sergents*, three *caporaux*, three *anspessades*, 41 grenadiers and a drummer. Finally, each company of grenadiers postiches was composed of three *sergents*, three *caporaux*, three *anspessades*, 51 grenadiers and a drummer, commanded by a *capitaine* and a *lieutenant*.

During the following years, from 1759 to 1762, there was no new mass levy of militia, but all permanent leaves were suspended. After the last attempt of forceful incorporation of detached militia companies into regular regiments in 1758, the publication of the decree of 25 November 1760 marked a complete change in doctrine: 'His Majesty considering that these special levies of militia were harmful to the countryside and deprived it of the arms necessary for farming, has preferred to raise voluntary recruits in each province … Neither seduction, nor ruses, nor violence must be used to surprise the good faith or force the dispositions of the subjects.'[7] A series of decrees and regulations followed, published in the middle of the war, which radically modified the recruitment system of the French regular army with the creation of battalions of volunteer recruits, raised in the provinces by the

7 Acte royal, 12 November 1733, *Ordonnance du roy concernant les milices du 12 novembre 1733* (Paris: Imprimerie Royale, 1733).

intendants in the name of the King, and which would constitute a reservoir of manpower for the regular regiments. These texts were the prerequisites for two decrees: that of December 1762 which removed the responsibility of recruitment by *capitaines*, then the decree of 1 February 1763, which created 32 regiments of recruits. The main consequence of this reform was that, in the future, the *capitaines* of the French infantry were relieved of the burden of recruitment which fell to the State.

Finally, the decree of 1 November 1761, applicable from 1 January 1762, once again modified the organisation of the 105 militia regiments. The battalions were reduced to six fusilier companies, one grenadier company and one grenadier postiche company, for a total of eight companies instead of 10. The fusilier and grenadier companies retained the same strength and organisation as before, except for the addition of a *capitaine en second* in the company of grenadiers postiches. From 1762, the militia companies were gradually released.

In November 1765, faced with the difficulty of raising entire regiments of recruits by enlistment, it was decided to draw lots to form these regiments.

The real militia strength presented in the various muster rolls were, as with the regular army, a far cry from theory. Thus, the muster roll of the militiamen of the battalion of Brioude arriving in Landau in November 1759 gives a strength of 491. Similarly, the marquis Montalembert, responsible for organising the defence of the Island of Oléron, received in July 1761 the Figeac militia battalion. He indicated that during the last review, the strength was only 405 men out of the theoretical 720.[8]

Particular Militias

The general provisions described in the previous section did not concern certain border regions which, before 1688, already had a system for levying soldiers drawn from the local populations in the event of conflict. This was the case of the militias of Boulogne, Roussillon, Béarn, Briançonnais, Metz Country and many others. These militias retained their own recruitment methods and were commanded by the nobility of the country.

The Province of Boulonnais provided six infantry regiments of 13 companies each, including one company of 45 grenadiers and 12 companies of 40 fusiliers. These six regiments were: Boulogne, Marquise, Wissant, Samer, Desvres and Étaples. This province also maintained five cavalry squadrons of 100 men and two dragoon companies. These militias were mainly used to defend the ports of Boulogne, Calais and Dunkerque.

Since the decree of 1 May 1756, the Province of Roussillon provided 55 militia companies, forming the Milices ordinaires du Roussillon, de Conflent et de Cerdagne. Twenty of these companies, of 50 men each, made up the two battalions of the Régiment de Perpignan, while the remaining 34 companies of 40 men each were organised into three battalions and distributed in various places in the province. Finally, one company of 50 men formed the garrison of the Fort de Salces.

8 Marc René de Montalembert, *Correspondance de monsieur le marquis de Montalembert* (Londres: publisher unknown, 1777), vol.2, p.578.

The Province of Béarn, whose Gouverneur Général was the duc de Gramont, provided three regiments raised according to the decree of 13 April 1756, they formed the militias of Béarn, Gramont, Navarre and of the Labourd and Soule regions. Each militia regiment was commanded by a *lieutenant colonel* with an *aide major*, Régiment des milices du Béarn, whose *colonel* was the duc de Gramont, consisted of 13 companies: one grenadier company of 45 men and 12 fusilier companies of 40 men each. The Bandes Gramontaises the militias of Navarre, which constituted the two other regiments, each consisted of one battalion of 500 men, each organised in companies. They were all armed by the King and dressed and equipped by the province and the communities. The town of Bayonne was guarded by four companies from the Labourd region, five companies from the Gardes Gramontaise and five from Orthez. The place of Saint-Jean-Pied-de-Port was guarded by one company of the militia of Soule. Finally, the small citadel of Navarreins (Navarrenx) was occupied by a battalion of the militia of Béarn. The militias of Labourd had a particular history dating back to the English occupation of Aquitaine in the Middle Ages. To ensure their defence, its inhabitants formed an armed community, the 'Armandat', without a seigniorial or nobiliary hierarchy. It was placed under the authority of a bailiff, who directly represented the king, thus escaping the authority of the local lords. After its annexation to the Kingdom of France in 1451, the Labourd region obtained the right to preserve the independence of the organisation of its militia, a privilege which it would retain until the Revolution. This militia was composed of 1,000 men and was used to ensure the defence of the places and borders.

There were also very small particular militias, such as those of the islands of Sainte Marguerite and Saint Honorât in the Mediterranean. These islands were defended by a militia company, whose *capitaine* was M. de Montboisier, which consisted of a *capitaine*, two *lieutenants*, two *sergents*, a *caporal*, an *anspessade*, a drummer and 30 soldiers.

Ranking of the Militias

Regarding the ranking of militia battalions, article XXII of the decree of 25 February 1726 specified: 'the said militia battalions will take among themselves the rank of the regiments maintained under the name of the provinces from which they are drawn.'[9] However, what may seem simple was actually much more complex during the Ancien Régime. Indeed, the administrative divisions, between the Généralités which served as the basic administrative structure for the recruitment of the militias and the territories constituting the various Provinces overlapped very imperfectly. For example, the Généralité of Lyonnais included the provinces of Lyonnais, Beaujolais and Forez, while the Généralité of Montauban extended over two provinces: Rouergue and Quercy. Exceptionally, the Généralité of Bretagne corresponded to the territory of the province. As another consequence of this decree, the militia battalions marched before the regular infantry regiments created after 25 February 1726.

9 Montandre Longchamp, *État militaire de France pour l'année 1759* (Paris: Guillyn, 1759), p.293.

After the reform of December 1762, which changed the rank of certain provincial regiments, we find in order of precedence: the militia battalions of Picardie which marched first, followed by the militias of Champagne; then came the battalions of the Généralités of Rouen, Caen and Alençon at the third rank according to the rank of the provincial Régiment de Normandie; the militia of Bourbonnais occupied the fourth rank; that of Auvergne, the fifth; that of Flandre, the sixth; the battalions of the Généralités of Montauban, Auch and Pau, and Bordeaux, the seventh rank according to the rank of the Régiment de Guyenne which ranked twelfth in the infantry in 1762; the militias of Poitou, the eighth; that of Lyonnais, the ninth; that of La Rochelle, the tenth according to the rank of the provincial Régiment d'Aunis; the militia battalions of Touraine, the eleventh; the militia of Dauphiné, the twelfth; the militias of the city and Généralité of Paris, the thirteenth according to the rank of the Régiment d'Isle de France; those of Soissonnais the fourteenth; those of Limousin the fifteenth; the battalions of the Généralité of Orléans, the sixteenth, here it was the rank of the princely Régiment du Duc d'Orléans which gave them this rank; those of Bretagne, the seventeenth; those of Lorraine and of the Trois-Évêchés, the eighteenth according to the rank of the Gardes Lorraines; the militias of Artois the nineteenth; those of the Généralité of Bourges, the twentieth according to the provincial Régiment du Berry; those of Hainaut, the twenty-first; those of Alsace, the twenty-second, here again a peculiarity, the Régiment d'Alsace was not maintained as a provincial regiment but as a German foreign regiment ranking 36th, nevertheless the militias levied in this province inherited its rank; the militia of the Duchy of Bourgogne occupied the twenty-third rank; those of the Province of Languedoc, the twenty-fourth; those of the Franche-Comté of Bourgogne, the twenty-fifth; and the militia battalions of Provence, the twenty-sixth.

Provincial militia battalions wore the same colours as the infantry regiments bearing their name. It should also be noted that, just as for the three infantry regiments of Piémont, Champagne and Navarre as well as those of Bourbonnais, Béarn and Auvergne, whose turn of precedence alternated each year, the turn of precedence of the corresponding militia battalions followed the same rules. Finally, within a Généralité, the rank of each militia battalion was determined by the seniority of the commission of the officers who commanded it. The same applied to the ranks of the various companies within a battalion.

9

The Grenadiers Royaux Regiments

The Creation of the Grenadiers Royaux

Until 1744, all militia battalions were composed exclusively of fusilier companies. The decree of 25 August 1734 had created a grenadier company in each battalion, but this company was disbanded at the end of the War of the Polish Succession in 1735. It was the decree of 15 September 1744, which definitively established a grenadier company in each militia battalion. The decree of 10 April 1745 organised the 84 companies into seven Grenadiers royaux regiments, each consisting of a battalion of 12 companies. The grenadier companies each of 50 soldiers comprised: one *capitaine*, one *lieutenant*, two *sergents*, three *caporaux*, three *anspessades*, 41 grenadiers and one drummer. The staff of each Grenadiers royaux regiment was composed of one *colonel* and one *lieutenant colonel*, both without companies, one *major* and one *aide major*. The regiments then took the name of their respective *colonels*.

The companies of Grenadier royaux always having to be complete, the decree of 28 January 1746 created a company of grenadiers postiches from which the new grenadiers would be drawn. The company of grenadiers postiches, which had also to be always complete, took the required soldiers from the fusilier companies of its militia battalion. Each company of grenadiers postiches had 56 men: one *capitaine*, one *lieutenant*, three *sergents*, three *caporaux*, three *anspessades*, 46 grenadiers and one drummer. From 10 March 1746, the seven Grenadiers royaux regiments were each increased to two battalions, for a total of 8,904 men in seven regiments, each of two battalions of 12 companies of 50 grenadiers; and 12 companies of 56 grenadiers postiches. From their creation, the Grenadiers royaux distinguished themselves during all the military campaigns in Flanders and Italy. They served as a reservoir of recruits for the Grenadiers de France: 'it is a singular distinction and an honour that the King wanted to do to his Grenadiers royaux to admit them into a body such as the Grenadiers de France, which is made up of the elite of his troops.'[1] In February 1748, two new regiments were formed, but in August 1748, when the preliminaries of peace were signed after the War of the Austrian Succession, the nine Grenadiers royaux regiments were disbanded.

In 1750, the 107 grenadier companies of the militia were organised into 11 battalions: eight battalions of 10 companies and three battalions of nine companies. However, these battalions were not yet grouped into regiments and the grenadiers postiches were therefore not part of this reorganisation. During peacetime, one-month training camps were organised in various places to train the grenadiers in weapon handling and exercises. The first of these camps took place in March 1750 and they were renewed every year until 1755. These camps were organised in early winter or early spring, when men were least needed for farming.

From the beginning of 1756, with war imminent, the militia battalions were assembled and the grenadier postiche companies were increased to 60 men. The decree of 5 December 1756 brought together all the grenadier companies of the militias and the grenadiers postiches, drawn from the 107 militia battalions, to reform 11 Grenadiers royaux regiments, with a total of 11,880 men and 595 officers.[2] Each of these 11 regiments had two battalions in 20 companies, including 10 companies of Grenadiers royaux and 10 companies of grenadiers postiches. Each grenadier company consisted of two *sergents*, three *caporaux*, three *anspessades*, 41 grenadiers and a drummer and were commanded by one *capitaine*, with one *capitaine en second* from 1 January 1762, and one *lieutenant*. The staff of each regiment was composed of a *colonel*, a *lieutenant colonel*, one *major* and two *aide majors*, and the first two companies of grenadiers postiches of each regiment had a second *lieutenant* in charge of carrying a colour. Each company of grenadiers postiches was composed of three *sergents* (by the addition of third *sergent* from 1 February 1757), three *caporaux*, three *anspessades*, 51 grenadiers and a drummer and were commanded by one *capitaine*, with one *capitaine en second* from 1 January 1762 and one *lieutenant*. The staff of each Grenadiers royaux regiment comprised a *colonel*, a *lieutenant colonel* without a company, a *major* and two *aide majors*. All commissions, of the 11 *colonels* of the newly formed Grenadiers royaux regiments for the Seven Years War, were dated 16 February 1757.

By the decree of 15 April 1757, the Régiment de Solar included only 16 companies or 880 men instead of 1,100. The decree of 23 April 1762 created a twelfth regiment of Grenadier royaux for service in the colonies. It assembled in Brest where it embarked for Martinique, but the end of the war caused the project to be abandoned and this regiment returned to France and was disbanded by the decree of 20 January 1763.

1 Gebelin, *Histoire des milices*, p.157.

2 Acte royal, 5 December 1756, *Ordonnance du roy concernant les milices* (Paris: Imprimerie Royale, 1750)

The Ranking of Grenadiers Royaux Regiments

All regiments forming the Grenadiers royaux were designated by the name of their *colonel*. Here too, there was a hierarchical order of precedence between the 11 Grenadiers Royaux regiments. As we have seen, militia battalions took the rank of the regiment maintained under the name of the province from which they were drawn, which then made it possible to create a new hierarchy for the grenadiers. The companies of Grenadiers royaux drawn from the first 11 militia regiments formed the first company of the 11 Grenadiers royaux regiments, and gave them their rank. But everything was not so simple, at the beginning of the 1757 campaign, the regiments were composed from the grenadier companies closest to each other. In November 1759, *maréchal* de Belle-Isle, taking advantage of the winter break, partially recomposed the Grenadiers royaux regiments. However, the muster rolls, as well as the letters and memoirs of the *majors* of these regiments indicated that the battalions of Grenadiers royaux were never properly reorganised to respect this hierarchy. For example, the grenadiers of the militias of the Généralité of Riom or Auvergne, drawn from the fiscal regions of Riom, Clermont, Issoire, Brioude, Saint Flour and Aurillac could be found in various Grenadiers royaux regiments. The battalion of Riom was in the Régiment de Modène, the battalions of Aurillac and Clermont in that of Coincy/Cambis, and the battalion of Brioude in the Régiment de Grenadier royaux de Méhegan.

Furthermore, some *colonels*, by promotion, transferred to another regiment while still remaining *colonels* in the Grenadiers royaux. Thus, the Régiment des Grenadiers royaux d'Aulan of 1757 is not the same as the Régiment des Grenadiers royaux d'Aulan of 1760.

The Grenadiers royaux regiments, as well as the grenadiers postiches associated with them, were not assembled until February 1757, the date when the new *colonels* were appointed. Less than a month later, on 19 March, it was decided to assign to the four regiments with the Army of Germany (Chantilly, Modène, Bergeret and Aulan), a *colonel en second* drawn from the Grenadiers de France. Then, by another decree of 1 May 1757, published to regulate service during this campaign, the regiment was given to the marquis de Saint Pern, commander and inspector of the Grenadiers de France, the same attributions on the Grenadiers royaux assigned to Germany; so that they 'have a same mind, same discipline, and same service.'[3] During the war, decrees were published to designate the *colonels* of the Grenadiers de France as second in command of the Grenadiers royaux regiments. Let us mention, for example, the comte de Bethisy who was made *colonel en second* of the Grenadiers royaux de Cambis for the campaign of 1762. He took command of the regiment after the injury of M. de Cambis, during the diversionary attack on the bridge of Homburg, on 9 August 1762. Or the chevalier de Narbonne, assigned to the Grenadiers royaux de l'Espinasse, who was killed in June 1762 in the affair of Grebenstein.

As we have already seen, the grenadier battalions of the militia were reconstituted as early as 1750 so that they could take part in the various

3 Léon Clément Hennet, *Les milices et les troupes provinciales* (Paris: Beaudoin, 1884), p.139.

training camps. They were assembled in 11 regiments on 5 December 1756, and their colonels were appointed in February 1757. Most of them had already been colonels of militia or Grenadiers royaux during the War of the Austrian Succession, or had already taken command of a battalion as early as 1750.

Colonels of the Grenadiers royaux Regiments

Grenadiers royaux de Bergeret 1757–1759, de Narbonne 1759–1762: Jacques Antoine de Bergeret was *colonel* of this militia regiment from February 1757 to February 1759, when he was promoted to *maréchal de camp* and resigned. He was succeeded until the end of the war by François de Narbonne Pelet, vicomte de Narbonne. Prior to his promotion in 1759, he had served as *aide major général* of infantry with the Army of Germany. This regiment took part in all campaigns in Germany. It particularly distinguished itself in February 1761 at the defence of Fritzlar, which made it possible for *maréchal* de Broglie to save his army. As a reward, the King granted the comte de Narbonne-Pelet the right to bear the name of Narbonne Fritzlar. The vicomte de Narbonne was a nephew of Cardinal de Bernis.

Grenadiers royaux de Bruslart 1757–1759, d'Aulan 1759–1761, de l'Espinasse 1761–1762: Gaspard Robert de Guérin de Bruslart commanded this regiment from February 1757 to February 1759, when he was promoted to *maréchal de camp*. Afterwards, it was Henri de Suarez, chevalier d'Aulan who commanded this regiment until February 1761. The appointment of the chevalier d'Aulan deserves some attention. In 1757, he was colonel of the first regiment of Grenadiers royaux. This regiment was responsible, at the start of the war, for protecting the Île de Ré against British incursions. It was relieved in 1759 by the Régiment des Grenadiers royaux de Bruslart. Shortly afterwards, the chevalier d'Aulan left his regiment to be assigned in April 1760 to the command of Lille. But he was recalled to the Île de Ré in May 1760 due to his services and his knowledge of the island. He was then placed at the head of the Grenadiers royaux regiment which guarded the island. He was promoted to *maréchal de camp* in February 1761. In June 1766, he was entrusted with the government of the Île de Ré, vacant by the death of the comte de Razilly. He was also known by the title of Bailiff of Aulan, as Grand Cross and Commander of the Order of the Knights of the Hospital of Saint John of Jerusalem in Malta. In 1761, Étienne Joseph, marquis then comte de l'Espinasse Langeac succeeded him at the head of the regiment. He had previously served as *lieutenant colonel* of the Régiment de Le Camus. At the beginning of the war, the regiment served on the coasts of Aunis and Saintonge. In 1761, it was sent to Germany.

Grenadiers royaux de Modène 1757–1761, de Camus 1761–1762: Pierre Raymond, chevalier de Modène was *colonel* of this regiment from February 1757 until February 1761, when he was promoted to *maréchal de camp*. He then resigned in favour of the comte Le Camus. The latter was already *colonel* of a Grenadiers royaux regiment, for him the transfer was a promotion since he acceded to a regiment of more prestigious seniority and rank. The regiment took part in all campaigns in Germany. It was at Hastenbeck in

1757, at the conquest of Hanover and at Krefeld in 1758, at Minden inn 1759, and at Corbach and Warburg in 1760.

Grenadiers royaux de Coincy 1757–1761, de Cambis 1761–1762: Jean Baptiste La Rivière de Montreuil de Coincy was *colonel* of this regiment from February 1757 to February 1761, when he was promoted to *maréchal de camp*. He resigned in favour of François de Cambis, baron de Frons et de Serignac. The latter was severely wounded on 9 August 1762, at the diversionary attack on the bridge of Homburg and it was the *colonel en second*, the comte de Béthisy, who commanded this regiment until the end of the war. The comte de Béthisy was one of the *colonels* of the Grenadiers de France who had been assigned to the Grenadiers royaux regiments. This interim appointment was only possible insofar as it was hoped that M. de Cambis could recover from his injuries. The regiment served in Germany. In 1762, it formed part of the small corps placed under the command of the Prince de Condé.

Grenadiers royaux de Châtillon 1757–1759, de Longaunay 1759–1761: Étienne de Châtillon was *colonel* of this regiment from February 1757 to February 1759, when he was promoted to *maréchal de camp* and resigned in favour of Charles André, marquis de Longaunay. The regiment was stationed in Médoc from 1756 to 1760 and was then sent to Germany. In December 1761, it returned to France and was garrisoned in Toul.

Grenadiers royaux de l'Escotais 1757–1761, de Pontessan 1761–1762: Joseph des Escotais, chevalier de Chantilly was *colonel* of this regiment from February 1757 to February 1761, when he was promoted to *maréchal de camp* and resigned in favour of Charles Marie Camille, comte du Plessis d'Argentré de Pontestan, who had previously served as *capitaine* in the Régiment de Limousin. The regiment took part in all campaigns in Germany. It was at Hastenbeck in 1757, then at the conquest of Hanover and at Krefeld in 1758, at Minden in 1759, at Corbach and Warburg in 1760, and at Vellinghausen in 1761.

Grenadiers royaux de Pruges 1750–1757, de Rochefort 1757–1762: Joseph Augustin de Prugues had been placed at the head of one of the new grenadier battalions assembled in 1750, he retained his command when the unit was transformed into a regiment in February 1757. He died shortly afterwards, in May 1757, and was succeeded by Charles de Rochefort, chevalier d'Ally. The regiment initially served on the coasts of France; in 1761 it joined the Army of Germany; and in 1762, it formed part of a small corps under the command of the Prince de Condé.

Grenadiers royaux d'Aulan 1757–1759, de Camus 1759–1761, de Puységur 1761–1761, de la Roche 1761–1762: Henri de Suarez, chevalier d'Aulan was *colonel* of this regiment since February 1757 to February 1759. The new *colonel* was Charles Joseph Auguste, comte Le Camus, he had previously served as *lieutenant colonel* with the Grenadiers royaux de Bruslart. Then, in February 1761, Barthelemy Athanase Hercule de Chastenet, vicomte de Puységur took command of the regiment for a few months, until November 1761, when he obtained a regiment of regular infantry under his name. He had been a retired *capitaine*, formerly of the Régiment Royal Comtois, and had served as *aide major général* of the Army of Germany. Gabriel Armand Benoit, marquis de La Roche Lambert replaced him. At the beginning of the war, the regiment initially served on the coasts of Aunis, then it was sent to Germany. In 1762, the regiment served under d'Estrées and Soubise. Its *colonel* was wounded during the affair of Wilhelmsthal.

Grenadiers royaux de Chabrillan 1757–1759, de Moroménil 1757–1762: Joseph Toussaint de Moreton, chevalier de Chabrillan commanded this regiment from February 1757. He had been a retired cavalry *mestre de camp*, formerly of the Régiment de Marbeuf dragons, he was promoted to *brigadier* of the dragoons in February 1759. When the regiment returned from Minorca in 1762, it was given to Nicolas Thomas Hue, comte de Miroménil. During the war, in 1756, the regiment embarked aboard Richelieu's fleet and was transported to Minorca, where it remained until May or June 1762.

Grenadiers royaux de Tresne 1757–1762: Léonard Casimir Lecomte, chevalier then marquis de la Tresne had already been *colonel* of a Grenadiers royaux regiment during the War of the Austrian Succession, in 1746. He was once more appointed *colonel* of a regiment from February 1757 until July 1762, when he was promoted to *maréchal de camp*. This regiment served on the coasts of Médoc from 1756 to 1760, when it was sent to Germany to take part in the last campaigns. It was at Vellinghausen in 1761. During the winter of 1761–1762, it returned to France where it was garrisoned in Verdun.

Grenadiers royaux de Solar 1750–1758, de Méhégan 1758–1762: The chevalier de Solar was *colonel* of a battalion in 1750, and of a regiment in December 1756. In November 1758, Jacques Antoine Thadée de Méhégan until then *lieutenant colonel* of the regiment succeeded him. During the campaign of 1757, the Régiment de Grenadiers royaux de Solar was assigned to the headquarters of the Army of the Lower Rhine, where it formed the escort of the vanguard, entrusted with the protection of the engineers and cartographers. It later served with the army. In garrison at Minden in March 1758, the chevalier de Solar signed, with *lieutenant général* de Morangiés, a capitulation deemed dishonourable by the government. The Régiment de Solar was disbanded, but it was re-established on 25 November 1758, and entrusted to its former *lieutenant colonel*, M. de Méhégan, who had opposed the capitulation. The regiment was then sent to the coasts of Normandie. *Colonel* Solar thus named in contemporary texts was probably Joseph Vincent de la Fontaine Solare, chevalier then comte de Solare.

10

Coastguard Militias

At the beginning of the eighteenth century, most of the conflicts involving France took place on its eastern borders, in Germany or in Italy. Tensions did also exist France's coasts, as in September 1746 with a raid by the British at Lorient, but it was not a real second front. During the Seven Years War, the British threat against the French coasts became much more pressing. The British, who dominated the oceans, tried both to hinder trade and supplies to French colonies, and to create a second coastal front; forcing France to mobilize resources and troops. They bombarded Le Havre, Dieppe, Saint-Malo, and captured in these ports a large number of ships loaded with goods. They also occupied Belle-Isle from 1760 to 1763. But, after their failures at Rochefort in 1757, and at Saint Cast in 1758, the British contented themselves with harassing French maritime traffic. On the French side, despite the lack of control of the sea, preparations were even made for an expedition against England. Neglected until then, the coastguard militias regained importance in the military defensive system.

The origin of the coastguard militias predates the land militias of Louvois and goes back to the feudal law of ban and arrière-ban (general levy) of the fifteenth century. The first decree giving the name of militia to the coastguards dates from 1696. Until then the appointment of their officers was the reserved domain of the navy. However, Louis XIV, when he restored the office of *amiral de France* in 1696, reserved the right to appoint himself the officers of the coastguard militias, even though these officers continued to be registered with the Admiralty and to take the oath with the *amiral de France*. With the decree of 24 February 1759, the administration of the coastguard militias was transferred from Department of the Navy to the Department of War and thus under the authority of the provincial governors. But the conflicts over the prerogatives of each, between the Departments of the Navy and War, were not over for all that. As an example of this persistent duality, when a militiaman or an officer of the coastguard militias was fined, it was the *lieutenant* of the admiralty who established the fines, the funds of which were intended for repairs to the guardhouses.

Coastguard militias were reorganized at various times during the first half of the eighteenth century; by Louis XIV between 1701 and 1705, then under the Régence in 1716. In December 1755, *maréchal* de Belle-Isle was made commander on all the coasts of the ocean, then a few months later secretary of state for war. Through his reforms, he endeavoured to give a more military character to the coastguard militias, in particular to the detached companies. The 1758 *Mémoire pour servir d'instruction concernant les milices garde-côte* was a copy of the 1753 decree destined to the regular infantry. It gave rank in the infantry to the detached companies, and allowed former army officers, who served in the coastguard militia, to keep their ranks and the seniority of their patents.

> These militias, both infantry and dragoons, have been subjected to the same rules and discipline adhered to among the regular troops, and the decree includes the penalty of perpetual galleys against deserters and those who enlist in the regular troops during the time of their service in the detached companies. In consequence of the project formed to support the new establishment of the coastguard militias on the foot of regular troops, a decree has been issued which assimilates them to the infantry, and to mange to inspire them with military inclinations, one has dispatched, at the beginning of the campaign of 1758, the orders necessary to encamp them. The intendants of the provinces have been charged for this purpose to provide very promptly for the general clothing of the coastguards on a model of uniform, and to make purchases of all tents, pots and other camping utensils, as well as supplies of flour, wood and straw in the places which had been designated.[1]

The Seven Years War was the occasion for the publication of numerous decrees. However, despite their number, these sometimes confused texts did not propose a thoughtful and global vision of a maritime border defence system. Two of these decrees had an important influence on the organisation of the coastguard militias; those of June 1757 and February 1759. The other decrees were more specific characters, adapted to the geographical and demographic situations of each territory, and to local rights and privileges. Like those of 5 June 1757 and 9 and 14 April 1758 for Provence; and those of 21 April 1746, 1 May 1748, 10 August 1756, 30 June 1759 and 2 July 1759 for Bretagne; the decree of 25 February 1756 and the regulation of 10 August 1756 for Belle-Isle; the decrees of 26 May 1755, 5 June 1757 and 21 October 1758 for Guyenne; the regulations of 5 June 1757 and 13 August 1757 for Normandie; the decree of 5 June 1757 and the regulation of 15 February 1758 for Picardie; the decree of 5 June 1757 for Aunis and Saintonge; and the decrees of 9 June 1757, 15 May 1758 and 25 February 1759 for Languedoc. All these decrees, even those subsequent to 24 February 1759, were signed by the King, the duc de Belle-Isle and the duc de Penthièvre, *Amiral de France*.

General Organisation

The defence of the coasts was organised as captaincies bringing together a set of parishes along the coast. They were headed by a *capitaine général*, assisted

---

1 Acte royal, *Mémoire pour servir d'instruction concernant les milices garde-côte* (Paris: Imprimerie royale, 1758).

by a *major* and a *lieutenant*; the latter took the title of *aide major* from the decree of 5 June 1757. There were also a *capitaine général du guet* and a *lieutenant général du guet* who dealt specifically with the service of the look-out companies. The *capitaine général* was a general officer, he had to perfectly know the topography, the means of communication and the resources of the parishes within his jurisdiction. There were more than a hundred captaincies spread over the French coasts.

Each look-out company and each detached company was under the command of a *capitaine*, a *lieutenant* and an *enseigne*. These officers provided with a commission by the King did not report to the admiralty. The first criterion to choose them was their place of residence which, in theory, had to be less than six lieues from the coast. They were chosen among the local nobility and retired army officers, but also more generally among people living nobly.

The composition of each company varied according to the captaincies. It comprised 50 to 100 men with two to four *sergents*, two to four *caporaux*, two to four *anspessades* depending on the size of the companies, but always only one drummer per company. In some captaincies the gunners were part of the companies, in others they were organised in separate companies.

In June 1757, when he reorganised the coastguard militias, Louis XV put in place 10 inspector generals in charge of controlling the proper organisation of the batteries and signals departments. By another decree of 12 March 1759, he reorganised the service of general inspection, leaving only two inspector generals under the authority of the *amiral de France* with, in each province, a particular inspector. They were the chevalier de Mirabeau, *colonel* of infantry and the comte de Beaujeu, *brigadier* of infantry, the first was responsible for Picardie, Normandie and Bretagne, the second for the provinces of Poitou, Aunis, Saintonge and Guyenne. Then, on 19 April 1760, a third inspector general was appointed: M. de Surlaville, *colonel* of infantry for the provinces of Languedoc, Roussillon and Provence. These three inspector generals only had a short existence, they were abolished by the decree of 16 March 1761. Only the particular inspectors of each province were retained.

Recruitment

These militiamen came from the coastal parishes, which were required to provide recruits by drawing lots. The age groups varied according to the periods and prescriptions: they went from 16 or 18 years old to 45 or 60 years old. The minimal height, without shoes, was five pieds (1.62m). The length of service was five years for fusiliers and six years for dragoons, renewed by the fifth or sixth each year. The inhabitants of parishes located up to two lieues from the shore (about 8km), were subject to recruitment. In 1701, the extent of the coastguard territory increased from half a lieue to two lieues, but the lists of the parishes subjected in 1756, show that, over the geographical reorganisation of the captaincies, recruitment areas could sometimes extend up to 12km. While the regular infantry and dragoon regiments were quartered in the places, the coastguard militia companies, by their location and proximity, ensured the first defence at the scene of a landing, while awaiting the arrival of regular troops. This is how the decree of 1746 considered it: 'It seems that we can still extend their usefulness, and that very often, not having enough troops within reach of the coasts to resist the landings that the enemies could make, it would be very essential to put the coastguard militias in a position to make up for it, provided they were supported by regular troops.'[2] The need for this organisation of small units scattered all along the coast was largely due to the lack of coastal roads. To get from one port to another, it was often necessary to go deep inland and then move on to the next one, which made each port relatively isolated. From the Seven Years War, the intendants and *lieutenant généraux* of the provinces set out to develop a whole network of communications, allowing them to quickly march reinforcements from one port to another, and this led to the disappearance of the coastguard militias in favour of gunner companies. The development of coastal roads dates largely from this period.

In return, this servitude exempted these same parishes from supplying men to the provincial militias and from a certain number of corvées. It even forbade them to enlist in a regular unit. But with the navy sorely lacking in sailors, who were mainly recruited in the coastal regions, they were authorised, if they were between 16 and 35 years old, to enlist as a sailor. Once incorporated into the detached companies, the militiamen could not be absent for more than eight days from their parishes without having written permission from their *capitaine*. The exemptions concern those whose activity was related to the sea: sailors, cabin boys, bargees, carpenters, and workers in the construction, refitting and maintenance of commercial or war vessels. But, as for the provincial militias, the exemptions were much broader, with many abuses tolerated by the intendants. Unlike provincial militias, replacement of recruits was permitted. They also benefited from a special right: a tenth of the wrecks washed up on the coast was shared between the companies of the captaincy where the grounding had taken place.

Service of each type of companies

Look-out Companies

The primary mission of the coastguard militia was to watch the coasts and give the alarm as enemy ships approached. For this reason, the militiamen were posted in guardhouses scattered along the coast, and they patrolled between these outposts. This service was not constant but was done only in case of war or military tension. Guardhouses were built in locations able to monitor the movements of the ships, and they were sometimes paired with an artillery battery. Men learned to give the alarm with smoke signals by day and fires and beacons at night. These signals were the same as those regulated by the decree of 1517. The 1716 decree also introduced

2 Eugène Fernand Magnan de Bornier, 'Notes sur les milices garde cotes au 18e siècle', *Carnet de la Sabretache, revue militaire rétrospective*, p.571.

alarm signals with flags hoisted on a mast or with cannon shots. Unlike the detached companies; which were usually assembled and encamped like the regular infantry, the militiaman of a look-out company did not carry out a permanent service, but a tour of duty, 'so that there is only one man from each household ordered on the same day for service', and 'His Majesty wishes that the Coastguard Militia have the freedom, in ordinary times, to attend to their particular labours and businesses.'[3] The theoretical strength of the look-out companies or parish companies represented 110–120,000 men. However, this did not prevent them having great difficulty in obtaining a regular service, as evidenced by the exchanges between the inspectors and the governors. All guardhouses were 'provided with a rack for laying down arms, a camp bed, a table and a bench, a lantern and an iron candlestick, and wood and lights will be provided.'[4]

Gunner Companies and their Batteries

Some of the militiamen were gunners capable of using the naval artillery pieces of the coastal batteries. These gunners were organised differently from one captaincy to another. Sometimes they were in separate companies of gunners as prescribed by the decree of March 1759 for Poitou, Aunis and Saintonge. In other cases, as mixed detached companies, as organised in the decree of June 1759 for Bretagne: 'Each detached company will be composed of 25 gunners; a *sergent*, a *caporal*, an *anspessade*, two master gunners and 20 assistant gunners; of a *sergent*, two *caporaux*, two *anspessades*, a drummer and 19 fusiliers.'[5] This role became the main activity of the coastguard militias and these companies of gunners multiplied on all the coastal islands of the Atlantic coast. The gunner companies were reorganized in 1778 under the name of coastguard gunners. Trained by naval officers at the start of the war, these gunners were, after 1759, trained by officers of the Royal artillerie: '...during this campaign [1760] a body of gunners was formed in each captaincy, who went by detachment to the places indicated to be trained in cannoning by the gunners of the Corps royal. Independently of these schools, the coastguard gunners on duty at the batteries continued to be instructed in gunmanship by the gunners.'[6]

The cannon and mortar batteries were installed in redoubts and forts of various sizes. Fortification engineers and naval officers made regular rounds of inspection 'to observe locations more or less suitable for landings, designate platforms to be built in time of war, and determine the locations of guardhouses and stores for ammunition to be distributed in the case of an alarm.'[7] This duality of authority was often a source of dissension. But already in 1753, the duc d'Aiguillon, newly appointed military commander

---

3 Acte royal, 15 May 1758, *Ordonnance du roi concernant les milices garde-côtes de Languedoc* (Paris: Imprimerie royale, 1759), p.13.

4 Briquet, *Code militaire*, vol.7, p.25.

5 Acte royal, 30 June 1759, *Ordonnance du roy concernant les milices garde-côtes de la province de Bretagne* (Paris: Imprimerie royale, 1759), p.3.

6 Célestin Hippeau, *Le gouvernement de Normandie au XVIIe et au XVIIIe siècle* (Caen: Goussiaume de Laporte, 1863), p.146.

7 Magnan de Bornier, *Notes sur les milices garde cotes au 18e siècle*, p.561.

in Bretagne, supervised the construction of redoubts and forts on the coast and coastal islands such as Fort Penthièvre on the Quiberon peninsula or Fort de Ré on Dumet Island. In February 1759, *maréchal* de Belle-Isle transferred the administration of the batteries from the Navy to the Secretary of State for War, with the exception of those in the harbours of Brest and Toulon. The inhabitants of the coastal communities participate, in the form of corvées, in the construction of the guardhouses, the battery platforms or the entrenchments.

The *État général des batteries de côte et de leur armement* of 1754 mentioned 622 batteries scattered on the coasts, armed with 3,219 guns. This same document allows us to know the manpower necessary for their service: 10,324 men. These pieces were cast iron naval pieces of all sizes; of 6, 8, 12, 16, 18, 24, 36 pounds even rampart pieces of 48 as at the Tour de Camaret, and mortars of 12-pouces. For their maintenance the officers of the land artillery could obtain supplies from the arsenals of the Navy 'as much as the intendants of the Navy can provide without disturbing the service of the vessels of His Majesty.'[8] Similarly, naval officers could, if necessary, be assigned to coastal batteries, alongside officers of the Royal artillerie. These batteries protected ports, roadsteads and other bays from landing, but even more, they made it possible to secure coastal trade and protect anchorages. In the absence of a coastal road network, these coastal shipping routes were a vital mode of communication.

The firepower of a battery was determined by the draft of the warships who could approach it. Thus a 10-gun corvette needed three meters of draft; a 44-gun frigate, six meters; and a 74-gun vessel, seven and a half meters. This depth was determined at the highest tide. The height of some batteries was determined to produce ricochet shots on the water. A 12-pouce mortar could fire shells up to 4,000 meters, and even if the reliability of the shot was not that of a cannonball, a single shell exploding on a ship could destroy it entirely, through the damage and the fires it caused. There were also small mobile guns on carriages, to fire on the launches and landing troops. There were also grills in the battery stations to fire heated shot.

Detached Companies

In addition to the look-out companies and the gunners, the coastguard militias were also made up of so-called detached companies, which were the best trained elements. They were named after the parish where they had to assemble. The detached companies were always complete, when a soldier was missing in a detached company, a new soldier was drawn from a look-out company, who themselves replaced him with a new militiaman drawn from the population. The soldiers of the detached companies were exempted from guard duty on the coast. They were all armed, whereas for the look-out companies, there was only common armament, supplied at the expense of the community, which remained in the guardhouse. In November 1759 M.

8 Acte royal, 24 February 1759, *Ordonnance du roi pour réunir au département de la Guerre tous les détails concernant les milices garde-côtes, le service, l'établissement et l'entretien des batteries servant à la défense des côtes* (Paris: Imprimerie royale, 1759), p.4.

de Martené, inspector of the coastguard militias of middle Normandie, wrote to the duc d'Harcourt:

> …the captaincies are generally very neglected, badly kept, filthy, badly disciplined and very badly trained … the disorder still increases in the captaincies of Ouistreham and Bernières, caused by desertion; 63 men were missing; of the 17 who remain there is not one from the parish … It is a contagion that spreads; in the captaincy of Dives there are 15 or 16 missing per company; we have not found a complete one; I believe it is time for you to consider the means to repress these mutinies.[9]

The strength of the detached companies in Picardie totalled 1,050 men, to which the 6,000 strong Boulonnaise militias had to be added. The latter, although part of the provincial militias, enjoyed a special status and organisation, and took part in the guarding of the coast. Normandie had 15,200 men; Bretagne, 10,000 and for the island of Belle-Isle, 1,200 men; Poitou, 1,920 infantrymen and 100 dragoons; Aunis, 1,600 men and 100 dragoons, to which the 1,000 men of the Île de Ré had to be added. Saintonge had 1,760 men and 200 dragoons to which the 2,000 men of the Île d'Oléron had to be added. Guyenne had 2,500 infantrymen and 50 dragoons, who were increased to 900 in 1758 and organised in nine squadrons. On the Mediterranean coast, Languedoc and Roussillon had 2,000 men, and Provence 2,000. This gave a grand total of 45,000 men exclusively for the detached companies, the rest of the inhabitants of the parishes could all be incorporated into the look-out companies. But, as for the provincial militias, all these figures were very theoretical.

The correspondence between the inspector generals and the minister or the governors of the provinces, clearly reveal the importance of desertion, or rather of the non-presentation of recruits for duty, which considerably reduced the strength. One of the reasons explaining this situation is the relative leniency with regard to the coastguard militias, compared to the fate reserved for deserters of the provincial militias. Their assimilation to infantry regiments in May 1758 considerably aggravated the penalties incurred, at least in theory. Furthermore, to avoid having to pay these troops, they were requisitioned only for periods of four days, during which the militiaman had to provide for himself, beyond that the requisitioned militiaman had to receive pay.

The detached companies were fighting troops, like the provincial militias, they trained in weapon handling and exercised to oppose a landing and thus allow for the arrival of regular troops. In peacetime, they had to assemble and train once a month, and twice a month in times of war. They were not as seasoned as the provincial militias or the Grenadiers royaux, even if they valiantly opposed British incursions. To complete the infantry embarked aboard the naval squadron of *maréchal* de Conflans in 1759, a certain number of detached companies were requisitioned. Intended to escort the troops of the duc d'Aiguillon for a landing in Scotland or Ireland, this squadron was defeated at the Battle of Quiberon Bay on 20 November 1759.

---

9 Hippeau, *Le gouvernement de Normandie*, p.31.

The Dragoons of the Detached Companies

In April 1758 for Aunis, Poitou and Saintonge, then in October 1758 for Guyenne, the King created coastguard dragoons. The dragoon companies all had the same composition: a *capitaine*, a *lieutenant*, a *cornette*, a *maréchal des logis*, two *brigadiers*, a drummer and 46 dragoons. The staff of all detached dragoon companies consisted of a commander ranking as *colonel*, a *major* ranking as *lieutenant colonel*, and an *aide major* ranking as *capitaine*. In Aunis, there was a squadron of 100 men in two companies, in Poitou a squadron of 100 men, in the Province of Saintonge two squadrons or 200 men, and in Languedoc, nine squadrons of two companies, or 900 men. Their main function was to transport mail and messages from one post to another in the province. This service, which could also be done on foot, took the name of 'pedonage'. On this subject, the marquis de Montalembert wrote to *maréchal* d'Havrincourt:

> I have noticed since I have been here [Oléron] that my correspondence with you, M. the Maréchal, was very long because of the difficulty I have in getting my letters to Marennes ... I believe it would be good for the service if you were kind enough to order that there should always be two coastguard dragoons at Pointe Chapus, destined to carry the letters that I would have the honour to write to you, directly to Moize, to the posts of dragoons which I was told were posted there for communication with Saintonge.[10]

But the duc d'Aiguillon relativised the usefulness of these dragoons:

> The establishment of coastguard dragoons in the provinces of Poitou, Aunis, Saintonge and Guyenne, has been presented under the appearance of prompter help for the defence of the coasts; but M. de Beaujeu, who was charged with the inspection of these dragoons in 1759 and 1760, represented that their institution, from which no advantage would ever result, did the greatest harm to the cultivation of the lands and was a very heavy charge for the people; he even observed that this body of dragoons never existed in Poitou.[11]

It should also be noted that there were sometimes dragoons in certain look-out companies.

Company Officers

The militia officers' commissions could be purchased after the decree of February 1705. By the decree of 25 February 1756: 'His Majesty being informed that the service of the coastguard militias of Bretagne is entirely neglected ... His Majesty revokes, both the provisions and commissions with which the capitaines, majors and lieutenants are at present provided...'[12] From

10 Marc-Rene, marquis de Montalembert, *Correspondance de Monsieur le Marquis de Montalembert, étant employé par le Roi de France à l'armée Suédoise, avec M. le Marquis d'Havrincour,etc.* (London: publisher unknown, 1777), vol. 3, p.65.

11 Hippeau, *Le gouvernement de Normandie,* p.150.

12 Acte royal, 25 February 1756, *Ordonnance du roy concernant le service des milices garde-côtes de la province de Bretagne* (Paris: Imprimerie royale, 1756), p.1.

then on, the *capitaine général* proposed a list of officers to the Governor and the Inspector General who transmitted it to the Secretary of State for War for approval. For the selection of officers, preference was given to retired officers who had already served with the regular troops. The *capitaines généraux* of the coastguard ranked immediately after the general officers of the army, who were present in the province.

In May 1758, to put an end to quarrels between regular troops and the coastguard militias, it was determined that the coastguard militia regiments took rank with the French infantry regiments. The ranks of the officers were established as follows: a *capitaine général* had the rank of a *capitaine* commanding a battalion or *premier capitaine*; the *majors* of the captaincies and the *capitaines* of the detached companies had the rank of infantry *capitaine*; *aide majors* had the rank of infantry *lieutenant*; the same was true for the officers of the coastguard dragoons. But *maréchal* de Belle-Isle was aware of the difficulties of applying this measure:

> The decree of 15 May 1758, giving a rank in the infantry to the coastguard militias, is of a nature to be examined, since it has been represented that the officers of the detached companies have, for the most part, no experience and can only have a very confused idea of discipline. There are, however, some among them, who have served in the regular troops, but their number is not very considerable, if we except the officers of the staffs. The composition of the others is even very defective in some provinces where the difficulty, which has been experienced in filling vacant posts, has led to the admission of subjects whose profession is not compatible with the character of officers whom they carry.[13]

Coastguard Vessels

Since 1667, alongside these militias, the coastal provinces with the financial support of the bourgeois and shipowners of the port cities financially participated in the chartering by the King of coastguard vessels which provided maritime surveillance and protection of the convoys of merchant ships. leaving French ports. These vessels, like the long boats or the fire ships, were armed with 6- or 8-pounder guns, their shallow draft making them suitable for coastal pursuit. This protection against British corsairs was only done over a few miles. This service stopped as soon as the threat had passed, so, at the signing of the Peace of Ryswick, these vessels were disarmed: 'the intention is for you to disarm all the coastguard vessels in the port of Rochefort and in the roadsteads of La Rochelle…'[14] From the beginning of the century, the lack of maintenance of the fleet had led to its frequent immobilisation and need to repair its vessels. Thus, during the Seven Years War, even supplying the coastal islands became hazardous in the face of the recklessness of the British corsairs.

---

13 Hippeau, *Le gouvernement de Normandie*, p.148.

14 Jean Fleury Elie Viaud, *Histoire de la Ville et du Port de Rochefort* (Rochefort: Fleury, 1845), vol.2, p.145.

Bibliography

Books and Articles

Anon., *Instruction pour l'infanterie de l'armée du roi commandée par M. le maréchal prince de Soubise* (Publication details unknown)

Anon., *Instruction concernant le service de campagne* (Metz: veuve Brice Antoine, 1733)

Anon., *Code municipal* (Paris: Prault, Vallat Lachapelle, 1756)

Anon., *Lettres écrites à un ami* (Maëstricht: Jean Edme Dufour, 1765)

Anon., *Mémoires d'un militaire, depuis l'année 1735 jusqu'au quartier d'hyver de 1758* (Wesel et partout: Publisher unknown, 1759)

Anon., *Mémoire politiques et militaires pour servir à l'histoire de notre tems recueillis et publiés par Mr de V---* (Francfort, Leipzig: dépens de la Cie, 1760)

Anon., M.L.C.D.B., *Mémoires pour servir à l'histoire de la Campagne du Maréchal de Broglie en Westphalie* 1761 (La Haye, Francfort: Aux depens de la compagnie, 1762)

Alletz, Pons Augustin, *Manuel de l'homme du monde* (Paris: Guillyn, 1761)

Archenholtz, Johann Wilhelm von, *Histoire de la guerre de Sept Ans, commencée en 1756, et terminée en 1763, trad, de l'allemand par M, le baron de Bock* (Paris: Buisson, 1789)

Arcy, Patrick, chevalier d', *Recueil de pièces sur un nouveau fusil* (Paris: Couturier, 1777)

Argenson, René Louis de Voyer, marquis d', *Mémoire et journal inédit du marquis d'Argenson, ministre des Affaires étrangères sous Louis XV* (Paris: Jannet, 1857–1858)

Aulnay, Louis Dupré d', *Traité général des subsistances militaires* (Paris: Prault, 1744)

Audoin, Xavier, *Histoire de l'administration de l'armée* (Paris: Didot l'ainé, 1811)

Babeau, Albert, *La vie militaire sous l'Ancien régime* (Paris: Firmin-Didot, 1889)

Bacon, Pierre Jean Jacques Bacon-Tacon, comte de, *Manuel du jeune officier* (Paris: Jombert, 1772)

Bacquet, Louis Hippolite, capitaine d'infanterie, *L'infanterie au XVIIIe siècle* (Paris, Nancy: Berger Levrault, 1907)

Barbier, Edmond Jean François, *Chronique de la Régence et du règne de Louis XV (1718–1765) ou Journal de Barbier* (Paris: Charpentier, 1858)

Bardet de Villeneuve, P.P.A., *Cours de la science militaire: à l'usage de l'infanterie, de la cavalerie, de l'artillerie, du génie et de la marine* (La Haye: Jean van Duren, 1740)

Bardin Étienne Alexandre, *Dictionnaire de l'armée de terre* (Paris: Corréard, 1843)

Baudoin, Simon René, *L'exercice de l'infanterie françoise ordonné par le Roi le 6 mai 1755*, (Paris: Publisher unknown, 1757)

Belhomme, Victor, *Histoire de l'infanterie en France*, (Paris: Charles-Lavauzelle, 1893–1902)

Belidor, Bernard Forest de, *La science des ingénieurs dans la conduite des fortifications* (Paris: Jombert, 1729)

Belle-Isle, Charles Louis Auguste Fouquet de, *Lettres du maréchal duc de Belleisle, au maréchal de Contades ; avec des extraits de quelques-unes de celles de ce dernier ; trouvées parmi ses papiers, après la bataille de Minden* (La Haye: de Hondt, 1759)

Beneton de Morange de Peyrins, Etienne Claude, *Histoire de la guerre* (Paris: Le Mercier & Boudet, 1741)

Beneton de Morange de Peyrins, Etienne Claude, *Traité des marques nationales* (Paris: Le Mercier, 1739)

Bernis, François Joachim de Pierre de, *Mémoires et lettres de François Joachim de Pierre, cardinal de Bernis (1715–1758)* (Paris: E. Plon et cie, 1878)

Bilistein, André de, *Institutions militaires pour la France, ou le Végèce français* (Amsterdam: Harrevelt, 1762)

Billon, Jean de, *Les principes de l'art militaire* (Rouen: Berthelin, 1641)

Bohan, François Philippe Loubat, Baron de, *Examen critique du militaire françois* (Genève: Publisher unknown, 1781)

Bombelles, Henri-François, comte de, *Mémoires pour le service journalier de l'infanterie* (Paris: Delatour, 1744)

Bombelles, Henri-François, comte de, *Traité des évolutions militaires, les plus simples et les plus faciles à exécuter par l'infanterie ainsi que les divers feux* (Paris: Herissant, 1754)

Bombelles, Henri-François, comte de, *Minutes des lettres écrites par M. de Bombelles, commandant à Bitche: au maréchal de Belle-Isle ; au maréchal de Noailles ; à M. d'Argenson, ministre de la guerre ; à M. de Baligand ; à M. de Saint-André ; au prince héréditaire de Hesse ; au cardinal de Soubise, etc.* Archives départementales des Yvelines (manuscript)

Bonneville, Zacharie de Pazzi de, *Esprit des loix de la tactique* (Leipzig: Weidmann, 1762)

Bottée Claude, capitaine au régiment de La Fère, *Études militaires contenant l'exercice de l'infanterie* (Paris: Le Clerc, 1750)

Bosroger, Le Roy de, *Principes de l'art de la guerre* (Paris: Cellot et Jombert, 1779)

Boudriot, Jean, *Armes à feu modèles réglementaires 1717–1836* (Paris: Boudriot, 1979)

Bourcet, Pierre Joseph de, *Mémoires historiques, sur la guerre que les François ont soutenue en Allemagne depuis 1757 jusqu'en 1762* (Paris: Maradon, 1792)

Boussanelle, Louis de, *Observations militaires* (Paris: Jombert Cellot, 1761)

Boussanelle, Louis de, *Le bon militaire* (Paris: Duchesne, 1764)

Brézé, Argentero de, *Observations historiques et critiques sur les commentaires de Folard et sur la cavalerie* (Turin: Reycends, 1772)

Brézé, Argentero de, *Réfexions sur les préjugés militaires* (Turin: Reycends, 1779)

Briquet, Pierre de, *Code militaire ou compilation des ordonnances des rois de France concernant les gens de guerre par le sieur de Briquet* (Paris: Rollin fils, 1741)

Briquet, Pierre de, *Code militaire ou compilation des ordonnances des Rois en France, concernant les gens de guerre* (Paris: Nyon, 1761)

Broglie, Victor François, *Instruction pour l'armée du Roi* (Francfort: Van Duren, 1760)

Broglie, Albert duc de, *Le secret du roi, Correspondance secrète de Louis XV avec ses agents diplomatiques 1752–1774* (Paris: Calmann Lévy, 1878)

Broglie, Victor François, *Correspondance inédite de Victor-François, duc de Broglie, maréchal de France, avec le prince Xavier de Saxe, comte de Lusace, pour servir à l'histoire de la guerre de Sept Ans – campagnes de 1759 à 1761* (Paris: Michel, 1903–1905)

Carrion, Nissas Marie Henri François Élisabeth, marquis de, *Essais sur l'histoire générale de l'art militaire* (Paris: Delaunay, 1824)

Casgrain, Henri Raymond, *Lettres de la cour de Versailles au baron de Dieskau, au marquis de Montcalm et au chevalier de Lévis* (Quebec: Demers, 1890)

Chaligny, *Tableau militaire des drapeaux, étendards et guidons des troupes au service de la France, les années de leur création et les noms de MM, les mestres de camp de cavalerie et de dragons pour l'année 1771*, Archives des Yvelines à Versailles

Chaline, Olivier, *Les armées du Roi: Le grand chantier 17e–18e siècle* (Paris: Armand Colin, 2016)

Chabo, de la Serre Antoine comte de, *Réfexions critiques sur les differens systèmes de tactique de Folard* (Berlin: Neaulme, 1756)

Chennevières, François de, *Détails militaires dont la connoissance est nécessaire à tous les officiers et principalement aux commissaires des guerres* (Paris: Jombert, 1750)

Chesnaye Des Bois, François-Alexandre Aubert de la, *Dictionnaire militaire* (Paris: Gissey, Bordelet, David, 1745)

Chesnaye Des Bois, François-Alexandre Aubert de la, *Étrennes militaires* (Paris: Gissey, 1758)

Chesnaye Des Bois, François-Alexandre Aubert de la, *Dictionnaire militaire, portatif* (Paris: Gissey, 1758)

Chesnaye Des Bois, François-Alexandre Aubert de la, *Dictionnaire militaire ou recueil alphabétique de tous les termes propres à la guerre* (Dresde: George Conrad Walther, 1751)

Chevrier François Antoine, *Théâtre de la grande guerre commencée en 1756* (La Haye: Pierre Gosse, 1761)

Chevrier, François Antoine, *La Vie politique et militaire de M. le Maréchal Duc de Bell-Isle* (Bruxelles: Boubers, 1762)

Choiseul, Étienne François de, *Mémoire historique sur la négociation entre la France et l'Angleterre en 1761* (Paris: Imprimerie Royale, 1761)

Colin, Jean Lambert Alphonse, *L'infanterie au XVIIIe siècle: la tactique* (Paris: Berger Levrault, 1907)
Colombier, Jean, *Code de médecine militaire pour le service de terre* (Paris: Costard, 1772)
Corvisier, André, *L'armée française de la fin du 17e au ministère de Choiseul* (Paris: Presses universitaires de France,1964)
Corvisier, André, 'Un officier normand de Louis XV. Le lieutenant-colonel Jean-François Le Parsonnier du Landey d'après sa correspondance 1714–1785', *Annales de Normandie*, 9e année n°3, 1959
Cotty, Herman, *Dictionnaire de l'artillerie* (Paris: Agasse, 1822)
Daniel, Père, *Histoire de la milice française* (Paris: Coignard, 1721)
Crissé, comte Lancelot Turpin de, *Essai sur l'art de la guerre par le comte Turpin de Crissé (*Paris: Prault fls aîné, 1754)
Crissé, comte Lancelot Turpin de, *Commentaires sur les institutions militaires de Végèce* (Paris: Nyons, 1788)
Dangeau, Philippe de Courcillon, marquis de, *Journal du Marquis de Dangeau* (Paris: Firmin-Didot, 1858)
Daniel, R.P. Gabriel, *Abrégé de l'histoire de la Milice française: on y a ajouté un Précis de son état actuel* (Paris: Hôtel de Thou,1773)
Douazac, *Dissertation sur la subordination avec des réflexions sur l'exercice et sur l'art militaire* (Avignon: Aux dépens de la Compagnie, 1752)
Drummond de Melfort, Louis, comte, *Traité sur la Cavalerie* (Paris: Guillaume Desprez, 1776)
Du Bois, *Camps topographiques de la campagne de MDCCLVII, en Westphalie: commencée par Mr, le maréchal d'Estrées, continuée par Mr, le comte de Clermont: avec le journal de ses opérations, & quelques autres morceaux fort curieux* (La Haye: Chez la veuve Van Duren, 1760)
Du Bousquet, Louis, *Instructions militaires sur le service de garnison et de campagne* (Rouen: Besongne, 1769)
Dufresne, J., 'Lettres de Guillaume de L'Église de Lalande', *Revue de Gascogne*, 1896
Duhesme, Guillaume Philibert, *Essai sur l'infanterie légère, ou traité des petites opérations de la guerre, à l'usage des jeunes officiers* (Paris: Michaud, 1814)
Dumersan,Théophile, *Chansons nationales et populaires de France, accompagnées de notes historiques et littéraires* (Paris: G. de Gonet, undated)
Dupain de Montesson, Louis Charles, *Les amusements militaires* (Paris: Desprez, 1757)
Dupain de Montesson, Louis Charles, *Vocabulaire de guerre, ou Recueil des principaux termes de guerre, de marine, d'artillerie, de fortification, etc.* (Paris: Publisher unknown, 1783)
Espagnac, Jean-Baptiste Joseph de Sahuguet d'Amarzit, baron d', *Essai sur la science de la guerre* (La Haye: Gosse, 1751)
Estaintot, Robert Charles René Hippolyte Langlois, comte d', *Saint-Valery-en-Caux et ses capitaines garde-costes du 16e au 18e siècle* (Rouen: Meterie, 1885)
Feuquières, Antoine de Pas, marquis de, *Mémoires de Mr le Marquis de Feuquières lieutenant général du roi contenans ses maximes sur la guerre et l'application des exemples aux maximes* (Londres: Pierre Dunoyer, 1736)
Garsault, François de, *Description des arts et métiers, Art du Perruquier* (Paris: Saillant et Nyons, 1767)
Gay de Vernon, Joseph, *Traite élémentaire d'art militaire et de fortifications* (Paris: Allais, 1805)
Gebelin, Jacques, *Histoire des milices provinciales (1688–1791). Le tirage au sort sous l'Ancien Régime* (Paris: Hachette, 1882)
Gebelin, Jacques, *Les milices provinciales de Nîmes d'après les archives nîmoises. Le tirage au sort à Nîmes au 18e siècle* (Nîmes: Librairie ancienne A. Catelain, 1886)
Girard, Pierre Jacques François, *Traité des armes* (La Haye: De Hondt, 1740)
Grimoard, Philippe Henri, chevalier de, *Essai théorique et pratique sur les batailles* (Paris: Desaint, 1775)
Grosley, Pierre Jean, *Mémoires sur les campagnes d'Italie de MDCCXLV, et MDCCXLVI, auxquels on a joint un journal des mêmes campagnes, tenu dans le Bureau de M, le Maréchal de Maillebois avec une explication de tous les passages et cols du Dauphiné versants en Savoie et en Piémont* (Amsterdam: Marc Michel Rey, 1777)
Grouchy, Emmanuel Henri de, J*ournal inédit du duc de Croÿ, 1718–1784* (Paris: Flammarion, 1906)
Grimoard, Philippe Henri, *Correspondance particulière et historique du Maréchal duc de Richelieu, en 1756, 1757 et 175H8, avec M. Paris du Verney … suivie de Mémoires relatifs à l'expédition de Minorque, en 1756, et précédée d'une notice historique sur la vie du Maréchal* (Londres, Paris: Buisson, 1789)
Guibert, Jacques Antoine Hippolyte de, *Essai général de tactique* (Paris: Magimel, 1803)

Guibert, Jacques Antoine Hippolyte de, *Défense du système de guerre moderne* (Neuchâtel: Publisher unknown, 1779)
Guignard, Pierre Claude de, *L'École de Mars* (Paris: Simart, 1725)
Hennet, Léon Clément, *Les milices et les troupes provinciales*, (Paris: Beaudoin, 1884)
Hennet, Léon Clément, *Les milices gardes-côtes* (Paris: Beaudoin, 1886)
Héricourt, Nicolas d', *Elémens de l'art militaire* (La Haye: J. Neaulme, 1739)
Héricourt, Nicolas d', *Elémens de l'art militaire* (La Haye: Pierre Gosse, 1748)
Héricourt, Nicolas d', *Elémens de l'art militaire* (La Haye: J. Neaulme, 1756)
Hippeau, Célestin, *Le gouvernement de Normandie au 17e et au 18e siècle* (Caen: Goussiaume de Laporte, 1863))
Joly de Maizeroy, Paul Gédéon, *La tactique discutée et réduite à ses véritables loix, avec les moyens d'en conserver les principes, & des remarques sur diverses parties de la science de la guerre: pour servir de suite et de conclusion au cours et au traité de tactique théorique, pratique et historique* (Paris: Claude Antoine Jombert fils aîné, 1773)
Joly de Maizeroy, Paul Gédéon, *Mémoires sur les opinions qui partagent les militaires* (Paris: Jombert ,1773)
Jomini, Antoine Henri, baron de, *Traité de grande tactique* (Paris: Magimel, 1805)
Jomini, Antoine Henri, baron de, *Histoire critique et militaire des guerres de Frédéric II* (Bruxelles: Petit, 1842)
Jomini, Antoine Henri, baron de, *Traité des grandes opérations militaires* (Paris: Tanera, 1851)
La Borde, Jean Benjamin de, Essai *sur la musique* (Paris: Pierres, 1780)
Lacour, René, *Les frères Prunelle de Vienne témoins oculaires de la guerre de Sept Ans* (Lyon: de la Guillotière, 1952)
L'Admiral, *Le petit dictionnaire du temps, pour l'intelligence des nouvelles de la guerre* (Paris: Bauche, 1756)
La Fontaine, sieur de, *Les devoirs militaires des officiers de l'infanterie contenant l'exercice des gens de guerre* (Paris: Loyson, 1775)
Laissac, capitaine de, *De l'esprit militaire* (Paris: Buisson, 1789)
Lamont, capitaine de, *Les Fonctions de tous les officiers de l'infanterie, depuis celles du sergent jusques à celles du colonel* (Paris: Quinet, 1669)
Lamont, capitaine de, *Les fonctions de tous les officiers de l'infanterie, depuis celle du sergent jusques à celle du colonel: la fortification offensive et défensive, la manière de construire toutes sortes de places régulières et irrégulières, l'usage du compas de proportion, le tout représenté par figures, comme aussi les évolutions militaires, l'exercice du mousquet et de la pique, telles que le roi le fait faire à ses mousquetaires et à son régiment des gardes, et l'abrégé de toutes les ordonnances et règlemens que Sa Majesté a fait faire depuis 1651 jusques en 1667 et aussi le rang de tous les régimens de France* (La Haye: Henry van Bulderen, 1688)
La Porterie, François de, *Institutions militaires pour la cavalerie et les dragons* (Paris: Guillyn, 1754)
La Roche, Aymon Antoine Charles Étienne Paul de, *Mémoires sur l'art de la guerre* (Paris: Corréard, 1857)
La Rue, Philibert Benoît de, *Nouveau recueil des troupes légères de France 1743–1746* (Paris: F, Chereau, 1747)
Le Blond, Guillaume, *Essai sur la castramétation ou sur la mesure et le tracé des camps* (Paris: Jombert, 1748)
Le Blond, Guillaume, *Elemens de tactique, ouvrage dans lequel on traite de l'arrangement & de la formation des troupes ; des évolutions de l'infanterie & de la cavalerie ; des principaux ordres de bataille ; de la marche des armées & de la castramétation, ou de la manière de tracer ou marquer les camps par règles & par principes* (Paris: chez Charles Antoine Jombert, 1758)
Le Blond, Guillaume, *Traité de la défense des places* (Paris: chez Charles-Antoine Jombert, 1762)
Legrand, l'abbé Paul, 'Livre des routes du baron de Plas capitaine au régiment d'infanterie Du Roi (1757–1759)', *Bulletin et mémoires de la Société archéologique et historique de la Charente*, année 1905–1906
Lemau de la Jaisse, Pierre, *Carte générale de la monarchie francoise, contenant l'histoire militaire, depuis Clovis premier Roy Chretien, jusqu'a la quinzième année accomplie du règne de Louis XV* (Paris: Publisher unknown, 1733)
Lemoine, Jean, *Sous Louis le Bien-Aimé, correspondance amoureuse et militaire d'un officier pendant la guerre de Sept Ans* (Paris: Calman Levy, undated)
Le Rouge, Georges, *Le parfait aide de camp, où l'on traité de ce que doit sçavoir tout jeune militaire qui se propose de faire son chemin à la guerre, avec des notes sur différens ouvrages de campagne, & sur les plans des principaux camps des guerres de 1740 & 1756* (Paris: Chez l'auteur, 1760)

Leroy, de Bosroger, *Principes de l'art de la guerre développés d'après les meilleurs exemples et appliqués, tant aux opérations d'un corps d'armée qu'à celle des détachements particuliers* (Paris: Cellot et Jombert, 1779)
Ligne, Charles Joseph, prince de, *Fantaisies militaires* (Kralovelhota: Publisher unknown, 1780)
Lloyd, Henry, *Introduction à l'histoire de la guerre en Allemagne en 1756* (Londres, Bruxelles: Pion, 1784)
Lombard, Jean Louis, *Traité du mouvement des projectiles, appliqué au tir des bouches à feu* (Dijon: Frantin, 1797)
Manesson Mallet, Allain de, *Les Travaux de Mars, ou l'Art de la guerre* (Paris: Denys Thierry, 1684–1685)
Marchant de Burbure, François, *Essais historiques sur la ville et sur le collège de La Flèche* (Angers: Pavie, 1803)
Margerand, Joseph, *Armement et équipement de l'infanterie française du 17Ie au 20e siècle* (Paris: Éditions militaires illustrées, 1945)
Martange, Marie Antoine Bouët de, *Correspondance inédite du général-major de Martange, aide de camp du prince Xavier de Saxe, lieutenant général des armées (1756–1782)* (Paris: Picard, 1898)
Mauvillon, Eléazar, *Histoire de la dernière guerre en Bohème* (Francfort: Paul Lenclume, 1745)
Mauvillon, Jakob, *Essai sur l'influence de la poudre à canon dans l'art de la guerre moderne* (Dessau: Société typographique, 1782)
Mauvillon, Jakob, *Essai sur l'influence de la poudre à canon dans l'art de la guerre moderne* (Lieipsicz: Haug, 1788)
May, Emmanuel, *Histoire militaire de la Suisse et celle des Suisses dans les différens services de l'Europe* (Lausanne: Heubach et Comp, 1788)
Mention, Léon, *L'armée de l'ancien régime de Louis XIV à la révolution* (Paris: L.H. May, 1900)
Mention, Léon, *Le comte de Saint Germain et ses réformes* (Paris: Clavel, 1884)
Mentzel, Elisabeth, 'Die französische und deutsche Komödie von 1759 bis 1703 und ihr Einfluss auf den jungen Goethe' in *Archiv für Frankfurts Geschichte und Kunst* (Frankfurt: Völker, 1882)
Mercoyrol, Jacques de, seigneur de Beaulieu, *Campagnes de Jacques de Mercoyrol de Beaulieu, capitaine au régiment de Picardie* (Paris: Renouard, Laurens, 1915))
Mesnil Durand, François Jean de, *Fragments de tactique* (Paris: Jombert, 1774)
Mesnil Durand, François Jean de, *Défense du système de guerre moderne* (Neuchâtel: Publisher unknown, 1779)
Monro, Donald, *Médecine d'armée* (Paris: Didot le jeune,1769)
Montbarrey, Alexandre, *Mémoires autographes de M. le prince de Montbarrey* (Paris: Eymery, 1826)
Montalembert, Marc Rene, marquis de, *Correspondance de Monsieur le Marquis de Montalembert, étant employé par le Roi de France à l'armée Suédoise, avec Mr le Marquis d'Havrincour, etc.* (Londres: Publisher unknown,1777)
Montigny, Claude Antoine Littret de, *Uniformes militaires où se trouvent gravés en taille- douce les uniformes de la Maison du Roy, de tous les régiments de France, les drapeaux, étendards et guidons* (Paris: Chez l'auteur, 1772)
Napoléon, *Précis des guerres de Frédéric II* (Paris: Hachette, 1872)
La Noue de Vair, Stanislaus Louis, comte de, *Nouvelles Constitutions militaires* (Francfort sur le Mayn: Knoch et Eslinger, 1760)
Pajol, Charles Pierre Victor, comte, *Les guerres sous Louis XV* (Paris: Firmin Didot, 1881–1891)
Perrin, secrétaire du maréchal de Belle-Isle, *Lettre d'un subdélégué à un intendant de province sur un projet du maréchal de Belle-Isle touchant à la substitution des légions aux régiments* (Paris: Publisher unknown, 1759)
Perrin, secrétaire du maréchal de Belle-Isle, *Réponse d'un major d'infanterie à un intendant de province sur la milice* (Avignon: Publisher unknown, 1760)
Pictet Gabriel, *Essai sur la tactique de l'infanterie* (Genève: Du Villard, 1761)
Pinard, *Chronologie historique et militaire, contenant l'histoire de la création de toutes les charges, dignités et grades militaires supérieurs, de toutes les personnes qui les ont possédés… des troupes de la maison du Roi* (Paris: Henssant, 1760–1778)
Poissonnier des Perrieres Antoine, *Mémoire sur l'habillement des troupes, Nouveaux mémoires de l'Académie de Dijon* (Dijon: Causse, 1772)
Pommelles Jean-Christophe Sandrier dit chevalier des, *Tableau de la population de toutes les provinces de France, Mémoire sur les milices, leur création, leur vicissitude et leur état actuel* (Paris: Publisher unknown, 1789)
Preval, Claude Antoine Hippolyte, vicomte de, *Du service des armées en campagne* (Blois: Aucher-Eloy, 1827)

Prieur-Duvernois Claude Antoine, *L'art du militaire ; ou Traité complet de l'exercice de l'infanterie, cavalerie, du canon, de la bombe et des piques ; une explication claire et précise des évolutions les plus ordinaires* (Paris: Dufart, 1798)
Pringle, docteur en médecine, *Observation sur les maladies des armées dans les camps et les garnisons* (Paris: Théophile Barrois, 1793)
Puységur, Jacques François de Chastenet, *Art de la guerre, par principes et par règles* (Paris: Jombert, 1749)
Quincy, Charles Sévin, marquis de, *Histoire militaire du règne de Louis le Grand, Roy de France, on y a joint un traité particulier de pratiques et de maximes de l'art militaire* (Paris: Mariette, 1726)
Quincy, Charles Sévin marquis de, *Maximes et instructions sur l'art militaire* (Paris: Mariette, Delespine, Coignard, 1726)
Ray de Saint-Geniès, Jacques-Marie, *L'art de la guerre pratique* (Paris: Jombert, 1754)
Richelieu, Louis François Armand, maréchal de, *Correspondance particulière et historique du maréchal duc de Richelieu en 1756, 1757 et 1758, avec M, Paris du Verney, conseiller d'État* (Paris: Buisson, 1789)
Roche-Aymon, Guillaume, marquis de la, *Mémoires sur l'art de la guerre* (Paris: Corréard, 1857)
Rochefort, *Ordonnances du Roy concernant l'infanterie françoise ordinaire* (Lausanne: Bousquet, 1744)
Rousse, Jacques de, *Essais historiques sur les régimens d'Infanterie, Cavalerie et Dragons, Béarn, Picardie* (Paris: Guillyn, 1765)
Roussel, Jacques de, (*Essais historiques sur les régimens d'infanterie, Cavalerie et Dragons, Dauphiné* (Paris: Guillyn, 1767)
Saint-Germain Comte Claude-Louis de, *Correspondance particulière du Comte de Saint-Germain avec M, Paris du Vernay* (London, Paris: Buisson, 1789)
Saint-Germain Claude-Louis, comte de, *Mémoires de M, le comte de St Germain, écrits par lui-même* (Amsterdam: Rey, 1779)
Santa Cruz de Marcenado, Alvaro de Navia Osorio de, *Réfexions militaires et politiques* (Paris: Jacques Guerin, Jacques Clousier, 1735–1738)
Sautreau de Marsy, Claude Sixte, *Le petit chansonnier françois ou choix des meilleures chansons sur des airs communs* (Genève, Paris: Vve Duchesne, 1780)
Sicard, François, *Histoire des institutions militaires des français* (Paris, Correard, 1831–1834)
Silva, marquis de, *Pensées sur la tactique et sur quelques autres parties de la guerre*, (Paris: Jombert, 1768)
Sionville, Prosper de, *Œuvres militaires* (Charleville: P. Thesin, 1756)
Soubise, Charles de Rohan, prince de, *Instruction pour l'infanterie de l'armée du roi commandée par Mr le Maréchal Prince de Soubise* (Publisher unknown, c.1761)
Surirey de Saint Remy, Pierre, *Mémoires d'artillerie* (Paris: Jombert, 1745)
Sparre, baron de, *Code militaire, ou compilation des réglemens et ordonnances de Louis XIV, faites pour les gens de guerre, depuis 1651, jusqu'à présent* (Paris: Mariette Delespine, 1709)
Sparre, Joseph Ignace Magnus, comte de, *Instructions militaires* (Paris: Briasson, 1753)
Susane, Louis Auguste Victor Vincent, *Histoire de l'infanterie française* (Paris: Dumaine, 1876)
Tronçon du Coudray, Guillaume Alexandre, *L'Ordre profond et l'ordre mince considéré par rapport aux effets de l'artillerie* (Metz: Publisher unknown, 1776)
Tuetey, Louis, *Les officiers sous l'ancien régime, nobles et roturiers* (Paris: Pion, 1908)
Valin, René Josué, *Nouveau commentaire sur l'ordonnance de la marine du mois d'août 1681* (La Rochelle: Legier, 1760)
Vaultier, commissaire d'artillerie, *Observations sur l'art de faire la guerre* (Francfort et Leipzig: Aux dépens de la compagnie, 1761)
Waddington, Richard, *Histoire diplomatique et militaire de la guerre de Sept Ans* (Paris: Firmin Didot, 1899–1904)
Warnery, Charles de, *Remarques sur la cavalerie* (Lublin: Publisher unknown, 1781)
Warner,y Charles, *Remarques sur l'essai général de tactique de Guibert* (Varsovie: Publisher unknown, 1782)
Zurlauben, Beat Fidel, *Tableaux de la Suisse* (Paris: Lamy, 1784)
Zurlauben, Beat Fidel, *Histoire militaire des Suisses, au service de la France: Avec les pièces justificatives* (Paris: Desaint et Saillant, 1752)
Zurlauben, Beat Fidèle Antoine Jean Dominique, *Code militaire des Suisses: pour servir de suite à l'Histoire militaire des Suisses, au service de la France* (Paris: Vincent, 1758–1764)

Decrees and Acts

Acte royal, 12 November 1733, *Ordonnance du roy concernant les milices du 12 novembre 1733* (Paris: Imprimerie Royale, 1733)

Acte royal, 20 April 1736, *Ordonnance du Roi concernant l'habillement de l'infanterie française* (Paris: Imprimerie royale, 1736)

Acte royal, 10 April 1737, *Ordonnance du roy qui enjoint aux officiers des troupes d'infanterie, cavalerie et dragons de porter l'habit uniforme pendant le temps qu'ils seront aux corps* (Paris: imprimerie royale, 1747)

Acte royal, *Règlement provisionnel pour le service de l'infanterie en campagne* (Paris: Imprimerie Royale, 1744)

Acte royal, 10 July 1743, *Ordonnance du roy, portant augmentation de trente-six mille hommes de milice du 10 juillet 1743* (Paris: Imprimerie Royale, 1744)

Acte royal, 6 August 1748, *Ordonnance du roy concernant les milices* (Paris: Prault, 1750)

Acte royal, 29 January 1747, *Instruction sur la façon et traitement d'un justaucorps de soldat* (Paris: Imprimerie royale, 1747)

Acte royal, 10 February 1749, *Ordonnance. du Roy concernant les régiments de son infanterie françoise du 10 février 1749* (Lyon: Valfray, 1749)

Acte royal, 15 February 1749, *Ordonnance du Roy pour la formation d'un régiment sous le titre de Grenadiers de France du 15 février 1749* (Paris: Imprimerie royale, 1749)

Acte royal, 1 May 1750, *Ordonnance du Roy, concernant l'habillement, l'équipement & l'armement de ses régimens de dragons* (Paris: Imprimerie royale, 1750)

Acte royal, 7 May 1750, *Ordonnance du roi sur le maniement des armes de l'Infanterie françoise & étrangère du 7 Mai 1750* (Lyon: Valfray imprimeur du Roi, 1753)

Acte royal, 1st March 1752, *Ordonnance du roi pour la levée d'un régiment Suisse du canton de Zurich du 1er mars 1752* (Paris: Imprimerie royale, 1752)

Acte royal, 23 May 1752, *Ordonnance du roi concernant le service des sujets de Sa Majesté qui s'étant engagés dans les régimens étrangers, sont réclamés et rendus à des capitaines françois du 23 mai 1752* (Paris: Imprimerie royale, 1752)

Acte royal,1st September 1752, *Ordonnance du roi pour entretenir le régiment suisse de Hallwyl au service de la marine du premier septembre 1752* (Paris: Imprimerie royale, 1753)

Acte royal, 1753, *Instruction pour l'infanterie concernant l'exécution de l'ordonnance du 7 mai 1750* (Paris: Imprimerie royale, 1753)

Acte royal, 17 February 1753, *Ordonnance du roi portant règlement sur l'infanterie en campagne du 17 février 1753* (Paris: Imprimerie royale, 1753)

Acte royal, 29 June 1753, Instruction sur l'exercice de l'infanterie du 29 juin 1753 (Paris: Imprimerie royale, 1753)

Acte royal, February 1751, *Instruction sur la milice, adressée par M. le comte d'Argenson le 27 juillet 1742, aux subdélégués de la généralité de Paris ; et par M. de Sauvigny, au mois de février 1751. Avec quelques nouveaux articles. Février 1751* (Paris: Pierre Prault, 1754)

Acte royal,1st May 1754, *Règlement pour la construction des espontons dont les officiers d'Infanterie doivent être armés ; et des fusils que doivent porter ceux des compagnies de grenadiers, en conséquence de l'ordonnance du Roi du 7 mai 1750, concernant le maniement des armes de l'infanterie du premier Mai 1754.* (Paris: Imprimerie royale, 1754)

Acte royal, 14 May 1754, *Instruction sur l'exercice de l'infanterie du 14 mai 1754* (Paris: Imprimerie royale, 1754)

Acte royal, 1755, *Commandemens de l'exercice de l'infanterie, en françois et en anglois, tirés de l'ordonnance du 6 mai 1755* (Paris: Imprimerie royale, 1755)

Acte royal, 1755, *Commandemens de l'exercice de l'infanterie, en françois et en italien, tirés de l'ordonnance du 6 mai 1755* (Paris: Imprimerie royale, 1755)

Acte royal, 6 May 1755, *Ordonnance du roi sur l'exercice de l'infanterie du 6 mai 1755* (Paris: Imprimerie royale, 1755)

Acte royal, 1756, *Mémoire pour servir d'instruction concernant le service aux batteries des côtes* (Paris: Imprimerie royale, 1756)

Acte royal, 25 February 1756, *Ordonnance du roy concernant le service des milices garde-côtes de la province de Bretagne* (Paris: Imprimerie royale, 1756)

Acte royal, 16 March 1756, *Ordonnance du roi concernant les milices garde-côtes de Picardie, Normandie, Poitou, Aunis, Saintonge et Guyenne du 16 mars 1756* (Paris: Imprimerie royale, 1756)

Acte royal, 20 September 1756, *Ordonnance du roi concernant les régimens écossois du 20 septembre 1756* (Paris: Imprimerie royale, 1756)

Acte royal, 6 December 1756, *Ordonnance du roi pour les troupes attachées au service de la Compagnie des Indes du 6 décembre 1756* (Paris: Imprimerie royale, 1756)

Acte royal, 8 July 1756, *Ordonnance concernant le régiment des grenadiers de France du 8 juillet 1756* (Paris: Imprimerie Royale, 1756)

Acte royal, 6 December 1756, *Ordonnance du roi pour les troupes attachées au service de la Compagnie des Indes du 6 decembre 1756* (Paris: Imprimerie royale, 1756)

Acte royal,18 January 1757, *Ordonnance du roi portant création d'un régiment d'infanterie de deux bataillons sous le titre de Bouillon du 18 janvier 1757* (Paris: Imprimerie royale, 1757)

Acte royal, 20 January 1757, *Ordonnance du Roi portant établissement d'une pièce de canon à la suédoise à la suite de chacun des bataillons de son infanterie, tant françoise qu'étrangère du 20 janvier 1757* (Paris: Imprimerie royale, 1757)

Acte royal, 29 January 1757, *Ordonnance du roi concernant les régiments Royal Italien et Royal Corse du 29 janvier 1757* (Paris: Imprimerie royale, 1757)

Acte royal, 20 March 1757, *Ordonnance du roi pour le rétablissement des régimens Royal-Lorraine et Royal-Barrois du 20 mars 1757* (Paris: Imprimerie royale, 1757)

Acte royal, 1st October 1757, *Ordonnance du roi concernant neuf bataillons de milice que Sa Majeté a destinés à être employés à ses armées en Allemagne du 1er octobre 1757* (Paris: Imprimerie royale, 1757)

Acte royal, 30 December 1757, *Ordonnance du roi pour le remplacement des officiers prisonniers de guerre du 30 décembre 1757* (Paris: Imprimerie royale, 1757)

Acte royal, *Mémoire pour servir d'instruction concernant les milices garde-côte* (Paris: Imprimerie royale, 1758)

Acte royal, 29 April 1758, *Règlement que le Roi a jugé à propos de faire sur l'ancienneté de service que devront avoir les officiers qui seront proposés pour commander les régiments du 29 avril 1758* (Paris: Imprimerie Royale, 1758)

Acte royal, 1st May 1758, *Ordonnance du roi portant augmentation de quatre onces par chaque ration de pain de munition, dont la fourniture sera faite tant en campagne que dans les garnisons, à commencer du 1er juillet prochain, aux troupes de sa majesté ; à l'exception des officiers, auxquels le pain continuera d'être fourni, en campagne, sur le pied de vingt-quatre onces par ration du premier mai 1758* (Paris: Imprimerie royale, 1758)

Acte royal, 15 May 1758, *Ordonnance du roi pour donner un rang dans l'infanterie aux milices garde-côtes et aux officiers qui les commandent du 15 mai 1758* (Paris: Imprimerie royale, 1758)

Acte royal, 15 May 1758, *Ordonnance du roi concernant les milices garde-côtes de Languedoc* (Paris: Imprimerie royale, 1759)

Acte royal, 1st June 1758, *Ordonnance du roi 1758 portant augmentation de traitement aux troupes d'infanterie françoise pour l'entretien du linge et chaussure du 1er juin 1758* (Paris: Imprimerie royale, 1758)

Acte royal, 8 July 1758, *Ordonnance concernant le régiment des grenadiers de France du 8 juillet 1756* (Paris: Imprimerie Royale, 1756)

Acte Royal, 12 September 1758, *Ordonnance du roi concernant l'armement et l'équipement des compagnies de fusiliers de ses troupes* (Paris: Imprimerie royale, 1758)

Acte Royal, 31 October 1758, *Ordonnance du roi concernant l'armement des officiers et des sergents des compagnies de fusiliers* (Paris: Imprimerie royale, 1758)

Acte Royal, 9 December 1758, Ordonnance du roi concernant l'armement des officiers et des sergens des compagnies de fusiliers de ses troupes, et des cartouches ou demi-gibernes dont ils doivent être pourvus du 9 Décembre 1758 (Paris: Imprimerie royale, 1758)

Acte royal, 24 February 1759, *Ordonnance du roi pour réunir au département de la Guerre tous les détails concernant les milices garde-côtes, le service, l'établissement et l'entretien des batteries servant à la défense des côtes* (Paris: Imprimerie royale, 1759)

Acte royal, 12 June 1759, *Réglement que le Roi a jugé à propos de faire, pour donner aux commissions de capitaine et de lieutenant-colonel, une valeur qui assure à ceux qui en sont ou seront pourvus, un avancement plus prompt lorsqu'ils seront parvenus à des régimens du 12 juin 1759* (Paris: Imprimerie royale, 1759)

Acte royal, 30 June 1759, *Ordonnance du roy concernant les milices garde-côtes de la province de Bretagne* (Paris: Imprimerie royale, 1759)

Acte royal, 18 January 1760, *Ordonnance du Roi, concernant les régimens d'infanterie allemande qui sont à son service du 18 janvier 1760* (Paris: Imprimerie royale, 1760)

Acte royal, 18 January 1760, Ordonnance *du Roi, concernant les régimens d'infanterie allemande qui sont à son service du 18 janvier 1760* (Paris: Imprimerie Royale, 1762)

Acte royal, 1st February 1761, *Ordonnance du roi concernant quelques bataillons de son infanterie françoise 1er février 1761*(Paris: Imprimerie royale, 1761)

Acte royal, 25 November 1762, Ordonnance du roi pour réformer plusieurs régimens de son infanterie françoise du 25 novembre 1762 (Paris: Imprimerie royale, 1762)

Acte royal, 10 December 1762, *Ordonnance du roi, concernant l'infanterie françoise du 10 décembre 1762* (Paris: Imprimerie royale, 1762)

Acte royal, 20 December 1762, *Ordonnance du roi concernant la vente des chevaux de canons et de pelotons et la suppression du supplément de solde, à commencer du 1er janvier 1763, aux sergens et soldats canonniers attachés au service des pièces de canons à la suédoise du 20 décembre 1762* (Paris: Imprimerie royale, 1762)

Acte royal, 21 December 1762, *Ordonnance du roi concernant le régiment royal-italien du 21 Décembre 1762* (Paris: Imprimerie royale, 1762)

Acte royal, 21 Décember 1762, *Ordonnance du roi, concernant les régimens d'infanterie allemande du 21 décembre 1762* (Metz: Collignon, 1763)

Acte royal, 21 Décember 1762, *Ordonnance du roi, concernant les régimens d'infanterie irlandoise du 21 décembre 1762* (Metz: Collignon, 1763)

Acte royal, 25 April 1767, *Règlement arrêté par le roi pour l'habillement et l'équipement de ses troupes* (Paris: Imprimerie royale, 1767)

Journals and Encyclopaedia

Carnet de la Sabretache, revue militaire rétrospective, 1895–1937, <https://gallica.bnf.fr/ark:/12148/cb34449073t/date>

Encyclopédie Méthodique, Art militaire (Paris: Briasson, David, Lebreton, Durand, 1751–1757)

Encyclopédie Méthodique, Art militaire (Paris: Agasse, 1784–1797)

Encyclopédie ou Dictionnaire raisonné des sciences, des arts et des métiers (Paris: Briasson, 1751–1765)

From Reason to Revolution – Warfare 1721-1815
http://www.helion.co.uk/series/from-reason-to-revolution-1721-1815.php

The 'From Reason to Revolution' series covers the period of military history 1721–1815, an era in which fortress-based strategy and linear battles gave way to the nation-in-arms and the beginnings of total war.

This era saw the evolution and growth of light troops of all arms, and of increasingly flexible command systems to cope with the growing armies fielded by nations able to mobilise far greater proportions of their manpower than ever before. Many of these developments were fired by the great political upheavals of the era, with revolutions in America and France bringing about social change which in turn fed back into the military sphere as whole nations readied themselves for war. Only in the closing years of the period, as the reactionary powers began to regain the upper hand, did a military synthesis of the best of the old and the new become possible.

The series examines the military and naval history of the period in a greater degree of detail than has hitherto been attempted, and has a very wide brief, with the intention of covering all aspects from the battles, campaigns, logistics, and tactics, to the personalities, armies, uniforms, and equipment.

Submissions
The publishers would be pleased to receive submissions for this series. Please email reasontorevolution@helion.co.uk, or write to Helion & Company Limited, Unit 8 Amherst Business Centre, Budbrooke Road, Warwick, CV34 5WE

You may also be interested in:

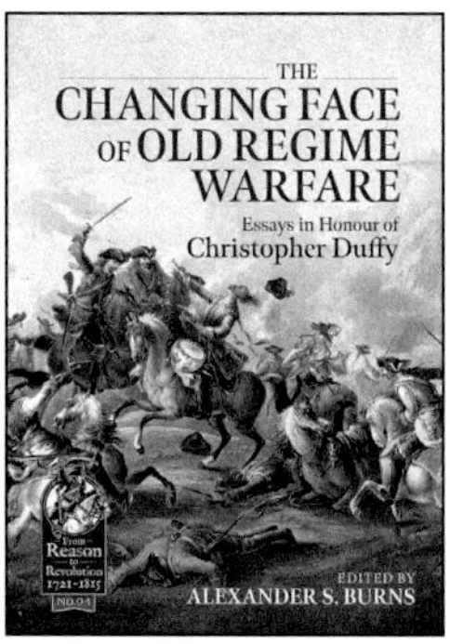

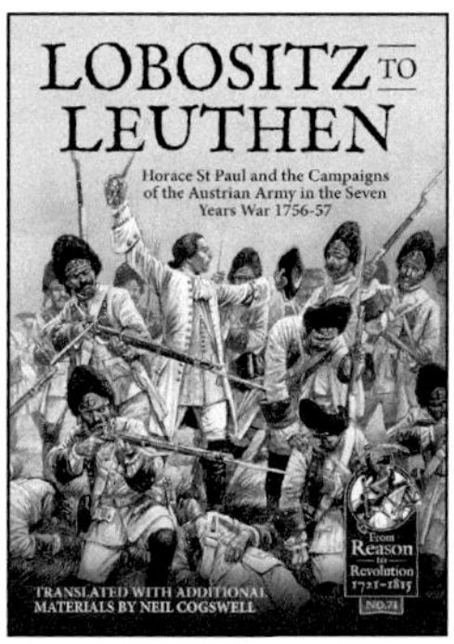

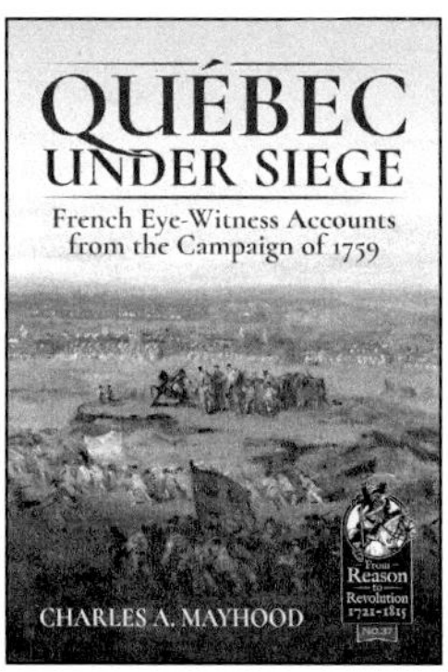

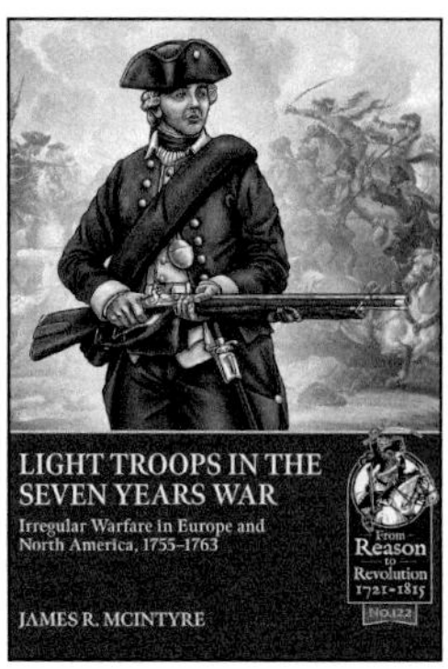

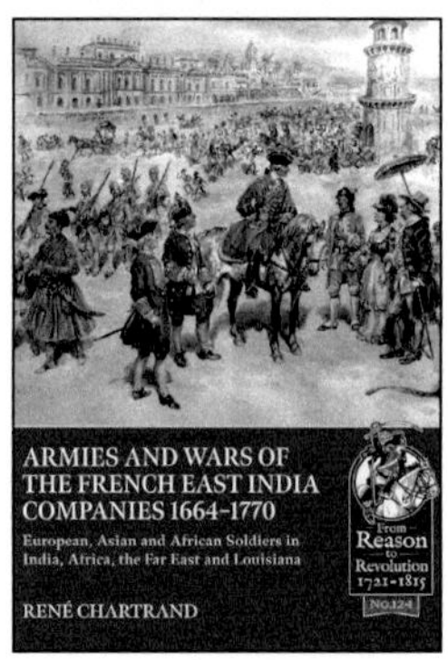